Eye of the Phoenix

Eye of the Phoenix

Mysterious Visions and Secrets
of the American Southwest

Gary A. David

Adventures Unlimited Press

Eye of the Phoenix: Mysterious Visions and Secrets
of the American Southwest.

Adventures Unlimited Press
P.O. Box 74
Kempton, Illinois 60946 USA
www.adventuresunlimitedpress.com

ISBN 978-1-931882-80-4

Earlier versions of some the information in this book appeared as articles
in the following publications: *Ancient American*; *Atlantis Rising*; *Canadian
Communicacator*; *Fate*; *Four Corners*; *Underground! The Disinformation Guide
to Ancient Civilizations, Astonishing Archaeology, and Hidden History*; and
World Explorer. A small portion of the material was also published in
The Orion Zone (Adventures Unlimited Press, 2006).

Cover art and design: by Jack Andrews
www.jackandrewsart.com

Photographs and illustrations: by Gary A. David
or non-copyrighted Internet sources unless otherwise noted.

Acknowledgments

I would like to thank Nancy Cannon and Ginger Johnson of the Smoki Museum in Prescott, Arizona, for their assistance in researching this manuscript. Thanks go as well to the Pioneer & Military Memorial Park and the Smurthwaite House in Phoenix.

I am indebted to the following Websites for publication of my work or interviews and notices regarding it: Tim Binnall at binnallofamerica.com, Michael Bourne at book-of-thoth.com, Walter Cruttenden at healthylife.net, Mike Hagan at mikehagan.com, Graham Hancock at grahamhancock.com, William Henry and Whitley Strieber at unknowncountry.com, Henrik Palmgren at redicecreations.com, Greg Taylor at dailygrail.com, and Gary Vey at viewzone.com.

I also commend the following people who have helped in various ways: T. L. Subash Chandira Bose for his enthusiasm about archaeo-symbology and the Hindu Mother Goddess, Amanda Laoupi for her astromythological research in Greece, octogenarian Gene D. Matlock for his verve and provocative writing, Rob Milne for his work on the Orion Correlation in South Africa, Jeff Nisbet for his role as a true colleague, and my publisher David Hatcher Childress for his alternative perspectives and for being an absolute pleasure to work with.

Heartfelt gratitude is extended to my benefactors and dear friends for their support: Susan Anway and Jack Andrews, Kim Anway-Anastasia and Ron Anastasia, Terry Bailey, Gary Creighton, Douglas McEdwards, and a few anonymous good souls.

My wife, Anita S. Descault, proofread the manuscript and offered invaluable suggestions. I cannot thank her enough.

This book is dedicated to my mother, Gloria P. David,
who encouraged me all along the way, and
to the memory of my father, Donald W. David (1923 – 1999),
who gave me the fortitude to get there.

It is also dedicated to the Hopi grandmothers and grandfathers,
whose ceremonies keep the world in balance.

Contents

Trading post at Santo Domingo Pueblo, New Mexico, 1991.

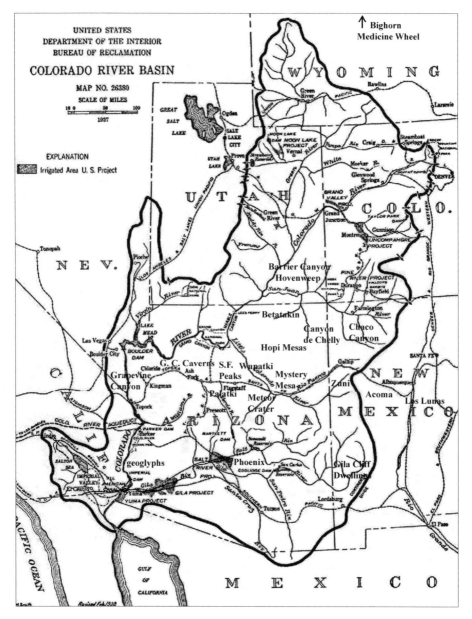

The American Southwest

Introduction: Spiraling To the Center of the World

"The Hopi land is the Hopi religion. The Hopi religion is bound up in the Hopi land."

Andrew Hermequaftewa

"Every month we have ceremonies to keep our people balanced. We still live here in the center of the world."

Thomas Banyacya

Keeping the World In Balance

The landscape of the Southwest seems hauntingly familiar. Is it merely the result of all those Westerns where director John Ford spuriously used Monument Valley as a backdrop? Or is it something more? If so, it may be the echo of some unfathomable dream—a cellular memory bubbling up from some ancient past.

This subtle yet unequivocal aura of the numinous is best felt at twilight—the crack between worlds, some say. I am sitting at Desert View on the eastern end of Grand Canyon. The last rays of the sun airbrush a few cirrus clouds salmon pink and saffron. Just before the Colorado River turns west into Grand Canyon proper, it flows out of Marble Canyon from the north. Looking like what T. S. Eliot has called a "strong brown god," this watery serpent glides over chocolate-colored slabs of Precambrian Vishnu schist and intrusions of Zoroaster granite.

Other exotically named geologic features further accentuate the Romantic nature of this unique formation: Shiva Temple and Buddha Cloister, Manu Temple and Ottoman Amphitheater, Osiris Temple and Cheops Pyramid, Isis Temple and Tower of Ra, Confucius Temple and Dragon Head, Thor Temple and Wotans Throne, Solomon Temple and Angels Gate.

Monument Valley, northern Arizona.
Copyrighted © photo courtesy of JCardaci.

As I perch on the south rim of the canyon with legs dangling over the abyss, waves of tranquility issuing from far below wash over the shores of my inner being. I am thoroughly relaxed here, partly because of my earlier hike down Bright Angel Trail. This was a day spent exulting in the cleansing sun and wind. As I trekked down the dusty path, elemental wonder and vertiginous awe had astounded me at every switchback. Profusely sweating, I had paused to take a drink, tipping back my head for the simple pleasure of cool canteen water. The cerulean river above bathed my relief.

Now it is evening. Indigo shadows grope their way across the Little Painted Desert. Some are lost in the Little Colorado River Gorge. Others flow east like dark water through the dry washes past their namesake Shadow Mountain and beyond. Somewhere from deep within all this eroded distance, I sense an echo from another lifetime—a vague yet powerful presence this boundless landscape somehow evokes.

The violet shade of crepuscular earth reposing against the royal blue of nightward-tipping sky distills an impression of timeless existence: the rituals and prayer-chants in half-remembered canyons, all those migrations through sacred precincts where sun-charged sand and Milky Way stardust merge. Through the dusky labyrinth of mesas and scattered bones a life of austere dignity and primal yet complex spirituality once emerged. It rose to walk the earth, patiently tending dry fields of blue corn, making offerings of corn meal and breath-feathers that kept the world in balance.

Perhaps this ancient life intimated to me now is keeping the world in balance still.

Spiraling Across Hopiland

Arizona is a land of diversity and contrast. A great deal more exists here than the stereotypic images of the massive saguaro cactus and the red-blossomed ocotillo. This story also involves the area north of the narrow range of these two low desert species. The southern edge of the Colorado Plateau is called the Mogollon (pronounced muggy-own) Rim. This geologic fault of Kaibab limestone curves across the state from northwest to southeast. The Colorado Plateau also extends northward through the Four Corners region into the three other states of New Mexico, Colorado, and Utah.

A good place to begin, however, is in the vicinity of the San Francisco Peaks, where native spirits live for half the year. The Hopi name for these mountains is Nuvatukya'ovi, or Snow Peaks. The Diné (Navajo) call them Dook'o'oosliid, or West

Mountain.

A warm vanilla scent of ponderosa pine greets me, bringing back the essence of sacred mountains elsewhere. The mid-September sun is hot on my skin, though the slight chill in the air is welcoming. (This is one of the contrasts of the high desert: Step into shade and you freeze, step into the sun and you broil.) Creating an Impressionist masterpiece, the visual explosion of purple asters and red Indian paintbrushes splatters the dominant yellow hue of wild sunflowers, mullein, gumweed, and goldenrod. Slanted sunlight filters through the forest, infusing the morning with the season's typically melancholy joy.

To the northeast gray clouds shroud the upper portion of the basaltic cinder cone named Humphreys Peak, highest point in Arizona, 12,633 feet in elevation. While I drove from the west, the mountains looked almost pyramidal on the horizon: Humphreys at the north, the slightly lower Agassiz Peak (12,356 feet) about a mile and a half due south, and Fremont Peak (11,969 feet) a mile southeast of the latter. Oddly reminiscent of the ceremonial structures on the Giza Plateau a half a world away, these mountains are home to the Hopi spirits called *katsinam* (plural of *katsina*, sometimes written *kachina*), to which they return each July. (See photo on the bottom of 33.)

I linger here awhile, reveling in the sunshine but cognizant of the possibility that a sudden fall blizzard could dust these peaks white, making the uplifts stand against the horizon even more prominently until they seem to float in mid-air, much like the world's other great volcanic mountains such as Fujiyama or Shasta.

Following Interstate 40 east through the Coconino National Forest, I travel through the middle of what naturalists call the Transition Zone. This ranges between 6,500 and 8,000 feet in elevation. The dominant plant species is *Pinus ponderosa*, the western yellow pine, occupying one of the largest areas of such in the country (and rivaling that of the Black Hills of South Dakota.) As expected, the mountains attract moisture from the clouds, so precipitation here is an average of eighteen to twenty-six inches annually—twice that of the desert. A lack of understory shrubs creates the characteristic broad, park-like land-scapes covered with brome and foxtail grass beneath the tall boles of pines that rise as impassively silent as meditating monks. Larger trees reach a height of 125 feet or more and may be over 500 years old.

An occasional stand of Gambel oaks is tinged a tannish orange by the increasingly cool nights. Along the highway bright yellow signs warn of elk crossings. If it were evening, a white-tailed deer or two –or even a group– might dart across the highway. Yet now to our left the peaks suddenly free of clouds point toward a blue noon, over 5,000 feet above us.

If I were to go higher along the road to the Arizona Snow Bowl –a ski lodge that desecrates the home of the *katsinam*– , I would be driving through what is called the Canadian Zone at over 8,000 feet, where Douglas fir and aspens are the major tree species. (It is commonly acknowledged that every rise of a thousand feet in elevation is the equivalent of traveling 300 miles north.) In the autumn sunlight whole hillsides of these golden-leafed aspens flash like ripples on a lake, while their flat-stemmed leaves tremble and dance on a mere whisper of a wind. Up close their white trunks wide as an embrace shine like ruined columns.

If I were to go even higher still, I would traverse the Hudsonian Zone above 9,500 feet. Here is the domain of Engelmann spruce and blue spruce along with a few bristlecone and limber pines. Englemann spruce is greatly affected by the prevailing wind, displaying either a "banner" type growth with branches only on the leeward side or a "wind timber" growth that forms a matted, savage-looking mass.

Finally, I would have to abandon my vehicle altogether and hike above the tree line on Humphreys Peak in order to reach the Alpine Zone at 11,500 feet. At these towering heights such arctic tundra wildflowers as the yellow-blossomed cinque-foil and the alpine avens spread out across the rocky terrain in low, dense carpets.

A land of contrasts indeed!

Although a detour in the cool mountain air seems inviting, I decide to stay focused on my goal. Continuing eastward, I pass the small college town of Flagstaff (population nearly 60,000). It is the only recognizable urban influence in northern Arizona.

In 1894 the pristine skies over the San Francisco Peaks prompted Percival Lowell, Massachusetts Brahmin and brother of the poet Amy Lowell, to build an astronomical observatory from which he could study the "canals" on Mars. In 1930 astronomer Clyde Tombaugh also discovered the planet Pluto with the observatory's telescope.

On the eastern side of the peaks, the rounder, more maternal Mount Elden spreads out to the left. A small ancient Anasazi (ancestral Hopi) pueblo ruin and burial site are nestled at her base. The modern motif now dominates, with radio antennae littering her summit.

Almost ten miles to the northeast Sunset Crater rises over one thousand feet. This dormant volcano began to smoke in the fall of 1064 AD and in the following year erupted with a lava flow from the eastern side of its base. (See photo on p. 199.)

Another thirteen miles in the same direction lies Wupatki National Monument with more pueblo ruins. You can also see a blowhole issuing from a system of underground limestone fissures as well a Maya-style ballcourt, which is the farthest north on the continent.

Still on I-40, I start to descend, driving the way the *katsinam* will travel after the winter solstice, back to the heart of Hopi country. Soon a sign for Walnut Canyon National Monument appears. At this site more pueblo ruins rest. These dwellings are strung out along the cliff side of a hoodoo island in the middle of the canyon. I reserve this pleasant setting of ancient Anasazi existence for another day, however, and continue eastward.

Now the landscape begins to change, as the ponderosa pine forest gradually gives way to the juniper-pinyon woodland. In this Upper Sonoran Desert Zone at an elevation of 4,500 to 6,500 feet, I notice that the air is getting warmer. In addition, the monolithic forest I had been traveling through opens up to shorter, less densely spaced trees and bushes. Here scraggly

Colorado pinyon and gnarled one-seed juniper are interspersed with the feathery-tailed cliffrose.

To the north I glimpse the low, rounded hills of the same Little Painted Desert that I saw from Grand Canyon—its pale gray-green, ocher, and maroon shale laid down originally as lakebeds in the upper Triassic period. As I gaze through binoculars, these mounds are spread out like folds on a piece of velvet thrown down upon the land. A maze of eroded buttes recedes into the distance, looking curiously like a village of Dogon huts with their conical roofs. In other places the terrain assumes a layer cake effect, frosted white with gypsum.

Flat-bottomed cumulonimbus clouds drift across limitless sky, casting watery blue shadows on the immense landscape. Driving eastward along the monotonous interstate, I meditate on the clouds until I am floating as well.

As I drop down even further, larger trees disappear almost entirely, except for a few stunted cottonwoods along dry arroyos. Cholla and prickly pear cacti scattered beneath giant toadstools of red Moencopi sandstone add a surreal effect to the environment.

This southeastern margin of the Great Basin desert scrub receives a mere seven to twelve inches of precipitation annually. It can support only such hearty species of vegetation as big sagebrush and four-wing saltbush or the oddly named greasewood, snakeweed, and mormon-tea. Western diamondback rattlesnakes and jackrabbits abound here. Grazing in the distance, small herds of pronghorns (more commonly called antelopes) are not an uncommon sight.

After passing the trading posts of Twin Arrows and Two Guns –the former still in business, the latter merely rubble– , I easily cross the concrete bridge over Canyon Diablo, a troublesome barrier to earlier expeditions.

Off to the right I see a sign for Meteor Crater. Approximately 47,000 years ago a large chunk of cosmic nickel-iron estimated to be about 150 feet across slammed into the earth at 40,000 miles per hour with a force greater than 20 million tons of TNT, creating a perfect bowl-shaped pit 570 feet deep and

4,100 feet in diameter. Pondering in silence at the crater's lip, the circumference of which extends almost two and a half miles, I am reminded of the fortuitous cataclysms the earth is sometimes subjected to. (See Chapter 3.)

In addition to scattering debris for miles in all directions, the crater recently has attracted a more modern sort of detritus: Meteor City, a single white geodesic dome with its attendant brightly painted tar paper teepees jarringly out of place here among all this desert sand and sky. A series of gaudy billboards visually hawks its dubious wares: Jewelry Made By Indians — Petrified Wood — Pottery — Moccasins — Kachina Dolls.

Tourists stop and gawk at "authentic" Western American knickknacks and plastic gewgaws (most likely made in Taiwan), while they suck down cold Mountain Dew. The middle-aged proprietors, however, are genuinely friendly in the tradition of the Old West. No doubt, the rugged, wind-burned couple finds that making a living in this lonely place can be a bit risky.

Behind the "city" a Santa Fe freight train with four engines blowing black diesel smoke to the pure air chugs west, hauling its heavy load and long history. On the other side of the interstate we see vestiges of Route 66 and remember Steinbeck's migrants from Oklahoma, who struggled across these harsh distances toward an uncertain destiny.

Now travelers to the Golden State pass motel rooms shaped like wigwams and the iconic golden arches of fast food modernity. Together these provide this remote Arizona vacation mecca with both a sense of exotic kitsch and a predictable ambiance of home—if not home cooking.

Here the eye might sweep over fifty miles from one horizon to the other. East and north of the Little Colorado River (whose headwaters flow from the White Mountains over a hundred miles to the southeast), the landscape becomes even more dramatic.

At the farthest reaches of this expansive vista float black nipples of volcanic rock. On the map their names are as exotic as those found in Grand Canyon: Montezumas Chair, Pyramid Butte, Sun Altar, and Star Mountain. Seemingly solid shafts of sunlight strike the earth, either right here in front of me or a dozen miles away. I might well be lost forever in this panorama as forlorn as the Pacific Ocean.

Breezing straight through the town of Winslow on the edge of the Navajo Reservation while humming the old Eagle's tune "Take It Easy," I pass the river at Sunset Crossing, once the only spot in the area you could safely ford. I stop briefly at Homolovi Ruins State Park. Here ancestors of the Hopi lived on the banks of the Little Colorado in a series of masonry and adobe pueblos from about the mid-thirteenth to the mid-fifteenth centuries. Refreshed by the small museum and well-organized visitors' center, I continue northward on the two-lane State Highway 87, also known as the Winslow-Toreva road.

Inching across the Navajo Reservation that completely encircles the Hopi Reservation and provides a buffer against the outside world, I enter the vestibule of some grand earth temple dedicated to the ancient spirits. An occasional octagonal hogan is swallowed up in the immensity of sacred space as I cross Tovar Mesa, headed straight for the heart of Hopiland. Alongside this traditionally Diné style of habitation frequently sits a trailer house with old tires on top to prevent its metal roof from popping and cracking in the fierce winds. Late afternoon shadows have brought the leviathan landscape into stark relief.

Finally I glimpse my destination. Extended from the giant hand of Black Mesa jutting down from the northeast, three great fingers of rock beckon. They are the three Hopi Mesas, isolated upon this high desert to which the Ancient Ones so long ago were led. (See map on p. 19.)

A whole cosmology along with an intricate religious cycle evolved here, grounded in the paucity of rainfall and the extremes of climate. Summer temperatures frequently exceed one hundred degrees. Winter winds blast down from the northwest, bringing snow and frigid air. Because no perennially flowing streams exist here, the people had to rely on local springs.

Gradually a number of villages grew, both at the bases and on the tops of the mesas. The pueblo of Oraibi located on Third Mesa (the one farthest west) is considered to be the oldest continuously inhabited community on the North American continent. It was founded about 1100 AD. (See photo on the bottom of p. 188.)

The ruins of even older villages are located in Canyon de Chelly, nearly seventy-five miles to the east. Over fifty miles due north of the Hopi Mesas, outlying communities were established. Known today by the Navajo names of Betatakin and Keet Seel, these cliff dwellings are located beneath spectacular archways of stone that frame and protect the Anasazi pueblos like massive, prehistoric proscenia.

Soon I'll make the ascent to the top of Second Mesa where are located the Hopi Cultural Center with its small museum, a tastefully decorated motel, and a restaurant that serves lamb and hominy stew along with traditional blue, paper-thin *piki* bread.

Yet for a few moments I stand below at the junction of Highway 264. The sun had set about an hour ago and Venus, a ball of liquid light on the western horizon, shimmers near the constellation Virgo. The huge orange globe of a full moon on the opposite horizon begins to push up into deepening shades of night.

High above in the old stone houses the lights are beginning to blink on. Some have been wired for electricity; a few others still use kerosene lamps. Nevertheless, the same language spoken in those rooms for nearly a millennium softly mingles with the fragrant pinyon smoke of evening fires.

I review the day's journey and the incredible diversity of landscape and resources. A simple yet inescapable question emerges: Why here? With all that this environment has to offer, why did the ancestors of the Hopi settle on these inaccessible mesas far from a regular, dependable source of that most precious element?

The Milky Way begins to arch overhead from south to north. A falling star glides across my field of vision as if the latter were a pool of water and the star an answer. I drink and feel a celestial wonder rising from deep within.

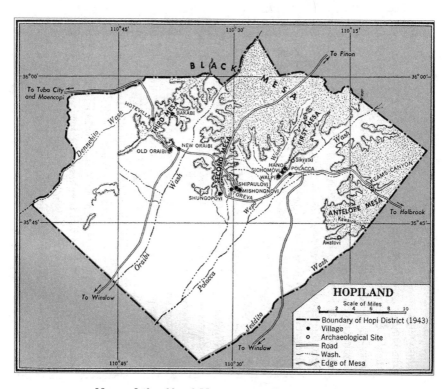

Map of the Hopi Mesas, northern Arizona.
[*From Laura Thompson,* Culture In Crisis]

Four Corners Region of the U.S.
with modern towns and major archaeological sites of the Anasazi (ancient Hopi and other tribes)
[from Wormington, *Prehistoric Indians of the Southwest*]

1. Ackmen	17. Keet Seel
2. Alkali Ridge	18. Kiatuthlana
3. Allantown	19. Kinishba
4. Aztec	20. La Plata River
5. Betatakin	21. Largo River
6. Butler Wash	22. Lowry Ruin
7. Canyon de Chelly	23. Mesa Verde
8. Canyon del Muerto	24. Pecos
9. Chaco Canyon	25. Piedra River
10. Durango	26. Puye
11. El Paso	27. San Juan
12. Flagstaff	28. Santa Fe
13. Gallina Creek	29. Taos
14. Governador Wash	30. Tyuonyi
15. Hopi Villages	31. Village of the Great Kivas
16. Kayenta	32. Zuñi

Chapter 1: Mystery Mesa—A Masonic Temple Beside An Ancient Hopi Village

"The primitive men met in no Temples made with human hands. 'God,' said Stephen, the first Martyr, 'dwelleth not in Temples made with hands.' In the open air, under the overarching mysterious sky, in the great World-Temple, they uttered their vows and thanksgivings, and adored the God of Light; of that Light that was to them the type of Good, as darkness was the type of Evil."

Albert Pike, *Morals and Dogma*

On top of the western edge of a low mesa located about a mile north of the Interstate 40 east of Winslow, Arizona, stands a huge white cross. (See map on p. 7.) I hop over a barbwire fence and begin walking over an abandoned cattle pasture, using the cross as a point of reference. In the distance to the west a windmill rises above a lone ranch house, a small clapboard structure that seems to belong to an earlier era.

Scrambling up the mesa without too much difficulty, I see that my destination is actually a Christian cross made of steel and painted white but now starting to rust. Measuring approximately thirty feet high and ten inches in diameter, it is positioned on the western end of an amphitheater at the top of seven steps leading up to it from the lower level. This oval-shaped amphitheater constructed of concrete is about 120 feet long, sixty feet wide, and a couple feet high, providing ample seating along its perimeter. At the eastern end is a three-tiered concrete platform with a single rose painted on it in white.

The platform and cross form an exact east/west axis. Also made of concrete, a shallow, tub-like depression measuring about six by eleven feet is positioned at the northwestern end of the amphitheater at an oblique angle to its axis. Many broken concrete pillars once held upright by rebar lie scattered in the

*Steel cross atop
the low mesa near
Homolovi State Park.*

*Right: amphitheater with
broken columns and tub.*

*Left: rose painted in white
on the concrete platform.*

*Foundation of the small
Cottonwood Creek Ruin.*

immediate area, emphasizing the sense of ruin. I surmise that this open-air temple was built before World War II, and it looks like a long time since anyone has been here.

Not more than twenty-five yards southwest of the cross, I come upon Cottonwood Creek Ruin, which the Hopi call Söhöptsokvi. (See the photo on the bottom of p. 22.) The Hopi, whose ancestors once lived in these villages now lying in ruins, have settled upon primarily three large mesas about fifty miles north of this site. The fifty-room pueblo village here was inhabited between about 1275 and 1375 AD. This masonry structure was relatively small in comparison to the Anasazi (ancestral Hopi) pueblo of one thousand or more rooms (known as Homol'ovi II) located nine miles to the northwest within the boundaries of Homolovi State Park.

The brown sandstone cliffs below the mesa top, however, abound in ancient petroglyphs. Rock art expert Sally Cole has found at least twelve examples of *katsina* iconography, which she meticulously records in a typically dry, academic style.

I found something more.

I recalled that Karen Berggren, the park manager at Homolovi, had simply mentioned that this was once a Masonic worship site. Park Ranger Kenn Evans, II, himself a Mason, later added that the site was constructed in the late 1920's or early 1930's by Winslow Masonic Lodge # 13 and its corresponding female organization, the Order of Eastern Star, Ruby Chapter # 6.

It is rather ironic that the outdoor gathering place for this secret society should be juxtaposed to a masonry pueblo. In fact, I've seen nothing like this in the entire Southwest. Sometimes mission churches were built next to ancient villages, like those in Pecos National Historical Park or Gran Quivira in Salinas Pueblo Missions National Monument, both in New Mexico, but otherwise this is an anomaly.

The petroglyphic evidence on the vertical cliffs below the pueblo ruin struck me as strange, even in the context of the Anasazi. (See the photos on the next page.) One petroglyph panel located within sight of the cross atop the mesa is particularly interesting. A figure with very large eyes and a crook or

Top photo: To the left are petroglyphs; to the right is a steel cross atop the mesa. Detailed photo below: At the far left is the alchemical symbol of Venus. Above that are three circles connected by two horizontal straight lines. Two circles connected by a line sometimes signify communication. The three circles may suggest communication between the three figures to the right. Zoomorphs do not necessarily represent horned animals but may instead connote direction. In this case the horns are pointed downward toward the snake. Does this mean that the three figures made a journey to the underworld? We probably will never know.

whip in its right hand holds hands with a smaller figure on the right, while a third figure farther to the right holds some kind of staff. To the left of this grouping is a sinewy snake juxtaposed with a clear alchemical symbol of the planet Venus (a circle surmounting a cross).

I also encountered a well executed checkerboard formed in an oval shape facing northwest—or more exactly, 300 degrees azimuth, the summer solstice sunset. The checkerboard pattern in Anasazi rock art is thought to symbolize the Milky Way, the pathway for the Warrior Twins.

In the context of Freemasonry, however, the black-and-white checkerboard found on the floor of each lodge represents night and day, or death and everlasting life. A checkerboard was also one of the ancient Egyptian hieroglyphs used to indicate a

Checkerboard petroglyph—the Milky Way?

scribe's palette, therefore connoting the wisdom of Thoth.

On one boulder I found an incised stick figure with a four-pronged headdress standing next to a lizard and perhaps a

scorpion. To the right and slightly above is a square divided diagonally with a crook carved into each section, each one facing opposite directions. The square represents "place" or "house," so this glyph may be expressing the House of the Two Crooks.

Humanoid with headdress, lizard, scorpion, and crooks inside square (pueblo symbol).

In Anasazi ideograms the crook or reed cane can symbolize fertility or the production of rain, and is frequently held by the ichthyphallic Kokopelli. The crook is also associated with the emergence legend, because the people had ascended through a reed from the previous Third World to the current Fourth World. (See Chaper 11.) In addition, it may symbolize either the ceremonial curved warriors' staff or the atlatl, the latter of which was the primary weapon used prior to the advent of the-bow-and arrow about 500 AD.

Although the Hopi word for shepherd's crook is *ngölö*, the semantically related word for "hooked" is *hewakna*. In Egypt *heq-t* referred to "shepherds crook," which represented divine sovereignty, rulership, and royal dominion or power. Osiris and other gods customarily held this crook, painted or inlaid with alternating dark and light horizontal bands. I might add that the striped pattern also mirrors the pharaoh's *nemes,* or royal headdress, similar to the one fashioned on Tutankhamun's coffin.

It is interesting to note that from the Hopi First Mesa village of Hano (Tewa) comes the Koshari, a figure with broad black-and-white bands painted horizontally on his body and a curved hoe somewhat resembling a crook in his left hand.

Simultaneously sacred and profane (like the aforementioned checkerboard dichotomy of eternal light and ephemeral darkness), this ritual clown participates with rowdy humor in the *katsina* dances. Known in his *katsina* capacity as a Koyaala, he is a singer to the Big-Horned Sheep *katsinam,* whose petroglyphic representation indicating rainfall I also found at the site. (See photo on the top of p. 27.)

On another panel nearby, a Mayan icon, the quetzal bird originating in the jungles over 1,500 miles to the southeast, has been carved next to a spiral. (See photo the in middle of the next page.) In Mayan symbology the feathered snake Kukulkan is associated with Venus as the Morning Star. The Aztecs called it Quetzalcoatl. Feathers and even whole birds were once part of an extensive trade network between Mesoamerica and the Four Corners region. Because of the light and shadow that fall across this stone, the petroglyph may be a solstice marker.

Spider Clan symbol (left), three bighorn sheep, Bear Clan symbol, and horned toad.

Petroglyph of quetzal and spiral.

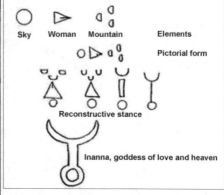

By Dr. Ali Akbar Bushiri, Bahrain University, 1989, Volume 18, ESOP (Epigraphic Society Occasional Publications.) [Thanks to Steven Bartholomew, from his article at: http://chargedbarticle.org/ phoenicians_in_utah.htm.]

Near the top of the aforementioned panel (on p. 24) are three circles arranged horizontally and connected with straight lines. These possibly represent three moons. Also depicted are a horned animal, a human footprint, and a stylized bird. Near the top right of the panel some sort of ritual artifact resembling a modern open-ended wrench has also been carved. (See photo on the bottom of p. 27.)

The fact that this petroglyph appears on the top of the same panel that has a Venus alchemical symbol reinforces the notion that this icon represents Inanna, goddess of fertility and love in Sumer and Dilmun (or Tilmun, now called Bahrain). Note what appears to be a triad of three natural holes above and slightly to the right of the petroglyph.

Although inverted from the usual position shown in Dr. Bushiri's work to represent "mountain," this triangle of holes may mean the same thing.

On yet another panel to the left of this grouping of glyphs are two more eerie figures. (See the photo below.) One has a rectangular body with geometric designs inside of it, clawed hands and feet, insect-like eyes and antennae. The figure on the left also has large eyes and a line coming out of the top of its head that ends in a circle. These two figures, both with upraised arms, are

Central figure with claws, antennae, large eyes, and rectangular body.

assuming what is known in Anasazi iconography as the prayer stance. In Freemasonry this posture with hands raised and elbows at right angles is referred to as the "Grand Hailing Sign of Distress." To the right of this pair are three "crows feet," representing the warfare motif consistent with the Warrior Twins previously mentioned.

Finally, I found an enigmatic petroglyph that may be a cross, a plumb line, the hilt of a Masonic sword, or even a stylized anthropoid. You decide. This rock art appears to involve three different periods. The most recent (and most crude) gives a scratched-in date of Jan. 7, 1915, roughly the time that the Masonic temple was constructed. The much older figure seems to be holding in its left hand (?) some sort of artifact. The head (or pommel) has an equilateral cross or star within it. Extended from the "neck" toward the figure's right side is a circle with what looks like horns on top. This figure is superimposed on a horizontal series of linked diamond shapes, which appear to be the oldest. These are thought to represent rattlesnakes, stars, or female puberty rites of passage. Again, you decide.

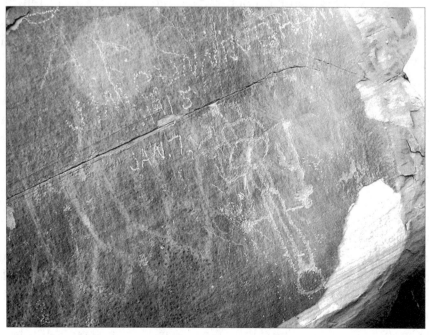

Cross-like figure over diamond shapes, "orb" in upper left corner.

Petroglyph (p. 29) enhanced.

Masonic sword

So what is going on here? We have a Freemasonry temple built in the early 20th century next to a pueblo constructed in the late 13th century. In the adjacent rock art we find Mayan, Egyptian, and possibly Middle Eastern symbology mixed with traditional Anasazi petroglyph designs.

Why did the Masons choose this particular mesa to erect their open-air worship center? Did the crumbling foundations of the village remind them of their sacred office? Did they recognize the non-indigenous iconography of this rock art, which resonated with specific elements in their holy ceremonies? Was an elite cabal operating within the rural Arizona Masonic lodge privy to arcane lore which dictated that the site be established precisely where we find its ruins today?

Remember that the Hopi name for this site means "cottonwood," whose root is used for the carving of *katsina* dolls. If one cuts crosswise into the limb of this tree, a perfect five-pointed star of Egyptian design is revealed. The Hopi word for cottonwood is *söhövi*. The Hopi word for star is *sohu*. Although

though the vowels are arbitrary, the Egyptian word for star (particularly those of Orion) is *sahu*. It is represented by the hieroglyph of a five-pointed star.

The deep mystery of this low mesa endures.

Above the painted "W" (for Winslow) on top of the mesa is the Freemasons' cross, where they once held open-air ceremonies.

Chapter 2: The Great Pyramids of Arizona

In the March/April 2001 issue of *Archaeology* magazine Farouk El-Baz of Boston University suggests that the three major pyramids of the Giza Plateau may have been modeled after the naturally occurring, conical hills found near the Kharga Oasis almost 150 miles west of Luxor. He also notes that the hieroglyph meaning "desert hills" has a pointed shape.

On the other side of the globe on the high desert of the American Southwest three great mountains rising out of the San Francisco Peaks eerily echo the Egyptian triad. The basaltic cinder cone of Humphreys Peak (12,633 feet in elevation, the highest point in the Arizona) dominates this arid landscape. The slightly lower Agassiz Peak (12,356 feet) is about a mile-and-a-half due south, while Fremont Peak (11,969 feet) rests a mile farther southeast.

These mountains are the winter home of the Hopi *katsinam*, intercessory spirits (rather than gods per se) that can take the form of any object or energy in the universe. Shortly after the winter solstice these divine beings travel to the three Hopi Mesas about 70 miles to the northeast.

There they assist in the germination and growth of corn, squash, beans and other crops during the spring and early summer. From late April until July Hopi men don *katsina* masks, not to impersonate these spiritual helpers but to actually become them. Dancing from dawn until dusk in the village plaza under the brutal desert sun, they coax moisture from the few clouds drifting overhead. Then upon the arrival of the monsoons in mid to late July, the *katsinam* return to their mountain habitat for the remainder of the year. (See Chapter 16.)

The relationship between the Egyptian desert hills and the three monumental pyramids may be similar to that between the volcanic mountains of Arizona and the three major Mesas where the Hopi settled about 900 years ago. Although the Mesas are natural landforms rather than human-made structures, the

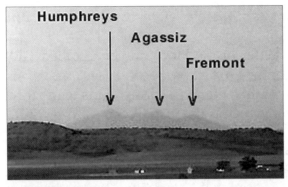

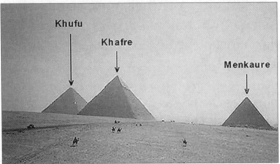

The San Francisco Peaks as seen from about 60 miles to the southwest. They are home to the Hopi spirit messengers called katsinam. The Hopi call these mountains Nuvatukya'ovi, which literally means "snow-butte-elevation."
They call Humphreys Peak (on the left) Aalosaka, to which the Al (Two Horn) Society prays. Agassiz Peak (in the middle) is called Pavayoykyasi, which literally means "water-rain." Fremont Peak (on the right) is called Omàuki, which literally means "cloud-home."

33

villages built atop them in effect sanctify the surrounding geography.

The center of the Hopi universe, called Tuuwanasavi, is comprised of the First Mesa, Second Mesa, and Third Mesa. Like the Giza pyramids, this area corresponds to the three stars in the belt of Orion, which is the visual focus and spiritual heart of the constellation. (See my book *The Orion Zone: Ancient Star Cities of the American Southwest*, Adventures Unlimited Press, 2006.) The Mesas function as natural ziggurats, lifting the supplicant even closer to the celestial forces that must be appeased in order to gain the blessing of rainfall. In his book *Pueblo: Mountain, Village, Dance*, scholar Vincent Scully explains the cultural significance of these landforms:

> "Once we see the mesas as more than simply man-chosen but almost literally man-constructed –at the very least, man-finished, as the Hopi see them– their true scale in Hopi culture opens to our understanding. We remember moreover that there is no semantic distinction for the Hopi between the works of nature and those of mankind. Hence the collaboration of the mesas is between commensurable beings. The Hopi are one with the rock."

For the Hopi the choosing and finishing of the Mesas is tantamount to the construction of the true pyramids of Egypt or the stepped pyramids of Mesoamerica.

The ancient Hopi petroglyph representing either "mesa" or "rain cloud" is the stepped pyramid, the exact copy of the Egyptian double staircase hieroglyph. The Egyptian word *Aatt* means both the necropolis of the pyramid region and the Other World. This word is formed by using both the double staircase hieroglyph and the pointed desert hills hieroglyph mentioned above.

The souls of the pharaohs took flight from their pyramids to the stars in the same way that the otherworldly *katsinam* soar upon terraced storm clouds. The Hopi word *aatsava* means "between" and the related word *atsva* means "above" or "on top," thereby stressing the verticality of the mesa/pyramid. Incidentally, the primary Egyptian example of the step pyramid is found at Saqqara. The Hopi word *saaqa* means "ladder" or "stepladder."

In both the Egyptian and the Hopi cultures, pyramids have an avian association. The Bennu bird, also known as the phoenix, was sometimes depicted as a gray heron perched atop a pyramid or obelisk. Periodically regenerated from its ashes, this sacred fowl is a primary symbol of eternal life. (See drawings on p. 70 and p. 133.)

The Bennu was even instrumental in the creation of the cosmos. The Shu Text describes "...that breath of life which emerged from the throat of the Benu Bird, the son of Rê in whom Atum appeared in the primeval nought, infinity, darkness and nowhere." [from R.T. Rundle Clark, *Myth and Symbol in Ancient Egypt*] Rising from the primordial abyss, the *hikê* (life-breath) is carried in the beak of the sacred bird of rebirth. It is perhaps more than a coincidence that the Hopi word *hik'si* echoes the Egyptian word *hikê* both phonetically and semantically.

The powerful image of a bird perched on the apex of a pyramid also appears on a Hopi artifact. In the early twentieth century near the present town of Winslow, Arizona, the renowned archaeologist Jesse Walter Fewkes unearthed a stone slab covering a grave at Chevelon Ruin. (See drawing on p. 36.)

On one side of the painted slab a white rectangular border with black on the outside encloses three isosceles triangles or pyramids of nearly equal size. On a yellow background each of these black pyramids contains a white square located near the base. A red bird, perhaps a macaw or parrot, is perched atop all three of these pyramids. Each of the stylized birds has a triangular body, the base of which forms its dorsal side. The body's apex (where its feet would be) touches each pyramid's apex. Only the bird at the center has eyes. Facing to the right, they all have bifurcated tails and curving beaks.

The four colors used on this slab are the traditional Hopi directional colors: yellow (northwest), black (southwest), red (southeast), and white (northeast).

Painted grave slab, Chevelon Ruin, Arizona.
[Twenty-Second Annual Report to the Bureau of American Ethnology]

What is the meaning of these figures? Fewkes suggests that the triangles are simply rain clouds. The white square at the heart of each pyramid signifies inner space, perhaps an Underworld of sorts. The three pyramids possibly designate the three major promontories in the San Francisco Peaks as well as the three Hopi Mesas.

The exotic parrot or scarlet macaw represents the moisture of the tropical jungles far to the southeast, the direction symbolically implied by their redness. This is also the region of the Mayan stepped pyramids. Used in prayer-stick making and other ceremonies, the multi-hued feathers of these birds may symbolize the nadir, the Underworld direction of "many colors." Whole bodies of both parrots and macaws have been found in burial sites throughout the American Southwest.

Fewkes also discovered other grave slabs at Chevelon with circular holes worn into them, ranging in size from a broomstick to an arm's width. Somewhat condescending vis-à-vis the modern Hopi, he remarks on their purpose: "Explanations more or less fanciful have been suggested for these perforated stones, one of which was that the rock had been placed above the body and the hole in it was for the escape of the soul or breath-body." [*Twenty-Second Annual Report to the Bureau of American Ethnology*, 1900-1901] Given this evidence, the three birds atop their pyramids in Arizona most likely performed same function as the journeying soul of the Bennu in Egypt did—that is, the omnipresent quest for immortality.

The Bennu iconography is also associated with the Benben, a black conical stone, possibly meteoric, used as a pyramidion, or apex of a pyramid. The Egyptian word *ben* denotes both the nominative "seed" or "semen" and the infinitive "to copulate" or "to impregnate"—all particularly apropos of the phallic obelisk.

In addition, the cognate *ben-t* means "cincture, belt, girdle," and might refer obliquely to Orion's belt. Alnitak, the most eastern star of the belt (corresponding to the Great Pyramid, or Khufu), literally means "the Girdle," while Mintaka, the most western star (corresponding to Menkaure) is called "the Belt."

As with every truly divine omnipotence, the positive aspects are counter-balanced with the negative. Hence the word *ben* also means "evil, wickedness," and the words *ben-t* or *benut* can also refer to "pustule, boil, abscess, or pus"—all of which are attributes of the Hopi god of the Underworld and death, Masau'u. (See drawing on p. 107.) No "b" sound exists in the Hopi language, but the related word *poengoe* means "boil" or "abscess."

Whether or not the pyramid-shaped hills of the Sahara served as models for the massive structures at Giza is still debated. Because the winter and summer homes of the *katsinam* are the San Francisco Peaks and the Hopi Mesas respectively, this tribe most likely acknowledged the relationship between the three natural mountains and the three ceremonialized Mesas. Similarly, these Mesas reflect the three belt stars of Orion.

Correlations abound, both on earth and in heaven. To live between the two realms upon this vast desert is to feel deep in one's bones the hermetic maxim "As above, so below."

Chapter 3: Meteor Crater—Arizona's First Bonanza?

Aerial view of Barringer Meteorite Crater, northern Arizona.

Deep Impact déjà vu

DATELINE: 47,000 YEARS BP, ARIZONA

As the fiery bolide streaked toward its terrestrial destination, the end of the world must have seemed imminent. This mass of cosmic nickel-iron measured 150 feet across and weighed 300,000 tons—nowhere near the size that caused the extinction of the dinosaurs at the end of the Cretaceous period. Nevertheless it slammed into the ground at 40,000 miles per hour with a force equivalent to 20 million tons of TNT. The impact and resulting explosion instantly created a bowl-shaped crater 570 feet deep and 4,100 feet in diameter with a circumference of nearly two-and-a-half miles.

The blast shook the ground and produced shock waves in the air for miles in every direction. Had the meteorite struck during the day, the eruption of ejecta, dust, and smoke would have risen high into the deep blue sky, obscuring the sun. If it hit at night, the blinding flash would have illuminated the landscape, turning darkness into broad daylight. Without warning, this bizarre astro-geological formation suddenly loomed more than 150 feet above the plane of high desert, much as it does today.

Barringer Meteorite Crater was named after Daniel Moreau Barringer, a Philadelphia lawyer and mining engineer who staked his claim in hopes of making a profit from this desolate stretch of sagebrush and red sandstone in northern Arizona. White settlers had already found meteoric iron in the form of spherules scattered over an area more than eight miles in diameter. Even larger meteorites had occasionally been discovered at the impact site and in nearby Diablo Canyon. One rock weighing 1,406 pounds is now housed in the Meteor Crater museum. (See photo on p. 41.)

Unfortunately for Barringer, no extractable meteoric metal was ever obtained. He and his Standard Iron Company had spent over $600,000 drilling test holes from 1903 until work was halted in 1929 with very little to show for his effort.

Based on these disappointing results, a majority of scientists have concluded that most of the nickel-iron of this meteorite was vaporized in the devastating explosion caused by the impact. Barringer's final hole, however, did show some promise but had to be abandoned due to poor drilling conditions. Moreover, some sources report substantial finds prior to his venture.

During the last decade of the 19th century both meteorite dealers and scientists were showing interest in Meteor Crater and Diablo Canyon. O. Richard Norton in his book *Rocks From Space* writes:

> "Meanwhile, miners hauled away tons of iron meteorites, loaded them on railroad cars, and shipped them to smelters in El Paso, Texas, where they were melted down and made into various iron products. Probably more than 20 tons were collected. There must be tools and machines still in use today that are made of celestial iron."

Nonetheless, this exploitation failed to exhaust the supply of meteoritic iron and nickel. Until the area was closed recently, meteorite hunters with metal detectors were still finding numerous specimens.

Did the estimated twenty to thirty tons of meteoric iron that had been collected equal the amount actually deposited by the deep impact? Or was this amount merely the remnants of an earlier recovery of sacred sky metal by the Anasazi?

Radiocarbon Dated Flyer

Perched on the lip of this natural wonder, we find it easy to grasp the immensity of the natural catastrophes our planet must sometimes endure. On the other hand, it's not so easy to imagine how we might have reacted to such an enormous event. Although many archaeologists believe that no humans could have witnessed the devastating creation of Meteor Crater, some recent findings point to the contrary.

About 330 miles to the southeast near Orogrande, New Mexico (about thirty miles south of the town of Almagordo), R. S. MacNeish of the Andover Foundation for Archaeological Research has uncovered evidence of human habitation that even predates the 47,000 YBP (years before present) window for Meteor Crater.

In Pendejo Cave, MacNeish found hearths, clay-lined pits, cordage, awls, serrated knives, pendants, and animal bones (including bison humeri) worked by hammer stones. He also unearthed a spear point embedded in the toe bone of an extinct species of miniature horse. Even traces of human hair as well as finger and palm imprints in fire-hardened clay were discovered. Radiocarbon dating of 171 samples consisting of charcoal, wood, bone, leaves, fiber, seeds, nuts, and feces indicate a range from a mere 350 YBP to an astounding 55,000 YBP, the earlier date being 8,000 years before the Meteor Crater impact.
[www.umass.edu/anthro/chrisman]

Could any of the Paleolithic peoples who ranged across what is now the Southwestern United States have seen the meteoric juggernaut crashing down from the heavens? The explosion caused by this massive chunk of space rock striking the Earth was a thousand times more powerful than the bomb dropped on Hiroshima. If humans

The Holsinger Meteorite is the largest discovered fragment of the 150-foot (45-meter) meteor that created Meteor Crater.

were anywhere near the impact forty-seven millennia ago, the colossal force would have surely provoked an overpowering awe.

It may even have caused the sort of numinous dread Rudolf Otto in his book *The Idea of the Holy* has termed *mysterium tremendum*, or "...'wholly other', that which is quite beyond the sphere of the usual, the intelligible, and the familiar, which therefore falls quite outside the limits of the 'canny', and is contrasted with it, filling the mind with blank wonder and astonishment."

In addition to temporarily changing the weather patterns, a detonation of this magnitude would have had an even more lasting effect. It would have radically altered the religious belief system of both those who actually experienced the cataclysm and those of succeeding generations who merely heard tales of it. A similar theological and mythological case occurred nearby with the milder Sunset Crater volcanic eruption less than a thousand years ago. The pervasive influence of meteoric lore and ritual connected with the more potent event would have been even profounder.

Either consciously or subconsciously, Meteor Crater's enduring presence has had a major impact (pun intended) on the religious system of those who eventually settled in this region. This crater is certainly one of the most recognizable geomorphologies in American Southwest. The Hopi call it Yuvukpu, which literally means "cave-in" or "sink"—essentially, a depression in the landscape.

The Hopi also have a Meteor Crater *katsina* akin to the Sunset Crater *katsina*, though the latter landform located thirty-six miles to the northwest is, as previously stated, volcanic in nature. (See photos on p. 199.) These two *katsinam* in turn are similar to another *katsina* called the Roast Corn Throwing Boy. This figure that frequently distributes roasted corn to the spectators at a dance ceremony wears feathers crossed horizontally atop his mask, which is half red and half yellow and is divided down the middle with a vertical white-and-black stripe. Carrying an *aaya*, or "moisture rattle," in his right hand (see photo on p. 224), he wears a bobcat costume with a spruce ruff, the latter worn to attract rain. As we shall see, storms and meteoric phenomena are mystically connected.

Meteor Cult Classics

A meteorite is a term designating a meteor, or shooting star, that has fallen to the ground. Throughout the ages meteorites have been the source of religious veneration for many different cultures worldwide.

Located in Mecca adjacent to the eastern corner of the rectangular Ka'ba, for instance, is the so-called Black Stone. An object of much obeisance, it is mounted within the foot-long, oval-shaped orifice of a large silver frame. This stone is most likely a meteorite. Legends say that this is the stone that God gave to Adam. It was once white, but the sins of countless pilgrims have turned it black.

Even earlier the Benben Stone was worshipped at Heliopolis in Egypt. According to Robert Bauval and Adrian Gilbert, co-authors of the provocative bestseller *The Orion Mystery*, meteoric iron was represented in the Pyramid Texts (some of the world's oldest writings) as both "the 'bones' of the star kings" and "the seed that is Osiris." The conical-shaped meteorite of the Benben Stone served as a prototype for the pyramidion placed at the apexes of both obelisks and pyramids. (It is interesting to note that the Hopi sky god Sótuknang is usually depicted as wearing a conical hat or peaked headdress. See drawing on p. 99.)

At another famous provenience, the Valley of the Kings, a gold-hilted sword with a blade of meteoric iron was found among the treasures of Tutankhamun. The mummified body of the young pharaoh also had a headrest made of the same celestial metal.

The Egyptian phrase for meteorite is *baa en pet*, or "iron of the sky," whereas *baa nu ta* means "earth-iron." (The similar-sounding Hopi word *paa-* means both "water" and "wonder.") The Egyptians conceptualized the sky, or the "floor of heaven," as a rectangular plate of iron, presumably of the celestial variety, held up by four pillars marking the cardinal points. Even the sun god Ra was thought to sit upon a throne of iron and not upon a throne of gold as one might suppose.

From this we can deduce that ancient Egyptians considered meteoric iron more valuable in both a spiritual and a material sense than the auriferous metal, at least in the pre-Dynastic Era. In fact, nine tubular beads of meteoric iron from 3500 – 3300 BC were found at El Girza north of Maidum.

From a slightly later period the Sumerians apparently esteemed both celestial and tellurian iron. V. Gordon Childe in his book *New Light on the Most Ancient East* observes:

"An object from the Royal Cemetery of Ur [2800 BC] turned out to be of meteoric iron. But a dagger blade from Khafaje had been smelted from terrestrial ores. It seems, however, to have been imported ready made, probably from Armenia. There, it can be deduced from later events, some barbarian tribe had discovered an economical method for smelting iron, but kept it secret successfully till the end of the IInd [2nd] millennium."

These "barbarians" must have been at least somewhat metallurgically proficient in order to work with ferrous metals over fifteen hundred years before the beginning of the Iron Age.

The oldest word for meteorite we know of is the Sumerian term KÙ.AN, which literally means "iron from heaven." An Assyrian text from 1900 BC describes a group of traders in Anatolia who apparently dealt in the precious metal. If we break down this word, KÙ means "field" or "earth" while AN relates to "sky"—thereby indicating the dual realms of meteorites. Surprisingly, the Hopi homophone *Kwan* refers to the One Horn Society, which is directly associated with their sky god. A synonym of KÙ.AN is the Sumerian *amutu*. The Hopi word *amu* means "they" or "them," while the suffix *-tu* is a dual indicator. "Many of them" could refer to those strange metallic sky creatures—the quintessential Other.

Meteoric iron was traditionally considered a celestial metal whereas copper was known as a terrestrial one. Both of these metals were known in the antediluvian era. In Genesis 4:22 Tubal-cain, the son of Lamech and grandson of Methusael (Methuselah), is described as "an instructor of every artificer in brass [a copper-zinc alloy] and iron..."

The first century Jewish historian Flavius Josephus says this about the original blacksmith: "But Tubal, one of his [namely, Lamech's] children by the other wife [Silla], exceeded all men in strength, and was very expert and famous in martial performances. He procured what tended to the pleasures of the body by that method, and first of all invented the art of making brass."

Whether or not Tubal Cain wears a conical hat like his Greek counterpart Hephaestus (or, as previously stated, the Hopi sky god), Josephus does not reveal.

Incidentally, the name Tubal is said by some to be the secret password of the Master Mason, the Third Degree of Freemasonry. In addition, the crude pun "Two Balls and Cane" is seen as a genital representation on a Masonic lapel pin, thus reinforcing the connotation of fertility.

The Old Testament also anachronistically refers to the

metal "steel." For instance, II Samuel 22:35 relates David's praise of the Lord: "He teacheth my hands to war; so that a bow of steel is broken by mine arms." Surely this does not refer to the same alloy we know today. Could this instead denote meteoric iron? If God gave him supernatural strength to defeat his enemies the Philistines, this is possible. In addition, the Hebrew word *paldâh* used in Nahum 2:3-4 refers to the steel or iron of chariots but is translated as "torches." Many cultures use the latter term to indicate falling stars.

America's Great Balls of Fire

Atlantean scholar Ignatius Donnelly claims that even the Mound Builders of North America, who were also disparaged by the term "barbarian," forged implements out of meteoric iron.

Among the now-extinct Skidi Pawnee of Nebraska, meteorites comprised the principal items of sacred medicine bundles, mainly because these celestial orphans were considered the children of Tirawa, the Supreme Being. (This name is similar to the Hopi sun god Tawa, or the Great Spirit. The Pawnee tribe is thought to have once lived in the American Southwest and shared many cultural and linguistic traits with the Hopi.) The Pawnee word for meteorite is *tahu:ru'*, but it also refers to "flint," "projectile point," and "tough skin" or "scalp." (The Hopi word *tahu'at* means "sinew" or "cartilage.") From this we may infer that the Pawnee conceptualized these obdurate sky children as having a hardened skin of iron.

The Hopi phrase *to'kpela owa*, literally "sky stone," specifically refers to a meteorite. For ceremonial purposes the Hopi grind up this fallen celestial metal as a pigment to paint their winter solstice prayer-sticks, to which eagle feathers are frequently attached. It makes sense, then, that Diablo Canyon (in Hopi, Ötöpsikvi, Canyon of the Strong Plant), where many round nodules of meteoric iron ore were found, is also one of the places where sacrificial golden eaglets are annually gathered. An eagle, of course, is conceptualized as an intermediary to the sky world, whereas a prayer-stick is an embodiment of its maker's direct petitioning of the gods.

The Anasazi also treated meteorites with reverence. One such sacred stone was discovered at Clear Creek Ruin atop a mesa in Arizona's Verde Valley. It was wrapped in a feather cloth and deposited inside a stone cyst on the northeast corner of a building, which is the direction of the summer solstice sunrise. Similar to the type used for infant burial, the grave of this fallen "sky child" also contained considerable pottery.

The meteorite itself, which weighed over 135 pounds, was determined to originate at Meteor Crater nearly 53 miles *to the northeast*. The fact that these ancient people hauled such a ponderous idol all that distance over rough terrain proves the spiritual importance of such objects.

Another example of the divine type of meteorite was found at the Casas Grandes pueblo ruin in Chihuahua, Mexico. Ritualistically wrapped up like a mummy, the meteorite obviously was a repository of great sanctity.

Some meteorite fragments also apparently served a more pragmatic or profane purpose, such as the well formed iron ax unearthed from a ruin in New Mexico. However, this is probably the exception rather than the rule.

A number of pit houses are reputedly located on the southwestern side of Meteor Crater, the direction from which the meteor apparently came. (I cannot report further on these structures because during my onsite investigation, two young men in a big pickup truck quickly chased me away from the privately owned area.)

The pit house is a pre-puebloan type of isolated domicile built prior to the 12th century in Arizona. (See the diagram on the top of the next page.) The circular or oblong structures were typically dug three to five feet deep and were about eight to twenty-five feet in diameter. Cut down with stone axes (or perhaps those of meteoric iron), four upright main timbers were imbedded in the floor to support cross-beams upon which rested a cribbed roof made of smaller sticks covered with brush, bark, grass, and mud. Earthen benches stretched around the

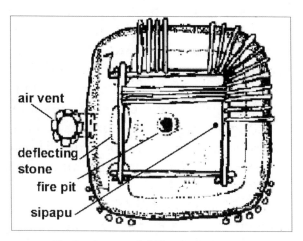

Early Anasazi / Hopi pit house.

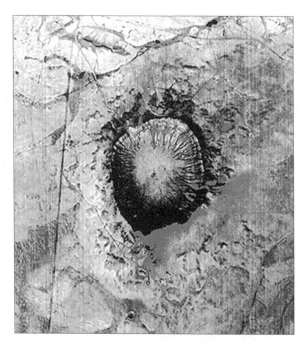

Meteor Crater as seen from directly above.

inner circumference of the pit house, and upright stone slabs sometimes lined the walls. Aligned on a south-to-north axis along the packed dirt floor were the following items: a ventilator shaft with a deflector stone, a fire pit, and a *sipapu*, or small hole symbolically leading to the underworld. Entry was by way of a ladder through the smoke hole in the roof.

Meteor Crater is not a perfect circle as one would expect but is instead a square with the corners rounded off. (See aerial photo on the bottom of p. 47.) The rounded corners of pit houses resemble the rounded corners of the crater. Thus, it is possible that Meteor Crater provided the initial model for these early dwellings.

If the blinding flash and smoke clouds from the gigantic cosmic rock plowing into *terra firma* were an arresting visual display, then its deafening roar must have been an equally arresting auditory one. Dr. E. C. Krupp in his book *Beyond the Blue Horizon* writes: "Sonic booms and the explosive flames of fragmentation accompany the object's descent. It lands with thunder. Even from a distance, fireballs are sometimes accompanied by sonic booms, and that, too, may have helped associate meteors and meteorites with thunderbolts."

The Hopi were certainly not immune from these types of parallels. In discussing the ritual usage of the rhombus, or bull-roarer, one authority states that the Hopi associate sound with meteorites, and its production is a means of incantation to bring rain. Both thunderbolts and fireballs evoke rain, which in the desert is synonymous with fertility. It comes as no surprise, then, that the Hopi phrase for shooting star is *soohu l`ööqö—soohu* meaning "star" and *l`ööqö* referring to "a bride who goes to the groom's house for a wedding ceremony," thus connoting fertility.

Hubert Howe Bancroft's multi-volume treatise titled *Native Races of the Pacific States* relates that the Spanish chronicler Tozozomoc found the Tarascans of Michoacan, Mexico, wearing "steel" helmets. Researcher Jeff Lindsay comments:

"Actually, a material that could be called steel was available in Mesoamerica, namely meteoric nickel-iron alloys. I found several examples of meteoric metals that compared to man-made steel listed, including haxonite from Canyon Diablo in Arizona, a face-centered cubic carbide related to tool steels and stainless steels. The point is that at least some meteoric metals can be called steel with technical accuracy, and could certainly be called steel by ancient peoples or modern translators, who might easily call a broad range of iron alloys 'steel.'"
[www.jefflindsay.com/LDSFAQ/FQ_metals.shtml]

As we previously noted, steel is referenced many times in the Bible. Was "steel," or meteoric iron, once a highly coveted precious metal prospected and traded in the same manner as gold and silver? If so, did Meteor Crater in Arizona serve as a major source of such ore?

Adventures in the Stone Trade

Recent findings in the Arctic indicate an extensive trade network dealing in celestial iron, the source of which was presumably the Cape York meteorite impact in northwestern Greenland. Research suggests that prehistoric Arctic dwellers began using metal tools about 1,200 years ago. On Little Cornwallis Island nearly 375 miles west of the Cape York event, forty-five iron artifacts –blades, harpoon points, needles, fasteners, etc.– were found in two Dorset villages dating to 450 AD. However, the trade network may be considerably older.

Arctic researcher Allen McCartney, professor of anthropology at the University of Arkansas, wonders whether this trade might have begun after the Cape York meteorite shower –estimated at a total of some two hundred tons– fell to Earth. Meteorite expert Vagn Buchwald suggests that the Cape York meteorite plummeted to Earth at least 2,000 years ago but may even have impacted as much as 10,000 years ago. The Meteor

Crater event, of course, is much older than even the earlier date.

In this context the claim that the Hopi migrations included the Arctic Circle prior to their final settlement in Arizona about 1100 AD does not seem so far fetched. The desert-dwelling Hopi refer to the Arctic region as the "Back Door of the Fourth World" blocked by snow and ice. In addition, Hopi pictographs dating back as much as 1,300 years were recently found in Grotto Canyon near Calgary, Alberta. Some depict the Humpback Flute Player (a.k.a. Kokopelli). The Canadian Indian people known as the Stoney First Nation have a legend of a foreign "rattlesnake people" who once lived among them. [www.farshores.org/alberhop.htm]

The Hopi Snake Clan is one of this tribe's primary clans. The Snake Dance and the Flute Dance, which alternate every August, are major rituals in the Hopi ceremonial cycle. (See Chapter 12.) Did the ancestral Hopi travel north in part to exchange the older sacred metal of Canyon Diablo for that of Cape York?

A substantial portion of the Arizona meteorite was either vaporized or atomized into countless droplets of molten metal. The question remains: What percentage of its 300,000 tons was so reduced? The survival of merely one tenth of one percent would have provided enough metal for a viable trading operation. If the Cape York meteorite weighing only two hundred tons could furnish a rich source of extraterrestrial ore, then perhaps the Barringer meteorite was a veritable bonanza, even if most of it was destroyed in its descent through the atmosphere and impact with the Earth.

This would have been more than a mere exchange of commodities as seen in modern terms, however. These meteorite fragments would have been perceived as nothing less than the sky spirits' metallic flesh, imbued with the mysterious power of the celestial realm. Graced by a visitation from these blazing star beings, the ancient inhabitants of Arizona would have experienced the same mixture of awe and reverence that normally accompanied any biblical theophany.

Chapter 4: Chaco Canyon—Ancient City of the Dog Star

A Mystery of the Desert

Chaco Canyon is the jewel of all the ancient pueblo sites in the American Southwest. The people who one lived there were formerly known as the Anasazi, a Diné (Navajo) word for "Ancient Enemy." Now they are more correctly identified with the Hopi name Hisatsinom, or "Ancient Ancestors."

Located along Chaco Wash, an intermittent stream in the arid and desolate San Juan Basin of northwestern New Mexico, this awe-inspiring group of a dozen large pueblos reflects a high degree of cultural synthesis. As Edgar Lee Hewett, one of the early archaeologists at Chaco Canyon, remarks in his book *Ancient Life in the American Southwest*: "The mystery of the desert reaches its climax when, in the center of this area a hundred miles square without a flowing stream of any sort, we come upon a group of ruins such as Egypt and Mesopotamia and Asia Minor and Middle America have been supposed to monopolize."

Multi-room, multi-story masonry pueblos exhibiting impressive architectural styles and craftsmanship were built in Chaco Canyon. The "great house" later named Pueblo Bonito consisted of a D-shaped pueblo with over eight hundred terraced rooms, some of which were five stories tall. This pueblo surrounded by immense plazas could have provided shelter for 1,200 inhabitants. In fact, it was the largest "apartment house" in the world until a larger one was built in New York City in the 1880's.

The walls were erected using a core of rubble and an ashlar veneer designed with great skill and esthetic sensibility. Then, surprisingly, these walls were finished inside and out with a layer of plaster, hiding their exquisite quality.

**Trail approaching Pueblo Bonito,
the largest village in Chaco Canyon.
Behind it rock debris has fallen off the cliff.**

Pueblo Bonito: kiva in foreground, hikers high atop cliff.

Chaco windows demonstrate sophiscated construction techniques and an eye for aesthetics. Why, then, did they plaster over the walls?

Left: Note thick walls at Pueblo Bonito. Corner window faces winter solstice sunrise.

Right: The low wall of Pueblo Bonito (center of photo) is oriented almost precisely on a north-south axis.

Begun in the early 900's, construction in Chaco Canyon entered a boom phase sometime after 1030 AD. Some authorities cite the date 1055 as the beginning of a period called the Florescent Bonito Phase (named after the main pueblo). This was the year following a massive supernova explosion seen for weeks across the Southwest and depicted in the canyon's rock art. Whether or not the construction surge and the celestial event are causally related is moot.

Author and artist Thomas E. Mails at any rate claims that "...by A.D. 1050 the Chaco people had ascended to the peak of their golden age. Living conditions were in many ways better than those of the middle classes of Europe and at least equal to the best conditions in Mesoamerica." [*The Pueblo Children of the Earth Mother*]

An estimated 215,000 trees logged from forests located between twenty and fifty miles away were used in the construction of all the pueblos at Chaco. An estimated fifty million pieces of sandstone were quarried and transported in order to build just one of the major village structures alone, Chetro Ketl. Hence, a greatly efficient cooperative labor system must have been in place to accomplish such prodigious tasks.

A system totaling more than three hundred miles of ceremonial roads was also constructed. Resembling the Mayan *sacbes* ("white roads") of southern Mexico, some of these roads leading into Chaco were over sixty miles long and thirty feet wide, all for a people who did not know the use of the wheel.

Because religious ritual was omnipresent in the life of the Chacoans, many communal great kivas or tower kivas were incorporated into the architecture. A kiva is basically a semi-subterranean prayer chamber. The ladder protrudes from the kiva's overhead hatchway, allowing for entry and exit of the ceremonial structure. The kiva also has cosmological significance in that it represents the previous Third World. The Hopi conceptualize these serial worlds as being stacked one on top of the other with the First World at the bottom. (See photo on p. 115.)

One great kiva called Casa Rinconada is nearly sixty feet in diameter, providing an area where a whole community could

worship. (See photo on the top of p. 161.) In terms of the smaller clan kivas, a ratio of one kiva to every twenty-nine domiciliary
or storage rooms has been found, suggesting an exceedingly rich
ceremonial life.

As Above, So Below.

In my book *The Orion Zone: Ancient Star Cities of the
American Southwest* (Adventures Unlimited Press, 2006), I
describe a correlation between the stars of Orion and the pattern
of ancestral Hopi villages in Arizona. This "terrestrial" Orion
closely mirrors its celestial counterpart, with prehistoric "cities"
corresponding to every major star in the constellation. Its belt is
represented by the three Hopi Mesas, where the Hisatsinom settled about 1100 AD.
[Refer to The Orion Zone Website, second map:
www.theorionzone.com/maps.htm]
Near the top of the map, the blue-white supergiant Rigel
(Orion's left leg) correlates to Betatakin ruin at Navajo National
Monument, while the faint yellow star Saiph (his right leg) is
represented by the ruins in Canyon de Chelly National
Monument. The red supergiant Betelgeuse (his right shoulder)
corresponds to Homolovi Ruins State Park near Winslow,
whereas the blue giant Bellatrix (his left shoulder) is equated
with the ruins at Wupatki National Monument north of
Flagstaff.
Like the Orion Correlation at Giza in Egypt, this terrestrial Orion is upside down compared to the way we see Orion in
the sky.
Chaco Canyon is located nearly 140 miles east of First
Mesa, which corresponds to Alnitak in Orion's belt. In this
ground-sky pattern Chaco, the largest grouping of pueblos in
the Southwest, corresponds to Sirius, the brightest star in the
heavens located in Canis Major, the Great Dog.
Although it has only twice the mass and diameter of our
own Sun, Sirius is forty times more luminous. As a white dwarf,

its spectral type is A0 with a surface temperature of about 10,000 degrees K. It has a magnitude of minus 1.42 and is only 8.7 light-years from Earth. Sirius is a binary star; its companion Sirius B has a magnitude of 8.65 and is invisible to the naked eye.

Many cultures throughout the world associate both the star and its constellation with canines. For the Greeks Sirius was the head of the Great Dog who was always waiting behind Orion, ready to fetch the game that his master hunts; hence, it was called the Dog of Orion. This asterism was also deemed Janitor Lethaeus, the Keeper of Hades. In other words, it is Cerebus of the southern sky who watches over the lower heavens where demons reputedly live.

In Arabia, Sirius was known as Al Kalb al Jabbar, the Dog of the Giant. In an early Hindu myth it was Sarama, one of the Twin Watch-dogs of the Milky Way. The *Rigvedas* also referred to it as Sivanam, the dog who awakens the Ribhus (gods of the mid-air) and summons rain.

To the Nordic peoples Sirius was the she-wolf Greip, who bore the god Heimdall, the Shining One. The Assyrians recognized it as Kal-bu Samas, the Dog of the Sun, whereas the Phoenicians saw it as Hannabeah, the Barker. In Egypt this spiritually significant star was associated primarily with the goddess Isis, wife of Osiris (Orion), but was also linked to the jackal-headed god Anubis. The heliacal rising of Sirius (which in 3000 BC occurred during the summer solstice) coincided with the flooding of the Nile; hence, it was also called the Nile Star.

In China this star was known as T'ien-lang, the Celestial Jackal or Wolf of the East, while what we conceive of as Canis Major's hindquarters was called Hou-Chi, the Bow and Arrow. In another Chinese legend from the Sung Dynasty (which, incidentally, is contemporaneous with the span of residence in Chaco Canyon), the stars just mentioned represent Chang-hsien, the Patron of Child-Bearing Women, who offered up prayers to him for fecundity. If a woman conceives, it means that this white-faced, bearded figure customarily seen with a young boy by his side has shot the Heavenly Dog with his bow-and-arrow.

Paralleling this latter connotation, the Babylonians

referred to Sirius as Kakkab kasti, the Bow Star, while the Persians called it Tir, the Arrow. The Egyptian round Zodiac of Denderah depicts the goddess Sati (or Satis) with a bow-and-arrow riding in the celestial barque of Sothis (Isis/Sirius). In one version of Sumerian mythology, Sirius was called KAK.SI.DI., or the Arrow-Star. The sixth tablet of the Sumerian epic *Enuma elish*, however, refers to a "Bow Star," which is called the lordly brother of the Annunaki, a group of fifty celestial deities among whom he was placed by the great god of heaven Anu.

In another context Sirius was known as the Scorcher, referring to its prominence at dawn during the "dog days" of summer. This torrid season in particular was believed to bring fever, pestilence, and madness. The Assyrians furthermore saw the sidereal point as Su-ku-du, the Restless, Impetuous, or Blazing One. The Arabic Al-Shi'ra reflects the Sanskrit Surya, or Sun God, both literally meaning "The Shining One." Sirius was also known in many cultures as the Sparkling One, due to its brilliant scintillation. In former times, however, numerous references describe it as fiery red or ruddy, hence its name *rubra canicula.*

The extinct Skidi Pawnee of eastern Nebraska (a tribe with cultural and linguistic similarities to the Hopi) saw Sirius as the Wolf Star, god of war and death. Its name was *ckiri ti'u:hac*, or Fools-the-Coyotes, a reference to the star rising before the Morning Star, thereby tricking coyotes or wolves into premature howling. In fact, the name of the Skidi band of the Pawnee literally means "wolf."

The Hopi word *Ponotsona*, meaning "The One That Sucks From the Belly," is the name for Sirius. Although this term does not specifically associate the star with a canine, it clearly designates a mammal. For the Hopi and probably their ancestors, Sirius is apparently a guardian star involved with hunting magic and the burgeoning of the animal kingdom.

To sum up the archetypal connotations of this asterism, I have discussed a cross-cultural, global connection with two well-defined motifs: (1) the dog (or other mammals) and (2) the bow-and-arrow.

How does all this relate to the people who resided in or made pilgrimages to Chaco Canyon?

Sons of the Dog

The Gran Chichimeca was the Spanish name of the vast territory north of Mexico where putative nomadic barbarians lived. This generic term designates a group of people known as the Chichimecs, literally "Sons of the Dog." Instead of being a unified tribe, the Chichimecs were a loose aggregate of diverse bands whose character has been compared to that of the Germanic tribes who swept down from the north in the 5th century AD to attack Rome.

Eric R. Wolf (his name a coincidence?) states that:

> "'Chichimec'… means literally 'descendants of the dog,' and was used in one sense to refer to the hungry nomads who inhabited the wide-open spaces north of the cultivated fields, the hunters and gatherers who used the *bow and arrow* [italics added], dressed in deer skins, and ate raw meat." [*Sons of the Shaking Earth*]

As the bellicose group from which the Aztecs are believed to have later descended, the Chichimec hordes migrated down from the north, eventually reaching the Valley of Mexico sometime between the 11th and the beginning of the 14th century.

The Chichimecs are frequently contrasted with the Toltecs, whose primary urban center was Tula (north of Mexico City in the State of Hidalgo) and who in that specific region and time period were considered the epitome of refined civilization.

Eventually the Chichimecs and the Toltecs forged an alliance, each helping the other. Basically the Chichimecs provided military aid and the Toltecs contributed the amenities of relative cultural refinement. According to legend, the figures of Mixcoatl and Xolotl were both attributed as the first to use the bow-and-arrow in Mesoamerica rather than the less accurate atlatl.

Mixcoatl, or "Cloud Serpent," was the chieftain-made-god of the Toltecs whose son founded Tula (also called Tollan, or "Place of Reeds"). This city's life span exactly corresponds to that of Chaco Canyon, about 900 – 1200 AD. The son was named Ce Acatl Topiltzin (a.k.a. Quetzalcoatl), who buried his assassinated father Mixcoatl at a site called the Hill of the Star, perhaps the snow-capped, extinct volcano named Orizaba. The presence of Topiltzin was frequently marked by an arrow that would pierce a tree, thereby creating a cross.

Xolotl was the likewise apotheosized chieftain of the Chichimecs who invaded the Valley of Mexico in 1224 AD (shortly after Chaco was abandoned). In his deific manifestation he was the dog-headed god who accompanied the dead to the Underworld, as well as the controller of lightning (arrows?).

Xolotl's son Nezahualcoyotl, which in the Nahuatl (Aztec) language means "Hungry Coyote," was the philosopher-poet-engineer-king who founded Texcoco (east of Mexico City). He erected a ten-zone pyramid with an exterior black roof covered with stars. In a style similar to the monotheistic reformations of the Egyptian pharaoh Akhenaton who reigned in the fourteenth century BC, Nezahualcoyotl dedicated this Mexican structure to an invisible god to whom no blood sacrifices were permitted. Hence, we see the motifs of both dog and bow ranging south of the U.S. border as well.

Given the above evidence, the Chichimec-Toltec contact with the Hisatsinom is self-apparent. Obviously the two groups had some connection, but the exact nature of the interface is unclear. Perhaps the foreign group merely traded with the Hisatsinom at Chaco Canyon, or possibly they played a more crucial role—that of adminstrator or even architectural director.

Many of the buildings there were constructed using strict archaeo-astronomical principles. In the less than favorable environment of Chaco Canyon, the Dog People may have managed to construct during the 10th and 11th centuries more than a dozen major pueblos, half of which are bow-shaped.

For example, the axis of Pueblo Alto is 1.1 degrees west of due north, while the axis of Tsin Kletzin to the south is one degree west of due north. Separated on a north-south line by about two-and-a-third miles, both of these bow-shaped structures are metonymically shooting their arrows –their spiritual energy– to the south toward the cosmological zenith, geographically represented by the ruins of Kin Ya'a, a Diné name meaning "House in the Sky." This was actually a four-story tower kiva located about thirty miles south of Chaco.

More perfectly though, the axis of the likewise bow-shaped (or D-shaped) Pueblo Bonito is only two-tenths of one degree east of due north, a geodetic exactitude approaching that of the Great Pyramid in Egypt. The cultural *sine qua non* of the bow icon is reinforced by a correlating petroglyph surmounted by a spiral found close to the "Sun Dagger" on nearby Fajada Butte. (See photo on facing page.)

In contrast to the southward emphasis of Pueblo Alto and Tsin Kletzin, Pueblo Bonito is shooting its arrow north toward the nadir, paralleling the Great North Road that leads to the Sipapuni, the entrance to the Underworld. In this case, I am talking specifically about Kutz Canyon located about thirty miles north of Chaco.

Whereas many of the Hisatsinom architectural structures in the Southwest are solstitially aligned, those at Chaco that were just mentioned reflect via their north-south orientation the vertical tripartite axis of the Underworld, earth, and heaven. As the sacred Center-place, or *axis mundi*, Chaco Canyon most certainly functioned as the ceremonial fulcrum between nadir and zenith, Underworld and starry realm.

A Welter of Words and Clans

A discussion of both linguistics and clan groupings might provide further light to traverse this shadowy terrain between the Chichimecs and the Hisatsinom.

The contemporary Hopi share the same language family with the ancient Chichimecs, specifically, Uto-Aztecan. As to the name of the latter group, however, the Hopi have no "ch" sound in their language; the closest phoneme is "ts-." The Hopi word *tsìit-si'rum* means "baring teeth." (*Tsìitsi* means "to divide" or "tear part.") The word *mak* means "hunt." If we combine these two Hopi words, the result sounds like the word Chichimec. "To hunt with bared

Fajada Butte, where the "Sun Dagger" and D-shaped petroglyphs are located.

teeth" clearly connotes a canine trait.

Incidentally, the Hopi term *tsìikwi* means "to straighten" (as in arrows). Hence, these Sons of the Dog are associated in the Hopi language with a specifically dog-like characteristic and possibly with the act of arrow-making. In yet another context we find a recurrence of the dual mythological motifs –dog and arrow– that are widely linked with the star Sirius.

What do the Hopi call Chaco Canyon, that most massive of Hisatsinom ruins? Both the ethnographic data and the contemporary Hopi are somewhat reticent in this regard. The word "Chaco" is apparently derived from the Spanish. For instance, the name *Chaka* was found inscribed on a Spanish map of the region dating from 1774. Did the Spanish get this term from the Diné, who in turn obtained it from the descendants of the Chacoans? At this point it is impossible to tell.

The meaning for the Spanish word does have some interesting resonances, however. *Chacal* means "jackal," and *chacoto* means "noisy mirth" or "racket"—the sound associated with the New World equivalent of the jackal, namely the coyote. In addition, *chacuaco* means "crude, boorish." *Chacra* (as in Chacra Mesa above Chaco Canyon) means "small farm," and *chagra* means "a person from the country, a peasant." All these connotations could certainly apply to the Chichimecs.

You recall that Chaco Canyon lies about 140 miles northeast of the Hopi Mesas. The Hopi terms *hopoq* and *hopqöy* both refer to the direction of northeast. Hópoko is known as the place of the summer solstice sunrise, at this latitude occurring at the azimuth of about 60 degrees. ("Azimuth" is the arc of the horizon measured in degrees from the north point.) The word *hopoqki* is the... "Northeastern Pueblo community or country where they bring back turquoise bracelets." Although this is a possible reference to the turquoise mine near the Rio Grande, it most likely refers to Chaco, especially since the Los Cerrillos mine is technically east-southeast of the Hopi Mesas. After all, Chaco Canyon was the undisputed clearinghouse for the turquoise trade in the Southwest.

More importantly, the proper noun Hopqöy means "a mythical place in the northeast where marvelous building was accomplished by *powaqam*, 'sorcerers'. The suggestion has been made that this may have to do with the Chacoan ruins." [Ekkehart Malotki, *Hopi Dictionary*] This term resonates with many of those found in the linguistic complex we have been describing. For instance, the Hopi word *pok* (or *poko*) means "dog," but it is also a homonym for "shoot arrows." *Hoohu* (pronounced "ho-o-hu") means "arrow" (and, metaphorically, "semen".) In addition, *hopaqa* refers to a small reed used in making arrows.

The only term for any of the Chacoan ruins that appears to have a Puebloan origin is Hongo Pavi. (The others are either Navajo or Spanish.) As a possible corruption of the Second Mesa village name Songòopavi, or "the place by the spring where the tall reeds grow," the word for this small ruin in Chaco Canyon is related to the Hopi word *hongap*, or "arrow material." (*Hongaptsikwànpi* is the grooved stone used for straightening arrows.) Although these numerous cognates create somewhat of a verbal blurring, they all enigmatically point to the Dog Star Sirius with its efficient weapon of choice.

Just as the Chichimecs should not be viewed as a discrete native tribe, what we know collectively as the Hopi is comprised of a number of sundry clan groupings, or phratries, and presumably the Hisatsinom society was structured in the same manner. In other words, the clan system has been an integral part of the Hopi polity since the first villages were constructed, and probably even before that time.

Prior to the 1906 split between Traditionals and Progressives at the village of Oraibi, there existed twenty-four separate clans grouped into nine different phratries. One phratry in particular seems to have all the thematic variations that we have been talking about. According to scholar Richard Maitland Bradfield, "The Reed-Greasewood-Bow grouping is evidently associated with the fall, with the waxing of Orion and the Pleiades in the night sky, with the onset of cold weather, with hunting (through the use of *bow and arrow,* and the link with *dogs* [italics added]), and, secondarily, with war." [*An Interpretation of Hopi Culture*] Of course, the contiguous Canis Major should be added to the configuration of prominent constellations.

The Reed-Greasewood-Bow phratry's *wuya,* or clan deity, is Pokonghoya, the Elder War Twin. Note the word *poko,* or "dog," in his name. As chief of both warriors and dogs, the Reed Clan sponsors a prayer-stick making ritual during Soyal, the Hopi winter solstice ceremony. On each of the four walls of its clan house, a totemic mural is painted. On the northeast wall –the direction of Chaco Canyon from the Hopi Mesas– a wolf is depicted. This contradicts the normal totemic associations: usually the wildcat is placed in the northeast while the wolf is found in the southeast.

In the tradition of the Reed Clan the legendary home of the Dog People is a village in the east (northeast?) called Suchaptakwi. (Possibly formed from *sutsep,* "always" and *taqyuwsi,* "warrior-like.") This is probably a reference to Chaco Canyon.

The Greasewood Clan refers to the wood traditionally used to make the phallic dibble. This prized item is ultimately placed upon a man's grave as a ladder whereby his spirit-breath may climb down to the Underworld. (Incidentally, the Hopi word for dibble is *sooya.* The related word *sootanta* means "to be having intercourse with a woman." Coincidentally, both words are cognates of *soohu,* or "star.")

The Bow Clan was the leader of the Hopi Third World,

which was destroyed because of its wickedness by an immense flood. According to the late Thomas Banyacya of the Coyote Clan in Oraibi, the chief of the Bow Clan was also father to a pair of sons who were given charge of the *owatutuveni*, or stone tablets: "Now the Great Chieftain who led the faithful one[s] to this new life and land was a Bow clan and he had two sons who were of the same mother.... It was to these two brothers [that] a set of sacred stone tablets were given and both were instructed to carry them to a place the Great Spirit had instructed them." [quoted in Rudolph Kaiser, *The Voice of the Great Spirit*] (See Chapter 17.)

The connection of the Bow Clan with the custody of the sacrosanct stone tablets illustrates the importance of this clan in Hopi history. Both the Bow Clan and the closely related Kokop-Coyote phratry are in charge of Wuwtsim, or the New Fire Ceremony, held in November. Originating from the northwest, this phratry includes such clans as the Gray Wolf, Fire, and Agave.

This section of this chapter has shown how the welter of words and clans that related to the Chichimecs of Chaco Canyon directly points both to dogs and instruments of archery, the same themes that recur vis-à-vis Sirius. The final section will reveal a more violent propensity of the people that once lived at Chaco.

A Meteor of Bloody and Brilliant Arrogance

Every society has its darker side (some more than others), and the Hopi tribe, despite its magnificent and complex religious rites, is no exception. This shadow-nature is specifically manifested in the canine context that we have been discussing. Again quoting Bradfield: "There is... an affinity of certain animals, notably wolf and coyote, with witchcraft. Both coyote and wolf are regarded as sources of *duhisa*, witch power." From the preceding section you will recall the connection between Chaco Canyon and sorcery.

The Yaya Ceremony was based on the shamanistic shape-shifting, or the ability to change into various animals. Those who performed this ritual obtained their power from the spirit people of the animal kingdom. Their abilities included fire-walking and seeing over long distances in the dark. In *Book of the Hopi*, Frank Waters writes: "About midnight a fog came in so thick the people could not see one another. 'This is a sign that your ceremony has been perfect,' said the leader of the animals. 'From now on your movements will be secret. Your protecting star will be Ponóchona [also spelled Ponotsona, or "Sucks From the Belly"—meaning a mammal], the star you must ask to increase the animal kingdom on earth." The star is, of course, Sirius.

The early ethnographer A. M. Stephen identifies the word *ya'yatü* as a Keresan word meaning "mother," thus emphasizing the nursing aspect of Sirius. He states that this was, on the other hand, a "phallic, wizard society" which performed many supernatural feats, such as falling off high cliffs without being harmed. Eventually, however, the Yaya ceremony was corrupted and a cult of sorcerers developed. Like practitioners of witchcraft the world over, these Southwestern sorcerers would frequently cause bad weather, personal misfortune, disease, or even death. In order to survive, some of these people would be forced to kill others, even their own relatives.

Recently a very dark scenario regarding Chaco Canyon has emerged. Archaeologist Christy Turner used osteological forensics to suggest that a cult of cannibalism centered on Chaco Canyon began during the time this ancient city was developing. In his book *Man Corn*, he states his theory:

> "...we propose that the majority of Chaco Anasazi cannibal episodes resulted from acts of violent terrorism, possibly combined with ritual, incited by a few zealous cultists from Mexico and their descendant followers who possessed the deadly ceremonial knowledge of certain Mexican socio-religious and warfare practices. If we are right, then it follows that the strong spatial and temporal concordance between Anasazi cannibalism and Chacoan

great houses points also to a Mexican stimulus for rapid development of things Chacoan."

He believes that these warrior-cultists also gained the social control needed to direct the construction of the colossal buildings in Chaco by performing human sacrifice dedicated to the Mesoamerican gods Tezcalipoca and Xipe Totec. The former was the jaguar (or sometimes eagle) god of the sun who wore a smoking mirror on his chest by which he observed and judged the deeds of men; the latter was the maize god of spring who wore a flayed human skin. Needless to say, this controversial hypothesis infuriates many contemporary Puebloan people.

Ultimately, we can only speculate on the complex interrelationships and branching migrations of native groups that occurred over a millennium ago around the Four Corners area. Are the two contemporary Hopi phratries mentioned above –the Reed-Greasewood-Bow and Kokop-Coyote– either offshoots of or remnants of the Chichimecs, or were they merely influenced by contact with the latter? Did a small but imperious cult of Toltecs actually infiltrate the erstwhile egalitarian and relatively pacifistic Hisatsinom culture, thereby instituting a despotic regime that used a campaign of psychological terror and coerced labor to construct the great pueblos at Chaco Canyon?

As David Roberts' book *In Search of the Old Ones* eloquently asks: "Had the Chaco Phenomenon been a spectacular aberration, a two-hundred-year meteor of bloody and brilliant arrogance flashing and dying across the blank sky of centuries in which the Anasazi co-existed in harmony?"

Although many questions have been left unanswered, I can say with impunity that the Dog People once lived at the geographic point whose celestial correlative is the Dog Star Sirius. Whether or not the more grisly hypothesis regarding Chaco Canyon is accepted, the constellation of recurrent cultural motifs I have discussed –namely, canine, bow-and-arrow, and fire– nonetheless reflects the archetypal resonances of the constellation Canis Major.

*Architectural "echo"
at Pueblo Bonito,
the largest ruin
in Chaco Canyon.*

*Adjacent rooms
with windows
at Aztec Ruins Nat'l Mon.,
also in New Mexico.
This site 50 miles north
of Chaco Canyon is on
the same longitude.
In the foreground is
the author's daughter,
Zia Ann Descault David,
born in Santa Fe.*

Chapter 5: Phoenix—Masonic Metropolis In the Valley of the Sun

Skyline of Phoenix, Arizona, looking north toward urban mountains.

Turquoise swimming pools when seen from the air shimmer like a squash blossom necklace on a jet setter's tanned breast. Imported palm trees tower over a surrendering army of native saguaros, while skyscrapers of steel and glass gleam in the distance like mirages. This western metropolis pushes out more than up though, sprawling over 450 square miles.

With the sixth largest population in the U.S., the Valley of the Sun attracts all kinds: retirees golfing their way into oblivion, snowbirds fleeing subzero winters, young construction workers cashing in on frenzied economic growth. Shopping malls, parking lots, concrete clover leafs, subdivisions, and apartments relentlessly eat away at the mesquite and ironwood at the rate of "an acre an hour."

Summer temperatures routinely soar over 100 degrees. Before air conditioning, the Sonoran Desert must have been unbearable. Where once rattlesnakes, scorpions, centipedes, tarantulas, and Gila monsters reigned over the sand, now gang wars, drug money, prostitution, Mafia murders, and other urban amenities civilize the asphalt.

In other words, an aura of the foreign and bizarre pervades Phoenix. What exactly attracted early settlers to this hard and uncompromising landscape?

A Local Habitation and a Name

In the autumn of 1867 Bryan Philip Darell Duppa and other founding fathers of the fledgling city were picnicking on the platform mound at Pueblo Grande near what is now the intersection of East Washington and 44th Streets near Phoenix Sky Harbor airport. Someone asked what this future municipality should be named.

A Southerner in the party wanted to call it Stonewall, after the Confederate general. Another idly offered the appellation Salina, meaning "salt marsh," but that too was voted down. Then Duppa spoke: "This canal was constructed in an age now forgotten. Prehistoric cities lie in ruins all around you. A great ancient civilization once thrived in this valley. Let the new city arise from its ashes. Let it be called Phoenix."

Both the platform mound and the canal had been built by the Hohokam who inhabited the basin as early as 300 BC. The flat-topped mound (shaped like a Mayan pyramid) measures three hundred feet long, one hundred and fifty feet wide and twenty feet high. Lacking draft animals and wheelbarrows, these industrious Native Americans also dug five hundred miles of aqueducts to irrigate over 25,000 acres. The main channels were seventy-five feet across and twelve feet deep.

H. M. Wormington, one of the first archeologists in the region, believed that the construction of this extensive system rivaled the architectural achievements of the Egyptian pyramids or the Mayan temples. Duppa would have probably agreed.

Born into English landed gentry, "Lord" Darell Duppa was one of the best-educated men in the American West.

*"Lord" Darell Duppa, who named both
the cities of Phoenix and Tempe, Arizona.*

*Upper left: woodcut of phoenix.
Upper right: Egyptian Bennu.
Lower left: flag of the city of
Phoenix, Arizona.*

Classically trained in Paris and Madrid, he knew Greek, Latin, Italian, French, and Spanish. The library that he carried with him into the wilderness included Homer, Ovid, and Juvenal in the original. An eccentric and a loner, he occasionally was given to fits of eloquence and could quote Shakespeare by the hour, especially if facilitated by a shot or two of whisky.

Months earlier Duppa had been seen in Prescott, the new prospecting town a hundred miles to the north. His ostensible business was to check up on some gold mining claims owned by his prosperous uncle. Earlier Duppa had helped to establish this relative's sheep ranch in New Zealand. Before arriving in Arizona, Duppa had traveled throughout Australia and was the sole survivor of a shipwreck off the coast of Chile. Although he escaped water rather than fire, this event may give a clue to his personal choice for the name.

Duppa was alluding to the description of the mythical phoenix by the Greek historian Herodotus. At the end of each temporal cycle this brilliantly plumed male bird flies to a myrrh tree in Heliopolis, Egypt. There he builds a nest of cassia twigs as a pyre upon which he will be resurrected. Thus a new cycle is initiated. All this scholarship must have impressed the settlers, because the name began to be used officially. Or so the official story goes.

Birds of a Feather

Perhaps it is no accident that most of the first citizens of Phoenix, including Duppa, were Freemasons.

John T. Alsap, for instance, was an attorney, judge, first territorial treasurer, and first mayor of Phoenix. He also served as the first worshipful master of Arizona Lodge No. 2 as well as the first grand master of the Masonic Grand Lodge of Arizona. Even earlier, he had been first master of Arizona's first Masonic Lodge called Aztlan, located in Prescott, the first territorial capital. (A lot of "firsts" here.)

Aztlan is a Nahuatl word meaning "place of the heron."

The Aztecs inhabited this mythical land after emerging from the Seven Caves located in the bowels of the earth. The heron is thought to be the naturalistic model for both the phoenix and the Bennu bird. In the Egyptian sun cult the Bennu was found perched atop an obelisk or sometimes upon a pyramid-shaped stone of meteoric iron called a Benben.

As a primary symbol of morning and new life, the Egyptian heron passes with flying colors (pun intended). Likewise, the Bennu embodies the morning star Venus, appearing each dawn on the laurel tree in Heliopolis. This ornithological curiosity is also the incarnation of the heart (or *ab*) of Osiris and the soul (or *ba*) of Ra, two primary deities related by this simple word reversal.

The hieroglyph for *bennu* means both "purple heron" (*Ardea purpurea*) and "palm tree." One denotation for the word "phoenix" is "purple-red"; consequently, the Phoenicians were known as "red men." Even today residents of Phoenix, Arizona, are known as Phoenicians. The flag of the city is a stylized white phoenix on a purple background. (See picture on p. 70.)

In a tome called *Morals and Dogma of the Ancient and Accepted Scottish Rite of Freemasonry*, 33rd-degree Mason Albert Pike states that the phoenix was a quintessential alchemical icon. In this regard J. E. Cirlot's *Dictionary of Symbols* remarks: "In alchemy, [the phoenix] corresponds to the colour red, to the regeneration of universal life and to the successful completion of a process." A few Arizona prospectors may indeed have been seeking spiritual gold as well.

Is it more than mere coincidence, then, that the phoenix, whose center of worship was the Pre-Dynastic City of the Sun, should lend its name to what would become the largest city in the Valley of the Sun? Is the name something more than the whim of some erudite inebriate misplaced in the hinterlands of America?

Aztlan is furthermore conceptualized as an island. Some speculate that the name even refers to the legendary continent of Atlantis. According to comparative linguistics scholar Gene D. Matlock, the Aztlán of Nahuatl mythology was really called

Aztatlán, referring to the village of Nayarit on Mexico's western coast. The Sanskrit word *Asta* apparently means "Place of the Setting Sun." Matlock suggests that this could actually be the westernmost boundary of what was once Atlantis.

Did Lord Duppa and Judge Alsap consciously try to merge Egyptian and Mesoamerican mythologies in the wilds of Arizona? Alsap's Bachelor of Law and Doctor of Medicine degrees prove that he was no dummy himself. Was the establishment of Aztlan (Masonic Lodge No. 1) and Phoenix (Masonic Lodge No. 2) an attempt to symbolically merge Prescott (the heron) and Phoenix (the Bennu) in the same way they would soon actually be linked by stagecoach? Was it a clandestine Masonic intent that a new Atlantis (Aztlan) should rise in Arizona and a new Heliopolis (Phoenix) should be its heart?

Whose Story?

Other questions about the initial territorial capital come to mind. Why was Prescott named to honor the prominent 19th century historian William Hickling Prescott, who never set foot in the town? Were the run-of-the-mill settlers really all that interested in his book *History of the Conquest of Mexico*? According to its author, "The inhabitants, members of different tribes, and speaking dialects somewhat different, belonged to the same great family of nations who had come from the real or imaginary region of Aztlan, in the far north-west." In other words, the Arizona Territory. Is this why two major thoroughfares in the town of Prescott are named Cortez Street and Montezuma Street?

Why did the territorial capital suddenly shift in 1889 from Prescott to Phoenix? The mercantile owner, postmaster, and territorial representative John Y. T. Smith greatly influenced this movement. He too was another "pioneer Mason" of Phoenix. After governmental authority had finally rested with the southern city, spiritual symbolism superseded natural potency. Did secret powers dictate that the phoenix instead of the heron should arise?

Whatever the reason, Columbus H. Gray, who served as a territorial senator and member of Maricopa County's Board of Supervisors, began during Phoenix's early years to construct a Masonic hall at the corner of Jefferson and First Streets. Before it was completed, he sold it to Mike Goldwater, grandfather of Arizona Senator Barry Goldwater, himself a 33rd-degree Mason. Incidentally, both Phoenix and Tempe are located at 33 degrees north latitude. (See Chapter 6.) Even stranger is the fact that another Tempe, the name of a suburb of Sidney, Australia, is located at 33 degrees south latitude.

By 1890 a number of the fraternal organizations were operating in the city: Masons, Odd Fellows, Knights of Pythias, Ancient Order of United Workmen, Grand Army of the Republic, Chosen Friends and Good Templars.

Darell Duppa spent his last days in the Valley of the Sun and crossed the bar in 1892. He is buried in the Masonic section of Pioneer and Memorial Park in Phoenix.

Further evidence of Duppa's Masonic association comes from one source that connects him to Jacob Waltz, the famous Lost Dutchman, by identifying both men as Masons. This German prospector supposedly discovered a fabulous gold mine in the Superstition Mountains east of Phoenix. As with many lost treasures of the Wild West, its location remains a mystery. Waltz is buried in the same Phoenix cemetary. In addition, Columbus Gray (mentioned above) is also interred there.

One more relevant Phoenix character was laid to rest in the Pioneer and Military Memorial Park. Benjamin Joseph Franklin was the great-grandson of the famous founding father and Mason. (See facing page.) He served as Arizona territorial governor for a little over a year shortly before his death in 1898.

Masonic influence in Phoenix continued well into the twentieth century. Arizona's first governor, George Wiley Paul Hunt, served seven terms between 1912 (the year of statehood) and 1932. He was also a prominent and longstanding Freemason. As a populist and supporter of trade unions, he spoke and wrote in a simple and sometimes [continued on p. 77]

Duppa's tombstone in Masonic section of Pioneer and Military Memorial Park, Phoenix.
To the left of his photo is a phoenix, to the right a logo for the city of Tempe.
Older plaque below.
Note different spelling of his name on each of the grave markers.

Left: B. J. Franklin, born in Kentucky in 1839, also served as a U.S. Representative from Missouri, 1875-79.
Maltese Cross contains CSA (Confederate States Army) and Confederate flag inside wreath.
Note backward "J" in Franklin's name.

Left: George W. P. Hunt, first governor of Arizona. (Photo courtesy of Phoenix Public Library.) Below: family mausoleum of Hunt, a Freemason, in Papago Park, Phoenix.

grammatically incorrect style. Nonetheless, like Duppa, he loved classical literature, which gained him the moniker "Old Roman." A man of contradictions, Hunt had also been known to address Theosophical Society meetings.

His final resting place in Phoenix's Papago Park is within sight of an archaeo-astronomical observatory once used by the Hohokam but now called Hole-in-the-Rock. Oddly enough, Hunt's family mausoleum was an Egyptian-style pyramid finished with white tile to mimic the Tura limestone that onced made the Giza pyramids gleam for miles in the desert sunlight.

Alas, Poor Geronimo

Many local history buffs portray early pioneers as hardy, pragmatic individualists who were more concerned with prospecting, gambling, and imbibing red-eye than with studying arcane lore. In most cases, this is probably true. In the same sense, most Masons are ordinary businessmen who just want to further their careers while enjoying camaraderie and offering charity to the community at large.

However, inside each citizenry and each lodge exists a cabal of operatives who long to achieve power and further their own ultimate goals or those of their ancient organization. B. P. Darell Duppa and John T. Alsap may have been such men.

An even more insidious instance of power and wealth was Prescott Sheldon Bush (1895-1972). He was father of the forty-first U.S. president George Herbert Walker Bush and grandfather of the forty-third president George W. Bush. All three had been members of the notorious Skull and Bones Society, an elite, quasi-Masonic fraternity at Yale University.

Possibly the eldest Bush was named after his distant relative William Hickling Prescott, the historian noted above. In 1918 Bush allegedly purloined the skull of the famous Arizona Apache warrior Geronimo from its resting place at Fort Sill, Oklahoma and took it back to the secret society's meeting hall to be displayed in a glass case.

***Geronimo, Apache warrior,
at the St. Louis World's Fair, 1904.***

The motive for this savage act is unclear, but it may have involved retribution for the 1869 killing of settler James G. Sheldon from Maine by Apaches at Camp Willow Grove west of Prescott. Sheldon, after whom a major street in Prescott was named, is perhaps a relative of Prescott Sheldon Bush, or he may merely be a namesake whom Bush was trying to avenge.

Bush was later elected as a U.S. senator from Connecticut. His son and grandson, of course, each became president. The Bush vacation home is located in Kennebunkport, Maine. Geronimo's skull has never been recovered.

And Phoenix remains an enigmatic talisman whose Masonic roots reach deep into the desert of the American Southwest.

Two More Pyramid Tombs of Famous Arizonans

Geronimo (Goyaalé, "One Who Yawns") *was born in*

Arizona or western New Mexico. After fighting fiercely for his land and people, he surrendered on September 4, 1886, in Skeleton Canyon, Arizona. He died as a prisoner of war on Febuary 17, 1909, and is interred at Fort Sill, Oklahoma, far from his home.

Charles Debrille Poston *is known as the "Father of Arizona."*

In 1863 he named the Territory of Arizona and obtained the signature of President Lincoln for its authorization. Poston was also responsible for the enactment that created the territory. He was its first Congressional deligate as well.

During a trip to India he got involved with the Parsee religion and became one of North America's first Zoroastrians. He even wrote a book called The Sun Worshippers of Asia *(1877).*

Poston died in Phoenix (Valley of the Sun) in 1902. His remains rest in a pyramid-shaped monument at the summit of Poston's Butte near Florence, Arizona, where he had once hoped to build a sun temple.

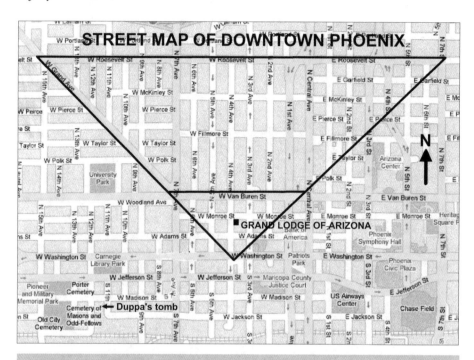

STREET MAP OF DOWNTOWN PHOENIX

N

■ GRAND LODGE OF ARIZONA

← Duppa's tomb

The slope of this inverted pyramid is formed by W. Grand Ave.
The base is W. Roosevelt St. and the apex is W. Washington St.
The Phoenix Masonic Lodge No. 2 (Grand Lodge) forms
the all-seeing eye of the capstone. (See p. 81.)
The east-west streets all are named for Masonic presidents
(although a few later became anti-Masons).

MASONIC TEMPLE

**Northern doorway of
Arizona Lodge No. 2, F. &
A. M., constructed in 1925.
To adorn the architrave
below the Masonic
emblem, the architect
seems to have favored
the nine-headed Naga
motif found in Cambodia.
(Read more about the
Nagas in Chapter 12.)**

Chapter 6: Along the 33rd Parallel— A Global Mystery Circle

What's In a Number?

The number 33 enigmatically stretches as a latitude line across many diverse cultures in many different times. Known in numerology as the Master Teacher, 33 is the most influential of all numbers, indicating selfless devotion to the spiritual progress of humankind. The other two master numbers, 11 (vision) and 22 (vision with action) form the base of a two-dimensional pyramid. Added together, they equal 33 (guidance to the world), the apex of the pyramid.

According to ritual Freemasonry, XXXIII is considered sacred because in most cases there is no higher degree or level to which a Mason may aspire. On the reverse of the Masonically inspired Great Seal of the United States is the pyramid with the all-seeing eye of divine Reason at its apex.

This is the Eye of the Phoenix.

In a biblical context we note that King David ruled in Jerusalem for thirty-three years, Jacob had thirty-three sons and daughters, and Jesus Christ was crucified at age thirty-three. Two interpenetrating triangles whose apexes point in opposite directions form the hexagram of the Star of David (3 + 3 = 6). On the other hand, 3 X 3 = 9, or the Ennead, the nine primal gods of Egyptian mythology.

The late thirteenth/early fourteenth century Italian poet Dante ended Canto XXXIII of the Purgatorio, or the second section of his *Divine Comedy*: "...perfect, pure, and ready for the Stars." Canto XXXIII of the Paradiso, or the third section, concludes with lines about the poet being turned "as in a wheel whose motion nothing jars— / by the Love that moves the Sun and the other stars." It is more than a coincidence that the 33rd canto of each section concludes with parallel lines regarding the celestial; it may instead be the code from a lost ancient tradition.

This number even permeates the biological realm studied by science: thirty-three is the number of turns in a complete sequence of DNA. A more ominous connotation appears in the 33rd element of the periodic table. Arsenic is a brittle, steel-gray substance that is actively poisonous. The Greek root *arsen* means "male, strong" or "virile," which suggests the active reach of this potent and potentially deadly number across the globe. Indeed, when we consider the northern latitude of 33 degrees, some intriguing synchronicities, or "meaningful coincidences," are found.

You Say Phoenix and I Say Phoenicia

The first stop on our tour along the 33rd parallel is the metropolis of Phoenix, Arizona, located at 33 degrees 30 minutes latitude. (See Chapter 5.) Few casual tourists realize that this was once the center of the ancient Hohokam culture.

The largest Hohokam site known as Snaketown was located about five miles north of the exact 33 degrees line, while the ruins of the astronomical observatory called Casa Grande still rest about five miles south of the line. The Hohokam inhabited the Valley of the Sun perhaps as early as 300 BC. At about the same time that Alexander the Great went on a conquering spree and the Ptolemaic Dynasties finished up their long history in Egypt, the Hohokam built one of the world's most extensive irrigation systems.

These ancient American Indians created an estimated total of five hundred miles of canals to irrigate over 25,000 acres in the Phoenix Basin—all constructed with mere digging sticks, stone implements, and woven carrying baskets. In fact, no wheelbarrows or draft animals were ever used. The main canals leading from the Salt and Gila Rivers measured up to seventy-five feet across at the top and fifty feet wide at the bottom.

As Southwestern archaeologist H. M. Wormington observes in his book *Prehistoric Indians of the Southwest*: "The scope of the canal project suggests comparisons with the erection of the huge pyramids of Egypt or the great temples of the Maya." Clearly this monumental technology was the key factor that allowed the desert dwelling people to inhabit their extremely harsh region for well over a thousand years.

Skipping across the Atlantic on the same parallel, we find a number of intriguing sites in the Old World. For instance, at a latitude of 33 degrees 19 minutes was located the primary Phoenician seaport of Tyre (now called Sûr), almost fifty miles south of Beirut. Dating back as early as 5000 BC, Tyre was renowned for a purple-red dye obtained from the snails of the genus Murex. The color is one of the meanings of the word "phoenix," which the ancient Egyptians sometimes associated with the purple heron.

Back in North America the "place of the heron" refers to Aztlan, the Nahuatl word for the mythical land that the Aztecs inhabited after emerging from Chicomostoc, the Seven Caves located in the bowels of the earth. Chicano folklore identifies Aztlan as that portion of Mexico taken over by the U.S. after the Mexican-American War of 1846—in part, the Arizona Territory, where the settlement of Phoenix arose.

The Masonic author Albert Pike states that Tyre was the

seat of the Osirian Mysteries after they had been imported from Egypt. Pike asserts that the two massive columns situated at the entrance of the Tyrian Temple of Malkarth were consecrated to the Winds and to Fire. This pair is thought to be the prototype of Jachin and Boaz, the two pillars found on the eastern wall of every Masonic temple in the world. On the right, or to the south, is Jachin, which means "He shall establish" and signifies an active, vivifying force. On the left, or to the north, is Boaz, which means "In it is strength" and connotes passive stability and permanence. The former may also represent the winter solstice sunrise, while the latter the summer solstice sunrise.

An alternate possibility is that Jachin represents the southern stargate between Sagittarius and Scorpius while Boaz signifies the northern stargate between Gemini and Taurus. (See my article: www.theorionzone.com/egyptian_stargates.htm.) This assumption is based on the fact that in the York Rite of Freemasonry a celestial globe symbolizing ex-carnation (that is, a spirit leaving its present body) is found atop Jachin, while a terrestrial globe representing incarnation is positioned atop Boaz.

During the tenth century BC King Hiram of Tyre supplied King Solomon with craftsmen, metallurgists, cedar wood, architectural design, and presumably the esoteric symbolism of these two columns for the construction of his temple at Jerusalem. (1 Kings 7: 13-22) In addition to being besieged at various times by Nebuchadrezzar, Alexander the Great, the Romans and others, the trade capital city-state of Tyre was conquered in the twelfth century AD by the Crusaders, who built a Knights Templar church there.

Some speculate that the orientation of the two pillars imitates obelisks placed before the pylons of Egyptian temples, especially those of the Heliopolitan temple of Thothmes (Tuthmosis) III, who reigned in the fifteenth century BC as the militarily expansionist pharaoh of the Eighteenth Dynasty. He is also thought to be founder of the Order of the Rosy Cross, or the Rosicrucians. The archaeologist Sir Flinders Petrie even found records in the Libyan desert that describe a secret Masonic guild meeting held around 2000 BC. William Bramley in his book *The Gods of Eden* comments:

> "The guild met to discuss working hours, wages, and rules for daily labor. It convened in a chapel and provided relief to widows, orphans, and workers in distress. The organizational duties described in the papyri are very similar to those of 'Warden' and 'Master' in a modern branch of the Brotherhood which evolved from those guilds: Freemasonry."

It seems that all roads lead to... Egypt.

Also of interest near the 33rd parallel is Byblos, a bit farther north of Tyre at the latitude of 34 degrees 08 minutes. The name of this city state is derived from the Greek *ta b blia*, which means "the book," or "bible." Indeed, the invention of a Phoenician alphabetic phonetic script occurred here and eventually spread to the Greek world.

A bit farther east at nearly the same latitude is Baalbeck, an ancient megalithic temple constructed with some of the largest stone blocks ever cut in the world. Extracted and hauled from a quarry many miles away, these megaliths include one block measuring 80 feet long and weighing 1,100 tons.

In this section we have seen how Phoenix and Phoenicia are linked by latitude. We shall continue eastward to encounter other significant ancient sites along the same parallel.

A Passage To China

A little over five hundred miles east of these Phoenician cities at 33 degrees 20 minutes is modern-day Bagdad in Iraq, with Babylon located about 55 miles to the south. This ancient capital of Mesopotamia on the banks of the Euphrates River was once the largest city in the world, encompassing over 2,500 acres.

The construction of Babylon began during the twenty-third century BC and included the Temple of Marduk (known as Esagila) as well as the legendary Tower of Babel (identified as Etemenanki). The latter structure was a seven-tiered ziggurat rising to a height of three hundred feet with a base on each side measuring the same distance. This measurement, incidentally, equals the length of the Hohokam platform mound at Pueblo Grande in Phoenix, Arizona.

On the eastern side of Babylon was an outer rampart of triple wall construction extending for eleven miles. A network of irrigation canals reminiscent of the Hohokam also once served the city. In addition, the terraced Hanging Gardens were one of the Seven Wonders of the Ancient World.

This "city and a tower" (Genesis 11:4) was known as Babel, the legendary site of the linguistic confounding. "The biblical interpretation of the name is fanciful. The Bible connects Babel with the Hebrew verb Bâlal, 'to confuse', whereas it really comes from Bâb-ili, which in Babylonian means 'Gate of God'." [Henri-Paul Eydoux, "The men who built the Tower of Babel," *The World's Last Mysteries*]

This terrestrial correlation to another sort of stargate is perhaps a reference to the Processional Way leading to Ishtar Gate, both of which were adorned with glazed blue enameled figures of lions, bulls, and dragons. Pike maintains that the temple contained a representation in silver of two large serpents. "The Greeks called Bel Beliar; and Hesychius interprets that word to mean dragon or great serpent. We learn from the book of Bel and the Dragon, that in Babylon was kept a great, live serpent, which the people worshipped." [*Morals and Dogma*]

This reminds us of the Place of the Snakes, or the Hohokam site of Snaketown, as well as of the Hopi biennial Snake Dance ceremony still performed with live rattlesnakes on the high desert of Arizona. (See Chapter 12.)

In more recent times Babylon played a significant role in the rituals of Freemasonry and continues to do so. For instance, the ceremony for the Royal Arch of Solomon Degree (13 degrees) entails the candidate and two others playing the roles of the three Master Masons of Babylon: Shadrach, Meshech, and

Abednego. According to the narrative told in the ritual, these children of the Babylonian captivity desire to assist in the rebuilding of the Temple of Solomon. Thus, Babylon's symbolic importance, which extends back to at least Knights Templar times and probably before, is reemphasized inside every Masonic lodge to the present day.

Traveling along the 33rd parallel from the Middle East to the Far East, we encounter the fabulous White Pyramid located about sixty miles southwest of X'ian (Sian or Hsian) in the Qin Ling Shan Mountains of China's Shensi Province. This city was made famous for the nearby discovery of the Terracotta Warriors. Resting at almost the same latitude as Phoenix's 33½ degrees, this massive stepped pyramid constructed of clay is estimated to be one thousand feet high and fifteen hundred feet at the base!

The current politics of the country have thus far prevented any detailed study of the structure, but it is thought to be 4,500 – 5,000 years old—the approximate age of the pyramids at Giza. The White Pyramid was built supposedly after the old emperors, known as "the sons of heaven," descended to Earth in their "fiery metallic dragons" and began to rule China. Its interior is rumored to be a model of this empire with a jeweled roof depicting the constellations and rivers of flowing mercury. The region also contains up to one hundred more pyramids.

Highway 33 Revisited

Back on the North American continent, if we journey somewhat over fifteen hundred miles east of Phoenix along latitude 33 North, we find the Moundville site lying exactly on the line. This city constructed by the Mississippian culture along the Black Warrior River in central Alabama from 1000 through 1450 AD had a population of over one thousand—second in size and complexity to ancient Cahokia in Illinois.

The twenty-six earthen platform mounds arranged in a circular pattern are similar in structure to those in Arizona's

Valley of the Sun, with temples and residences for the elite priesthood likewise built on top. One of the larger mounds is a ramped pyramid that rises to a height of fifty-eight feet. In addition, the town was protected on three sides by wooden palisades, much like the Hohokam villages along the Salt and Gila Rivers.

Did the earlier Hohokam culture of the American Southwest somehow influence the later development of this Mound Builder culture in the American Southeast? The many similarities between the two seem to point in that direction.

A few other Mound Builders cities were settled quite near the 33rd parallel. Approximately ten miles southwest of the town of Lake Providence (32 degrees 49 minutes) on the Mississippi River floodplain in northeastern Louisiana is Poverty Point State Historic Site. Constructed in 1800 BC (much earlier than even the Hohokam settlements), a C-shaped or perhaps a partial octagon-shaped earthwork three-quarters of a mile across was formed by six concentric ridges that are one hundred and forty to two hundred feet apart and four to six feet high.

To the west of this earthwork, Bird Mound rises seventy-two feet high and extends six to eight hundred feet at its base. Resembling some sort of fowl flying toward the sunset, this mound was constructed using 300,000 cubic yards of clay, or the equivalent to ten million fifty-pound baskets. To truly realize the shape of the bird, one needs to be at least a thousand feet or so in the air.

Poverty Point was almost entirely abandoned about 1350 BC, indicating over five centuries of cultural development, though minor construction on the earthworks continued until 700 A.D.

Even closer to the magic number 33 though not as impressive or as old are the Winterville Mounds, located six miles north of the town of Greenville in west-central Mississippi (33 degrees 25 minutes). Inhabited between 1000 and 1450 AD, the site includes twnty-three flat-topped mounds, with the main Temple Mound rising fifty-five feet.

About four miles south of Cartersville in northwestern Georgia (34 degrees 11 minutes) is Etowah Indian Mound State Park. The Creek tribe and the later Cherokee tribe called this site Itawa or Italwa, which means "high tower." It is interesting to note that the Hopi word for the sun deity is *Tawa*. Etowah was first inhabited in 950 AD and contains three major mounds. One is a ceremonial mound sixty-three feet in height and another is a burial mound in which were found numerous artifacts including copper ear ornaments, stone effigies, and seashells along with obsidian and grizzly bear teeth from the Rocky Mountains.

Closer to the home of the Hohokam on the western side of the Colorado River are located a number of geoglyphs (also called "intaglios"). These figures formed in the desert by removal of darker pebbles to reveal a lighter undersurface are sometimes hundreds of feet in length. One group (the Blythe complex) is positioned about sixteen miles north of Blythe, California (33 degrees 40 minutes), while another group (the Ripley complex) is located about twelve miles south of Blythe.

In addition to human and animal figures, snakes, spirals, stars, circles, and other geometric figures, a Knights Templar-like Maltese cross nearly ten feet in diameter has been found adjacent to a humanoid figure at the Ripley complex. (This geoglyph is discussed in greater detail in Chapter 15.) Another anthropoid geoglyph in the area has been associated with the Hopi Fire Clan deity Masau'u.

Hence, we find that many different tribes were apparently involved in these rituals dating from between eleven hundred and three thousand years ago. Because these earth forms, like the Nazca lines in Peru or Bird Mound at Poverty Point, are best appreciated from the air, they were probably intended to be an homage to the sky gods.

The geoglyphs together with other cairns, stone circles, and cleared dance paths may be ritually associated with the huge network of interconnected trails found in the low desert upon which the ancients made pilgrimages. One such pilgrimage called the *keruk* is performed even today by the Yuman speaking tribes (namely, the Yuma, Mohave, Cocopa, and

Maricopa) in a four-day trek to Avikwa'ame, the sacred mountain to the north, in order to celebrate the cosmogony.

According to David S. Whitley in his book *A Guide to Rock Art Sites*:

> "The route ran from Pilot Knob, or Avikwal [near Yuma, Arizona], the spirit house where the dead dwell at the southern end of the river, to Avikwa'ame, or Spirit Mountain, where the Earth was created, in the north. This pilgrimage was intended to honor the creation, and ritually retrace the path of Mastamho [the creator-deity, whose name echoes the Hopi god Masau'u mentioned above] in his mythic adventures."

Here we find a north-south dichotomy similar to that found along the Nile, with the "Mound of Creation" (i.e., Heliopolis) located to the north. Atop Avikwa'ame, legends say, was a great house name Aha-avulypo, or literally "Dark Round House." The north-south road itself was named Kwatcan, the "first trail to the homeland." The Hopi word for "track" is *kuku'at*, but the word for "grandfather" is the near homophone *kwa'at*. Perhaps the suffix *-can* is a variant of *"ka,"* part of the word *katsina*. Either "spirits of the track" or "spirits of the grandfathers" may be the intended meaning. Midway on this spirit road between the sacred mountain of the North and the mouth of the Colorado River are the aforementioned geoglyphs at the 33rd degree of latitude.

Also on this line is the Three Rivers Petroglyphs site, located on the western base of the Sacramento Mountains eighteen miles west of Ruidoso, New Mexico (33 degrees 19 minutes). One of the largest rock art sites in the Southwest, this park contains over 20,000 glyphs scattered over fifty acres. Carved atop a ridge by the Mogollon culture between 900 and 1400 AD (contemporary with the late Hohokam period), these figures include anthropomorphs, zoomorphs, *katsina* masks, star symbols, and various abstract or geometric designs, including a Maltese cross within a circle surrounded by a ring of seventeen dots. (See photo on p. 176.)

Rock art expert Polly Schaafsma states in *Indian Rock Art of the Southwest*:

> "Distinctive at Three Rivers is the circle-dot motif; one investigator who took the trouble to count found it to be the single most common element at this site. Interestedly enough, its presence elsewhere is negligible, and its symbolic content has not been determined, although it occurs in various contexts in Mesoamerica. Possibly it refers to Quetzalcoatl."

This deity, of course, is known as the Plumed Serpent.

Three Rivers Site is also unique because it is one of only a few places in the Southwest that were used primarily for rock art rather than it being merely an adjunct to the village. However, another site lying exactly on the 33rd parallel was also used expressly for this purpose. Near Gila Bend, Arizona, about sixty-two miles west of Snaketown (mentioned above) is Painted Rocks [sic] State Park, which has thousands of petroglyphs of similar designs—not "painted" but pecked into the boulders.

A fascinating site also in the general vicinity of Phoenix is called the Circlestone Observatory (33 degrees 28 minutes). High in the Superstition Mountains about fifty-four miles east of the metropolis lies an elliptical "medicine wheel" constructed of a stonewall three feet thick with a circumference of four hundred and twenty-seven feet. On his extensive and thoroughly detailed web site, New Zealand researcher Martin Doutré claims that this structure incorporates various navigational codes, including phi, or the Golden Ratio (1.618...). "Ancient astronomers mathematicians built sites like Circlestone as repositories of codes and places where initiates could be taught age-old principles."
[www.celticnz.co.nz/Circlestone/Circlestone1.htm]

Doutré further suggests that Circlestone was used by colonists from the eastern Mediterranean or Europe who may have operated a gold mine—perhaps the famous Lost Dutchman's Mine itself! Although American Indians may instead have constructed this site for an astronomical observatory similar to the one at Casa Malpais near Springerville, Arizona (34 degrees 10 minutes), Doutré's theory is nonetheless an intriguing one.

Four other ancient sites along latitude 33 N warrant brief mentions. Gila Cliff Dwellings National Monument (33 degrees 22 minutes) is located in a rugged and isolated region about sixty miles west of Truth or Consequences, New Mexico. Reminiscent of the seven Aztecan caves mentioned above, five caves in the Mogollon Mountains of southwestern New Mexico contain about forty masonry and adobe rooms built around 1280 AD, although semi-subterranean pit houses have been found nearby dating back to circa 100 AD.

In saguaro cactus country about fifty-six miles northeast of Phoenix is another site on the global mystery circle called Tonto National Monument (33 degrees 44 minutes), which also contains cliff dwellings within shallow caves. Constructed of unshaped quartzite and adobe mortar, these ruins inhabited in the mid-fourteenth century contained seventy rooms within three caves.

About forty miles due east of the small town of San Carlos, Arizona (33 degrees 24 minutes), is Point of Pines Ruin. Occupied between 1200 and 1500 AD, this huge masonry pueblo contained eight hundred rooms, a central plaza, a surrounding wall, and a great kiva.

The site is also one of the few in the Southwest that shows evidence of three different cultures living together: the Hohokam, the Mogollon, and the Anasazi—the last group named migrating from the Hopi country to the north. The population is estimated to have been between two and three thousand. Incidentally, five or so miles to the south is a hot springs called Arsenic Tubs, number 33 on the periodic table.

And finally, Besh-ba-gowah Archaeological Park located one-and-a-half miles south of downtown Globe, Arizona (33 degrees 25 minutes), was a granite cobble pueblo of over two hundred and fifty rooms inhabited between 1225 and 1450 A.D. The artifacts found include copper bells and macaw feathers from Mesoamerica as well as shells from the Gulf of Mexico and the California coast.

Besh-ba-gowah is an Apache phrase meaning "place of the metal," referring to the copious silver and copper deposits in the area. In fact, the town of Globe was so named because of the 1875 discovery of a globe-shaped mass nine inches in diameter made of 99 percent pure silver and valued at $12,000. Curiously, reports also stated that the continents of the Earth were etched upon its surface. The whereabouts of this artifact is currently unknown.

A Brief History of 33

Entering the historical period, we find hovering near the 33rd parallel a number of provocative synchronicities. For instance, the first Supreme Council of the Ancient and Accepted Scottish Rite of Freemasonry, Southern Jurisdiction of the United States, was established in 1801 at Charleston, South Carolina. This charming antebellum port city and hub of southern culture is located less than fifteen miles south of the 33rd parallel. Called the Solomon Lodge No. 1, the Masonic meeting place was known as the Mother Lodge of the world.

Shortly before the end of World War II Franklin D. Roosevelt died suddenly of a cerebral hemorrhage at Warm Springs, Georgia, which is less than ten miles south of 33 degrees latitude. This town, incidentally, is located about thirty-five miles northeast of Phenix City, Alabama.

It is noteworthy (no pun intended) that in the mid-30s FDR, a 32nd degree Mason and 32nd President of the U.S., initiated the printing of the reverse side of the Great Seal (the pyramidal eye mentioned at the beginning of this chapter) on the legal tender. Roosevelt was succeeded in April of 1945 by 33rd-degree Mason Harry S. Truman. (The "S." supposedly stood for Solomon.)

On July 16th of the same year, the first atomic device –the Gadget, as it was called– was detonated at Trinity Site, New Mexico: 33 degrees 41 minutes North latitude. Spanish explorers originally called this area La Jornada del Muerto, or "The

Journey of the Dead," but now the site is marked by a small stone obelisk erected twenty years or so after the explosion. (Was this monument Masonically inspired?)

A few weeks after the explosion at Trinity Site the 33rd president of the United States ordered the annihilation of two Japanese cities by nuclear bombs dropped from B-29 bombers. The 33rd parallel runs exactly between Hiroshima and Nagasaki.

In this context astrological Sabian symbols have relevance. These are a series of 360 brief vignettes –one for each degree of the zodiacal circle– received in 1925 by San Diego clairvoyant Elsie Wheeler and recorded by astrologer Marc Edmund Jones. The Sabian symbol for 33 degrees is the following: "Natural steps lead to a lawn of clover in bloom." [Dane Rudhyar, *An Astrological Mandala*] Clover's trefoil suggests the Trinity, while its flowering suggests new life or even resurrection.

Two years after the war ended, the modern "flying saucer" age began in earnest when *something* crashed near Roswell, New Mexico: 33 degrees 26 minutes North latitude.

Bringing us up to the present day, the so-called Phoenix Lights were witnessed by hundreds or perhaps thousands of people. On the evening of March 13th, 1997, an immense triangular UFO perhaps a mile wide flew over the American Southwest. First sighted over Henderson, Nevada, at 6:55 p.m. (Pacific Standard Time) traveling southeast, this virtually silent "craft" (for lack of a better term) had a number of lights evenly spaced on its leading edge.

It was next seen twenty-two minutes later over the village of Paulden, Arizona (nearly twenty-five miles north of the town of Prescott). It was then observed ten miles to the south in Chino Valley. It apparently streaked over my own house there, but I missed seeing the event by a matter of minutes. Just one minute after the Paulden sighting, it was reported over Prescott Valley, which is twenty-three miles south-southeast of the former.

By 8:23 (Mountain Standard Time) the object had reached the Phoenix metro area roughly seventy-five miles away, where it hovered for about four or five minutes over the vicinity of the

Indian School Rd. and 7th Avenue intersection.

Next the UFO entered Sky Harbor Airport's air space, where air controllers in the tower and the flight crew from at least one commercial airliner viewed it, although radar failed to detect it. The craft continued southeast above Interstate 10 and was sighted in the Tucson area about 8:45.

This series of sightings that occurred within a four hundred-mile stretch took just fifty minutes. The average speed of the craft was 480 m.p.h.

At approximately 9:50 p.m. an arc of amber "orbs" measuring one mile across appeared above the Estrella Mountains about twenty miles southwest of Phoenix. This range was named for the Spanish word meaning 'star' by conquistadors because of the pattern of deeply carved canyons radiating from the summit. The display of lights videotaped by scores of people in the Phoenix area was possibly related to the earlier sightings.

At the time of this latter UFO sighting the constellation Orion would have been seen hovering over the southwestern horizon, were it not for urban light pollution. In fact, at 9:49 p.m. when the final phase of the event was beginning, Alnilam, the middle star of the Belt, was 33 degrees above the horizon at an azimuth of 242 degrees. If a line is drawn from the State Capitol to the Estrella range's Monument Hill (the initial point for surveying of property in Arizona), the azimuth is also 242 degrees. At the latitude of Phoenix this is the exact point of the winter solstice sunset as well.

Thus, these orbs appeared at a significant archaeo-astronomical position in the sky and also in the precise region where Orion happened to be at that particular time. Above the right hand of Orion between the constellations Gemini and Auriga is the northern stargate previously mentioned, located at a declination (celestial latitude) of 33 degrees.

One odd aspect to the Phoenix Lights story is that, other than a few minor write-ups in local newspapers, it was not reported in any national media until June 18th, over three months later, when *USA Today* ran a front-page article picked up by the other media. In this sudden and unexpected frenzy,

Governor Fife Symington gave a spoof news conference with a Grey alien in costume.

Stranger still, on the ten-year anniversary of the event the former Arizona governor admitted to seeing the delta-shaped craft himself. On CNN's "Larry King Live" TV show, he said: "I think it was from another world. I've never seen anything like it. It was enormous."

In any event, one of the most intriguing UFO sightings in decades was focused upon the 33rd parallel—a paramount Masonic number.

Why are so many significant ancient and historic sites located along the 33rd parallel?

Perhaps the ancients discovered a ley line sort of dragon energy corresponding to this latitude, and constructed temples and sacred cities in order to utilize this terrestrial *chi*. Or perhaps the numerological and Masonic significance of 33 dictated that monuments to this sacred number be erected as a signal to future generations.

Whatever the rationale, the 33rd parallel is a path of power across the globe, a circuit that links both time and space in order to vitalize the dynamo of a mystery we are just now beginning to realize.

**Eye of the Phoenix:
Mars Descent Camera**

Artist rendition courtesy of NASA.

In May of 2008 the Phoenix Mars Lander is scheduled to touch down on the red planet's north pole and begin a search for extra-terrestrial life. Its robotic arm will dig into the icy arctic soil, looking for any trace of microbes. Dr. Peter H. Smith of the University of Arizona's Lunar and Planetary Laboratory heads the Phoenix mission. He claims that Phoenix has the scientific potential "to change our thinking about the origins of life on other worlds."

The University of Arizona is located in Tucson, North latitude 32.22° — less than one degree from 33.

Chapter 7: The Flying Shields
of the Hopi Katsinam

Ancient flying machines have long been a tradition of many cultures across the globe. Venerable Hindu texts such as the *Ramayana* and the *Mahabharata* describe airships called Vamanas that were used even for battle. Among the hieroglyphs on the wall of a 3,000 year-old Egyptian temple at Abydos are depictions of what appear to be modern airplanes and helicopters. Grooved stone discs found in caves on the Chinese-Tibetan border tell of an extraterrestrial race called the Dropas whose spacecraft fell to Earth 12,000 years ago.

The Hopi Indians have inhabited three large mesas in northern Arizona for over a thousand years. Their legends also refer to aerial vehicles. These magical flying shields called *paatuwvota* existed in the Third World, a previous epoch destroyed by an immense flood. This was a time when great cities and trade routes were built, and civilization was flourishing.

In an address delivered to the United Nations, Thomas Banyacya of the Hopi Coyote Clan said: "The people invented many machines and conveniences of high technology, some of which have not yet been seen in this age." We, of course, recognize this startling description as echoing Atlantis.

In one legend the flying shield is associated with Sótuknang, the Hopi sky god. (See drawing on facing page.) Apparently a devastating flood had destroyed Palatkwapi, "the red city to the south," possibly located in the red rock country near Sedona, Arizona. Shortly afterwards a brother named Tiwahongva and his twin sister Tawiayisnima who were forgotten in the chaos and left behind by their fleeing parents set out on a journey to find them.

In the evening they decided to make camp. They were just opening their bundle for dinner when they heard a great roar overhead. The children were very frightened, wondering what this strange thing could be. The brother held his sister tightly to his chest as a fantastic being descended from the heavens. He was wearing a costume that glittered like ice (silver?), while his head and face shone like a star. He spoke: "Do not be afraid. My name is Sótuknang. Because of my sympathy for your plight, I have come to help you. Get on my *paatuwvota* and let us be on our way."

He then took them on his flying shield up into the sky so that they could see for many miles around. Feeding the hungry children ripe melons, he told them

Hopi drawing of the sky god Sótuknang [Fewkes, Hopi Katcinas, Dover Publications, Inc.]

that they must have faith in him and in his teachings that would later arrive through their dreams. Finally he landed a short distance from the village in which their mother and father had settled, bid the young ones farewell, and flew up again into the clouds. Forever grateful to the sky god, the brother and sister walked into the village to be reunited with their parents.

Because the Hopis had no such thing as a saucer, flying or otherwise, they named it after the cultural accouterment closest to that shape, namely, the warrior's shield. The word *tuwvota* specifically signifies this type of shield. Oddly, the concept of war is connected in Hopi ideology with the stars. The use of *tuwvota* rather than the more common word for 'disk' or 'circle' thus suggests a celestial origin for the *paatuwvota*.

Since the Hopi term *paa* means 'water', *paatuwvota* possibly refers to the expanding concentric rings in water. This might be a metaphorical description for the way the peculiar airborne device

This petroglyph near Winslow, Arizona, may depict a triangular aerial craft.

appeared to function. The related word *patuka*, or 'spindle', may also describe the shield's spinning motion. In addition, the prefix *pa-* denotes wonder or awe. For the people of the desert, water equals wonder, but *pa-* perhaps suggests the reaction to this extraordinary means of transportation.

The tradition of the flying shield also appears in rock art. In his book *Mexico Mystique*, Frank Waters, a non-Indian expert on the Hopis, writes:

"On Second Mesa near Mishongnovi an ancient petroglyph depicts a dome-shaped object resting on an arrow which represent travel through space, and the head of a Hopi maiden who represents pristine purity. As the Hopis believe that other planets are inhabited, this petroglyph represents a paatuwvota or a 'flying shield' similar to a 'flying saucer' that came here in the Beginning. So now at the End the sacred ones will arrive from another planet, said to be Venus, by flying saucers. Many Hopi traditionalists recently have reported seeing flying saucers, all piloted by beings they call kachinas."

Some readers may be familiar with the wooden *katsina* (plural *katsinam*, singular form also spelled *kachina*) dolls that the Hopis carve. *Katsinam* are not gods per se but spirits that act as mediators between gods and humans. They may take the form of any animal, plant, celestial body, or otherworldly creature. During the spring and early summer the Hopis perform a ceremonial cycle of masked *katsina* dances as a plea for rain and the general well being of the tribe. (Also see Chapter 16.)

Much like the fallen angels (or the Watchers) of the Bible (see Genesis 6:1-4), the *katsinam* were sometimes known to mate with Hopi women. This prefigures the contemporary theme of alien abduction for the purpose of reproduction. One Hopi myth tells of a young bride who accompanies her handsome Ka'nas *katsina* husband back to her village of Mishongnovi on a flying shield.

> "As the shield lifted off, the kachinas all gave out a bois-terous yell. The spectacle was incredible; every sort of kachina conceivable was present. All of a sudden as the couple flew along, flashes of lightning were visible in the air and the rumble of thunder could be heard. When the shield rose higher, drizzle began to fall. The kachinas were now accompanying them... [Her] parents had headed to the edge of the mesa at this time to look out. Looking down from the rim of the mesa, they saw an incredible number of people coming across the plain. To their great amazement all were kachinas, singing and crying out their calls in a pandemonium."

This quotation is taken from a book called *Earth Fire: A Hopi Legend of the Sunset Crater Eruption* co-authored by Ekkehart Malotki, a non-Indian professor of languages at Northern Arizona University, and Michael Lomatuway'ma, a Hopi from the Third Mesa shrine-village of Hotevilla. The Ka'nas *katsina* is associated with the volcanic eruption starting in 1064 AD that created the now-extinct Sunset Crater located near the San Francisco Peaks. (See photos on p. 199.) Another sixty miles far-ther northeast a large rectangular rock below the village of Mishongnovi is also known as "the house of the Ka'nas *katsina*."

As the entourage advanced from the "*katsina*" peaks toward Second Mesa, it bore a huge quantity of corn and melons on their backs as gifts for the Hopis. This diverse group of divine messengers must have been a stunningly beautiful sight. In fact, the Hopis sometimes refer to *katsinam* as "the beautiful crea-tures." This designation emphasizes not only their esthetically

Eototo, *chief* katsina (left), *and* Aholi, *his lieutenant* (katsina *dolls at* Museum of Northern Arizona).

pleasing appearance but also their role as actual entities in a kinship system.

Long ago the *katsinam* were adopted into the clans along with various plants and animals during the migrations that took place after the Hopi emergence from the Underworld—the Third World previously mentioned. Their presence had clearly been physical or tangible as opposed to supernatural or ethereal. In other words, their influence was once felt directly on a material level. As time went on, however, social and religious corruption –a recurring motif in Hopi thought– forced these bizarre but benevolent "people" to abandon the American Southwest. From that period to the present, *katsinam* appear for the most part only in their spirit forms.

Some Hopis believe that *katsinam* still maneuver these mysterious aircraft. In his book *The Terra Papers*, the Hopi/Apache author Robert Morning Sky describes how his grandfather and five other men were camping in the desert in August of 1947, shortly after the infamous Roswell incident, when a flying disk streaked across the night sky and crashed. From the wreckage they recovered a silvery alien, unconscious but still alive, whom they named the Star Elder.

After they nursed it back to health, the ET then telepathically described by means of a crystal the galactic war raging above which had downed its spacecraft. This X-Files material with a Native American twist remains unconfirmed.

Unexplained sightings continue, however. In the summer of 1970 hundreds of UFOs were seen about one hundred and twenty-five miles southwest of the Hopi villages near the town of Prescott, Arizona. On the evening of March 13th, 1997, in the same vicinity a delta-winged craft perhaps as large as a mile across with lights on its leading edges was spotted drifting silently overhead before speeding off toward the south. It later became known as the Phoenix Lights. (See Chapter 6.)

In 1998 the radio talk-show host Art Bell interviewed two Hopi elders who stated that their very distant ancestors knew how to travel to other planets. They also said that during the End Times, we would be visited by "people outside" the Earth who have an advanced technology.

Many Hopi wisdom keepers believe that the increased presence of flying shields signals the end of the Fourth World, or our current era. (See Chapter 18.) In conjunction with biblical prophecies of the apocalypse, the *katsinam* may be trying to warn us of this dire state of affairs. By listening to these spirit messengers throughout the ages, the Hopis living on their isolated mesas have long known the global fate that now seems imminent. Some of the signs and portents are in the skies. We need only look up.

Sótuknang (Hopi sky god, left—see p. 99) with shaman (center) and four-pointed "star-bird" with tail feathers and claws (right). Petroglyph National Monument, New Mexico.

Chapter 8: Is the Starchild a Hopi God?

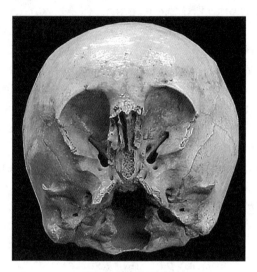

Starchild skull
(Courtesy of Lloyd Pye,
www.starchildproject.com.)

The Starchild skull stares back in eerie silence. We identify with its humanness. At the same time we are mesmerized by its strangeness. The skull has a certain symmetrical beauty that we don't find in other human deformities such as the Elephant Man. But is it really human?

This unique skull was found around 1930 in an abandoned mine tunnel near a tiny village one hundred miles southwest of the city of Chihuahua, Mexico. It was accidentally discovered by a teenaged girl from El Paso, Texas, who was visiting the original home of her parents.

While out wandering near the village, this girl found two complete skeletons deep inside the tunnel. One was a normal native woman about five feet tall. It was lying supine on the surface. The other skeleton about four feet tall was buried in a shallow grave. Its arm bone stuck out of the earth and was wrapped around the arm of the skeleton lying on top of the ground. The girl dug up what she called the "misshapen" skeleton and put the bones of both individuals in a large basket.

The Starchild skull had noticeably shallow eye sockets and an unusually broad shape at its back, or occipital region. It also had an uncharacteristic dent deforming the apex of its crown. As she put the skulls into the basket, she noticed that the larger one weighed only about half as much as the normal-sized skull. Surprisingly, the Starchild skull was later determined to be at least double the strength of normal human bone but only half as thick.

The girl then hid the bones in a copse of trees while she decided what to do with them. Unfortunately a huge rainstorm washed away most of the skeletons. She could only recover both skulls and a piece of the jaw from the "deformed" one, which she carried back into the U.S.

The young woman kept these skulls for the rest of her life. They have since changed hands twice. That's when Lloyd Pye* got involved.

Over an eight-year period, Pye has been the custodian of the skull and has directed an extensive series of osteological and DNA tests. Results show no signs of any congenital defects, such as hydrocephalus ("water on the brain"). The most recent DNA testing was reported in July of 2003.

The test on the mitochondrial DNA, which comes only from the mother, showed that the normal human adult female was haplogroup A, a typical Mesoamerican type. The mitochrondrial DNA of the Starchild skull proved to be haplogroup C, a rarer type of Mesoamerican but still human. This means that the normal female and the Starchild were not mother and child.

They were, in fact, not related at all. The normal human might have been a caretaker, friend, or even lover of the Starchild. Because the arms of the normal female and the Starchild were entwined, Pye speculates that the woman committed suicide after the Starchild had died and she had buried it. The mitochondrial test also proves that the mother of the Starchild was human.

The test on the nuclear DNA, which comes from inside the cell nucleus, again showed that the normal female was human. The same test on the Starchild skull, however, did not have any reading for human-only primers. This test was done six times and no human DNA coming from the father and the mother could be recovered at all.

Traditional scientists would say there must have been some sort of degradation for this to be the result. Lloyd Pye, on the other hand, claims that this is strong evidence that the father of the Starchild was an extraterrestrial. One final DNA test still needs to be done in order to verify that the Starchild was indeed a human-alien hybrid. Results from this new 454 Life Sciences technique of gene sequencing should be obtained by 2010. [www.454.com]

Analysis of part of the Starchild skull by a scanning electron microscope also revealed a strange durable fiber not found in any other species on Earth.

The normal skull and the Starchild skull were radiocarbon dated as well. The test shows that these two individuals died about 900 years ago, plus or minus forty years.

It just so happens that the time around 1100 AD was crucial for the Hopi Indians to the north. Most archaeologists believe this was the period when the tribe ended centuries of migrations and settled permanently on three large mesas in Arizona. They still live there today.

The place where the Starchild lived and died would not conceivably be out of the range of Hopi migrations. A great pueblo of ancestral Hopi was in fact located at Casas Grandes northwest of Chihuahua (not to be confused with Casa Grande Ruins National Monument near Phoenix).

The Hopi have a deity named Masau'u, also spelled Maasaw. Notice this description translated directly from the Hopi language in the book *Maasaw: Profile of a Hopi God* by Ekkehard Malotki and Michael Lomatuway'ma: "His head is so enormous and so bloody that it shines a little when light falls on it. His mouth is round and his eyes are hollow. Furthermore, his forehead bulges out in a large ridge."

*Petroglyph of cryptozoomorph
(on left) near Winslow, Arizona.*

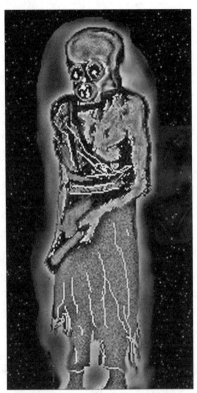

*Masau'u, Hopi god of death.
(Graphic adapted
from Petra Roeckerath.)*

*Masau'u katsina doll
(traditional style).*

*Pictograph of Tlaloc, Hueco
Tanks Historical Park, Texas.*

Masau'u is the god of the earth, fire, death, and the under-world. His head has also been described as being shaped like a summer squash, rather bulbous and bumpy. His eyes are goggle-like and close to each other.

This bizarre figure was there when the Hopi emerged from the previous Third World (or era) into the current Fourth World and began their migrations. He was also present at the end of their journey when they returned to their homeland in Arizona. Some say Masau'u himself directed these migrations across the continent.

He also has a *katsina* form and is represented by a corresponding doll. (See photo on p. 107. Hopi *katsinam,* also spelled *kachinas,* are masked beings that can represent any object or energy in the universe. Like angels, they are usually benevolent intercessors between the divine realm and the human realm.) The location of the eyes, absence of a nose, and the round mouth of this Hopi spirit messenger are very similar to those of the Starchild skull.

A pictograph (or rock painting) of the same figure has also been found at Hueco Tanks Historical Park just over thirty miles northeast of El Paso, where, coincidentally, the girl who found the Starchild skull lived. (See photo on p. 107.)

In addition, the rain god Tlaloc has goggle eyes and may be related. This was the main deity at Teotihuacán north of Mexico City.

Tlaloc, Teotihuacán, Mexico. Photo © by José Romelo Lagman.

The name of the god Masau'u is quite astounding. The Hopi root-word *mas* literally means "gray." If you look at artist rendition of Masau'u shown above, he does indeed look like contemporary versions of extraterrestrial Greys.

About five years ago I contacted Lloyd Pye and pointed out the similarity in form of the Starchild skull and the head of the Masau'u. He didn't really want to comment on that, and I respect his discretion. As he says in the Preface of his book: "Because the Starchild is so ripe with potential to change history, and so solidly documented, science must be –and must remain– at the forefront until the issue is resolved, one way or other, up or down, win or lose."

Still one has to wonder. Is there a link between the Starchild and a primary Hopi god? The Starchild skull and the head of Masau'u described in multiple Hopi oral accounts are strikingly similar. The shape of the head and the facial features closely correspond in each figure.

Also the slight frame of the Starchild's skeleton matches the spindly body that Masau'u is said to possess. (I use a present tense verb here because Masau'u apparently still visits the Hopi.) In legends Masau'u is sometimes called "Skeleton." This may refer to his very thin, ectomorphic body type. It may also symbolize his relationship to the land of the dead.

The approximate time when the Starchild died is the same period when Masau'u helped the Hopi establish the villages where they now live. Masau'u even directed the Hopi people to the exact locations where they should build their stone pueblos. In this sense he was both a helper and a teacher.

Also, the place where the Starchild died is only six hundred miles south of where the Hopi settled. Some believe that this distance would have been too far for the Starchild and/or the Hopi to travel. However, the discovery of parrots and macaws at many burial sites of ancient Hopi people contradict this notion. These birds are not native to the American Southwest but instead live fifteen hundred or more miles to the south.

The Hopi may have once traveled as far south as the

Maya territory in southern Mexico and Central America. An extensive trade network between the Hopi and the Maya surely existed in prehistoric times, so a walk of only five or six hundred miles would not at all have been out of the question.

The gloomy character of Masau'u in addition seems to parallel the numerous accounts we have of extraterrestrial Greys. The Hopi god is a nocturnal creature. His arrival is sometimes accompanied by balls of light or plasma dancing across the tops of mesas. He also travels between worlds. He rules this world but he is also the master of the spirit world. He is a dark and frightening figure whose presence is, at the very least, uncomfortable. He is sometimes even conceived of as a sort of judge in the underworld, a role similar to that of Osiris in ancient Egypt.

And like the Greys, Masau'u is known to have mated with human women. In one legend Masau'u goes to the house of a beautiful maiden. He does not, however, present himself in his horrific guise. Instead he appears as a handsome young man, finely dressed and wearing turquoise necklaces and long turquoise ear pendants. They soon get married and live together in the village "forever afterwards." Happily? The story does not say whether or not Masau'u ever showed his true appearance to her. [H. R. Voth, *The Traditions of the Hopi*, www.sacred-texts.com/nam/hopi/toth/toth034.htm]

The relationship between the Starchild and the Hopi god Masau'u remains a mystery, although comparisons between the two are certainly easy to see. The true nature of the nine hundred-year-old Starchild skull found in northern Mexico awaits the results of final genetic testing. The aura of the ancient Hopi god is shrouded in the memory of a very secretive people who still perform sacred rituals on the high desert of Arizona. Many in contemporary society continue to be inexplicably haunted by dream-like images of alien Greys.

Imagine that a celestial being from a star system light-years away came down to Earth and bred with a human female. This is not science fiction. This is exactly the story told in the Book of Genesis, when the "sons of God" mated with the "daughters of men."

Perhaps the Starchild was not really a child at all but a mature creature unlike any other on the planet. Is it possible that this alien/human hybrid or others like it was the same entity that the Hopi call Masau'u?

If the link between the Starchild skull and the ancient Hopi god could ever be proven, then our view of humanity and our place in the cosmos would be irrevocably changed. As Lloyd Pye remarks, we might be looking at "the most important relic in world history."

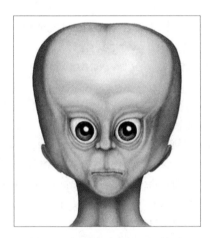

**Artist rendition of Starchild.
(Courtesy of Lloyd Pye,
www.starchildproject.com.)**

*For more details go to: www.starchildproject.com
and www.lloydpye.com.

Also see the newly published book by Lloyd Pye, *The Starchild Skull: Genetic Enigma or Human-Alien Hybrid?* (Bell Lap Books, Inc., Pensacola, Florida, 2007).

Drawing of the Hopi god Masau'u was adapted from Petra Roeckerath in *Maasaw: Profile of a Hopi God*

Chapter 9: The Ant People of Orion— Ancient Star Beings of the Hopi

All across the American Southwest we find rock art showing beings with spindly bodies, large eyes, and bulbous heads, some with antennae. These eerie figures are frequently shown in a "prayer stance," their elbows and knees at right angles, similar to an ant's bent legs. (See photo on p. 28.)

Do these rock drawings represent a race of Ant People? Do they record ancient encounters between humans and an alien species? Are the creatures truly "alien," like those of the 1947 UFO crash near Roswell, New Mexico? Or are they some strange zoological form from our own planet? If not, then are they merely projections from our collective unconscious? Let's examine the evidence.

The Hopi Indians of Arizona say that the Ant People played a primary role in the survival of their ancestors. These migrating Native Americans were another "chosen people" like the Hebrews. Only the good members of the tribe who followed a certain sacred star by night were able to find Sótuknang, the Hopi sky god. (See drawing on p. 99.) He eventually led them to the Ant People for protection.

The Ant People's caves provided sanctuary during both the destruction of the First World –the initial era– by fire (volcanism or asteroids) and the Second World by ice (glaciers). The Third World was destroyed by a deluge, though the Ant People did not help the Hopi that time. Instead the Hopi escaped the flood on bamboo rafts. Hopi elders say we are now at the end of the Fourth World.

The Hopi word for ant is *anu*, while *naki* means friend. The combination of these two words is *anu-naki* or "ant friend." This may be related to Zecharia Sitchin's Anunnaki. (See *The 12th Planet* and his other books.) Anu was also the name of the sky god of Babylon (modern-day Iraq). One Sumerian (pre-Babylonian) cylinder seal from around 2250 BC shows all the major deities wearing peaked hats. The Hopi sky god mentioned before also wears a pointed hat.

In addition, Anu was another name for Heliopolis across the Nile from the Great Pyramids. This Egyptian city contained a pointed structure called an obelisk with a "holy stone fallen from the sky" (a meteorite) sitting on top. In their book called *The Orion Mystery*, Robert Bauval and Adrian Gilbert claim that the three major pyramids at Giza reflect the pattern of Orion's belt.

The Maya share with the Egyptians and the Hopi a belief in Orion's importance. These Indians of southern Mexico also tell legends of ant-like men—peculiar beings who built stone cities and roads during the First Creation (similar to the Hopi First World). Their Ant People also possessed magical powers and could summon stones into proper architectural positions by just whistling. The Mayan word for these creatures means "the twisted men."

This reminds us of Kokopelli, or the humpbacked flute player, an insect-like figure found in rock art and tourist shops throughout the Southwest.

**Petroglyph of Kokopelli
near Winslow, Arizona.**

Many fans of Sitchin are familiar with the Nephilim, also spelled Nefilim. He translates the Sumerian letters NFL not as the football league but as "...those who were cast down upon the Earth!" Genesis 6:4 of the King James Bible calls them "giants in the earth." Before the Great Flood "the sons of God," interpreted as fallen angels or Watchers, mated with "the daughters of men" to produce these giants. It may be a case of synchronicity that the word Nephilim sounds like the Hebrew word *nemâlim*, which means ants. We are talking here about very, very big ants, or more exactly, humanoids with ant-like characteristics.

Masonic researchers Christopher Knight and Robert Lomas claim that the Aramaic word *nephîliâ* means "those that are of the constellation Orion." [*Uriel's Machine*] The name Orion is formed by dropping the "m" in the Indo-European word *morui*. Astoundingly, this word means ant. Perhaps the constellation was named that because its thin, human-like waist resembles the insect.

The Hopi call Orion by the name *Hotòmqam*, meaning either beads on a string or the number three. This could refer to the three stars of Orion's belt. It could also refer to the three shiny, bead-like sections of the ant's body: head, thorax, and abdomen.

Many of the Hopi's annual religious ceremonies are timed by the appearance of Orion through the overhead hatchways in what are called kivas. These partly subterranean prayer chambers actually look like anthills. Each February the Hopi perform the Bean Dance inside the kivas. Fires are kept continuously ablaze, turning these underground structures into superb hot houses. This ritual may commemorate a time when the Ant People taught the Hopi how to sprout beans inside caverns.

Ants resonate in our unconscious minds as inhabitants of both the surface of the earth and the underworld. Mythological and linguistic evidence indicates, however, that the image of ant-like humanoids is more than a mere psychological reaction to the tiny *Formicidae* (scientific name for ants) of the natural world. Why else would the mass media constantly give E.T.s the characteristics of bugs? Unlike the fantastic but vague images of our dreams, Ant People appear terrifyingly real.

If these creepy creatures are an extinct or isolated species from Earth like Big Foot or the Loch Ness Monster, we have yet to uncover any fossil or skeletal evidence of their past existence. (Lloyd Pye's Starchild skull is about the closest thing ever found. See Chapter 8.)

Were the Ant People (in Hebrew, *nemâlim*) actually the Nephilim, the children of women who mated with rebellious angels?

Did agents from Orion, whose name means ant, come to the southwestern United States to save the Hopi from two different natural cataclysms? Did these agents remember when they genetically manipulated the Hopi long ago and as a result felt some sort of responsibility?

When Orion dominates winter skies, the ants are deep in their own "kivas" (anthills). Were the caves in which the Hopi of Arizona found refuge really the anthills of ancient star beings?

These questions may never be fully answered. Nevertheless, they keep us intrigued.

Round kiva at San Ildefonso, New Mexico.

A Contemporary Sighting

"I made this sketch immediately after I recovered from the apparition of what I call an 'ant person' that appeared right in front of me at the foot of our bed when I walked into the room alone. This was at our home outside of Tucson, Arizona, just about two years ago. I stood there for a second in awe until my fear kicked in and said, 'What the hell is that?' I ran out of the room terrified and immediately told my wife Susan about it. It had been moving slightly as if it were a real physical form not two feet away, basically staring me right in the face. The creature I saw had "carapaces." It also had slight hairs on curving rows of lines on these carapaces, and the entire body had a black sheen, as one can see on a black ant, if observant." – Jack Andrews

Chapter 10: The Serpent Knights of the Round Temple

Round Towers Around the Globe

Like pyramids, circular towers of stone can be found on both sides of the Atlantic. The common figure linking these structures, however, proves to be the serpent or snake. Cultures as diverse as the Celts of Ireland and the Hopi of Arizona associate this religiously and psychologically charged reptile with those round temples reaching toward moisture-laden storm clouds.

Over sixty-five towers of exquisite masonry, some rising more than one hundred feet high, dot the green countryside of Ireland. The monasteries of Monasterboice, Domhnach, and Kilkenny were all built adjacent to earlier round towers. (See photo on top of p. 169.) Although they may have served as fire temples dedicated to sun worship, most of these commanding structures are located next to healing springs or holy wells issuing from the subterranean realm over which the snake rules. (Also see Martin Gray's "Places of Peace and Power" Website: www.sacredsites.com/2nd56/190.html.)

The Phoenicians may have spread this unique architectural feature globally in homage to Baal, the fertility deity of rain, thunder, and lightning. In his book *Jesus, Last of the Pharaohs*, Ralph Ellis avers that round towers were modeled after the Egyptian Benben tower located in the Phoenix Temple at Heliopolis. (The Phoenicians were named after the mythical bird that rose from its ashes. See Chapter 5.) Morphologically similar to round towers, the *djed* pillar was known as the "backbone of Osiris." This column symbolically channeled kundalini (serpent energy) up the vertebrae.

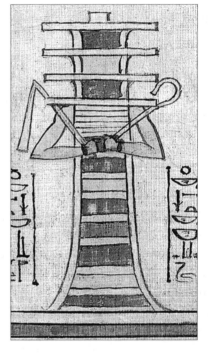

**Upper left:
East Indian stupa.
Upper right:
Egyptian djed pillar.
Lower left:
Temple Church, London.
Round section
completed 1185 AD.
[Picturesque England,
www.mspong.org/picturesque.]**

Over 7,000 circular towers called Nuraghi from the second millennium BC are found on the island of Sardinia north of the ancient Phoenician city of Carthage (modern-day Tunis). On the Maltese island of Gozo the Gigantija, or Giants' Tower, was constructed a millennium before the Great Pyramid. Its elliptical chambers at one time possibly supported towers. A stone relief discovered at the site depicts a serpent.

Perhaps serving as a model for the minaret, the Radkan Tower in northeastern Iran is circular with a conical cap. Archeoastronomer Manochehr Arian (Zia) has found solstice and equinox alignments for this structure, suggesting a sophisticated observation of the sky going back at least eight hundred years and probably more. [www.jamejamshid.com]

Moving from the Near to the Far East, we can easily see how the design of the Indian stupa or Chinese pagoda is another form of the round tower. According to the principles of *feng shui*, the pagoda traps negative *ch'i*, or dragon energy, located in the earth.

This belief stems from the popular legend of the celestial Lady White Snake, who enchanted a mortal with her beauty and gave birth to his son. A monk eventually discovered her true nature and summoned the elemental powers to imprison her inside Thunder Pagoda for a thousand years.

Most of Europe's Gothic cathedrals were constructed using designs uncovered by the Knights Templar in a 12th century excavation of Jerusalem's Temple Mount. A key architectural feature of this fraternal organization (which eventually gave rise to both the Rosicrucians and the Freemasons) was the round temple.

In his book *Sacred Geometry* Nigel Pennick explains the symbolism of this form: "Like the Pagan temples, the round churches were microcosms of the world. In the late Middle Ages, they became the prerogative of an enigmatic and heretical sect, the Knights Templar. The round form of church became especially connected with the order..." One example of this architecture is London's Temple Church, which was featured in Dan Brown's novel *The Da Vinci Code*.

Some believe that a group of Knights Templar even sailed to the New England coast in 1308 and erected a Romanesque round tower at Newport, Rhode Island. In their book *Templars in America*, co-authors Tim-Wallace Murphy and Marilyn Hopkins comment: "...the elders of the Narragansett Indians have a tradition that states that the tower was constructed by 'Green-eyed, fire-haired giants who came in peace, had a battle and then left.'"

Newport Tower in Rhode Island.
[Photo courtesy of Donald Sinclair, *www.caithness.org*]

The Serpent and the Circle

In a Christian context the serpent suggests the Devil and his minions who were "...cast out into the earth..." (Revelation 12:9) In his excellent book *From the Ashes of Angels*, Andrew Collins refers to an apocalyptic fragment from the Dead Sea Scrolls called the Testament of Amram. As father to Moses, Amram perceives in a dream-vision a Watcher named Belial. He is "terrifying in appearance, like a serpent..." and "his visage [is] like a viper..." The figure of Belial found in II Corinthians 6:15 means "lawlessness," "worthless," or "reckless" and is an appellation of Satan. The word "serpent," Collins adds, is synonymous with both the Watchers found in *The Book of Enoch* and the Nephilim. The latter denotes the "giants in the earth" from Genesis 6:4.

Contrary to the Latinate cross representing the body of Christ, a circular structure stands for the worldly or even satanic domain. In addition, it signifies a center called an *omphalos* where tellurian serpent forces accumulate. This Greek word literally means "navel" and refers to the oracular Stone of Splendor at Delphi, which had the ability to directly communicate with the gods.

The figures of the serpent and the circle are united in the Gnostic and alchemical symbol called the Ouroboros. This serpent biting its tail designates world-creating spirit hidden within matter.

Omphalos stone at Delphi, Greece.

Round Towers in the Four Corners

Numerous round towers built by the Anasazi can still be found in the American Southwest. At the Chetro Ketl pueblo ruin in Chaco Canyon, New Mexico, a round "tower kiva" rises three stories high. (See Gary David's book *The Orion Zone*, photo on p. 272.)

Circular towers at Kin Kletso and Tsin Kletsin in the same canyon are also found, and the Chacoan outliers of Salmon Ruin forty miles due north and Kin Ya'a Ruin twenty-five miles due south contain similar structures.

Round towers are located as well at the spectacular cliff dwellings in Mesa Verde National Park of southwestern Colorado. These include Cliff Palace, Sun Temple, Cedar Tree Tower, and Far View Community. The Cajon Group at Hovenweep National Monument in southeastern Utah also exemplifies this type of ceremonial structure. Circular buildings are found at Mummy Cave Ruin in Canyon de Chelly and at Wukoki Ruin at Wupatki National Monument. Both of these sites located in Arizona are traditional homes of the Snake Clan.

**Cliff Palace, Mesa Verde, Colorado.
Tree-ring dated from 1190 AD, five years after
Temple Church in London was constructed.
(Photo by Ansel Adams, courtesy of The U.S.
National Archives & Records Adminstration.)**

**Astronomical observatory
at Chichén Itzá, Mexico,
called El Caracol,
which literally means "snail."
This refers to its inner spiral
staircase made of stone.
The structure is aligned
to solstice sunrises and
sunsets, equinoxes, and the
motions of Venus.**

Incidentally, the astronomical orientations of Wukoki Ruin are akin to those of the circular Caracol observatory at Chichén Itzá built three hundred years earlier by the Yucatan Maya, who worshipped the plumed serpent Kukulkan. (See photo on the bottom of the previous page.)

The Hopi refer to round towers as "snake houses." A narrative describing the origin of the Snake Clan mentions that the wife of the culture hero Tiyo gave birth to a brood of venomous snakes, which kept getting loose. In one version of the myth, Masau'u (or Masau, Hopi god of death, the earth, and the Underworld) explains to the snake mother why her children no longer can have a house in which to live.

> "And Masau said, 'No, the snakes have no houses; because they have bitten and killed Hopi they should never again have a house, but should live under rocks and in holes in the ground.' But he also said the snakes houses (the round towers) which were built for them should never again be destroyed and that all coming generations of people should know the snake's doom, never again to have a house." [Stephen, "The Journal of American Folklore"]

We are obviously talking not about rattlesnake pens but either the temples or domiciles of a dangerous, snake-like race. They may even have been home to what we now call the Reptilians. The same Hopi myth concludes with a nocternal offering to the recovered snakes:

> "...they took the first snake they had found and washed its head and gave it the name Chüa (he of the earth) and decorated it with beads and ear rings. Then the Youth [Tiyo] opened a bag and gave the people cotton and beads and said as the snakes had brought rain the people should now be happy and content, and on every celebration of the Snake festival good things would be given to them."

Chüa is the Hopi name of the worshipped snake that initiated their biennial rain ceremony still performed on the high desert of Arizona. This name is similar to "Chna," an English transliteration of the Greek word referring to the Phoenician land of Canaan. The biblical Anakim were known to have hailed from southern Canaan.

The offerings of earrings and necklaces are particularly significant. Andrew Collins also states that the Nephilim were known as the sons of the Anakim. "The word Anak is generally taken by Jewish scholars to mean 'long-necked', or 'the men with the necklaces'..." In this context it is curious that the Hopi term *naaqa* means "turquoise necklace" or "ear pendant " and that *anaaq* means "ouch!", an interjection used to express extreme pain, such as that caused by snakebite.

In addition, Baal, the Phoenician rain god mentioned above, is similar in sound and sense to the Hopi word *paal*. (Because the Hopi have no "b'" sound, "p" is the closest approximation.) This word means "liquid," "tree sap," "juice," or "broth." Its root word *pa* (or *paa*) denotes "water," but it also has the sense of "wonder."

The Hopi legend previously mentioned might point to the Indo-European Nagas, those snake worshipping seafarers originating from the Indus River Valley. (See Chapter 12.) They are also known as the Long Ears, who stretched their lobes with earplugs. Coincidentally, archaeologists found an example of this artifact in an ancient pueblo ruin known as Snaketown near modern-day Phoenix.

The Black Plague and the Knights of the Round Temple

Around 1300 AD most of the villages on the Colorado Plateau that had been inhabited for a century or more were suddenly and "mysteriously" abandoned.

At least some archaeologists find this depopulation mysterious. If one takes a more a more global viewpoint, however, the concurrent Black Death provides a causal explanation. The bubonic plague killed as much as one-third of the populations of Europe, the Muslim world, and China during this time. The pandemic may have originally spread westward from Norway to Iceland and Greenland, and thence on Viking ships to the New World.

The southwestern U.S., with its dry climate and large rodent populations, make it particularly susceptible to the spread of disease. Larger pueblos were the norm after the beginning of 1100's. (At the same time the Templars back in the Old World were flourishing.) Those living in these villages must have been especially hard hit. The survival strategy would have been to seek conditions of decreased population density in smaller, more widely dispersed villages. John G. Bourke, aid to General Crook in the Apache campaign, writes in his book *Snake-Dance of the Moquis*: "The Navajoes say that the cliff-dwellers were carried off by a bad wind. He [an old Diné man] repeated this statement without explaining his meaning. Was this bad wind a pestilence or an epidemic? Such a supposition is not altogether unreasonable." If indeed a factor, this is yet another piece of evidence in favor of pre-Columbian contact.

Templar Testament

Did the Phoenicians, who might have assisted the Anasazi in building the round towers, come to the American Southwest and establish outposts in order to trade with the latter? Were the Knights Templar the recipients of this Naga/Phoenician legacy, carrying forth the ancient traditions bequeathed from Egypt? Do these structures form a global network centered upon ophidian fertility symbols?

To return to our starting point, were the Irish round towers also "snake houses," or phallic temples used by a race of serpent people whom St. Patrick in the 5th century AD ultimately had to chase into the sea?

Perhaps we are uncovering more questions than answers. Nonetheless, round towers survive as a testament to the awesome spiritual power of the Knights of the Round Temple. Their serpentine eyes gaze across the centuries, now and then sending a shiver up the spine.

Does this Utah petroglyph show a Knight Templar?

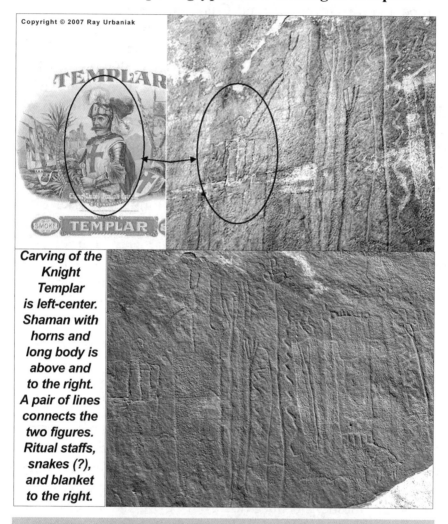

Copyright © 2007 Ray Urbaniak

TEMPLAR

SMOKE TEMPLAR

Carving of the Knight Templar is left-center. Shaman with horns and long body is above and to the right. A pair of lines connects the two figures. Ritual staffs, snakes (?), and blanket to the right.

"The panel is not widely known because it is hidden in plain sight in downtown St. George, Utah. It is an incredibly beautiful panel and is unique to the area, but very faint from patination and erosion. I would estimate its age to be around 3,000 years old from the early Anasazi Basketmaker period.

"When I first saw the small figure, which appears to be a projection from the head of the Shaman, it reminded me of a Knights Templar drawing I had seen. Could this have been a vision seen by a Shaman long ago?" –Ray Urbaniak, author of Anasazi of SW Utah: The Dance of Light and Shadow. Purchase this book on rock art at: www.naturalfrequency.net.

Chapter 11: Coming Up Through the Reed— Hopi Legends, Global Legacies

"He [the Creator] then gave them instructions according to which they were to migrate for a certain purpose to the four corners of the new land, leaving many footprints, rock writings, and ruins, for in time many would forget that they were all one, united by a single purpose in coming up through the reed."

Dan Katchongva, the late spiritual elder, Hopi Sun Clan

The current world we now live in is not the first world. According to the Hopi Indians of northern Arizona, the world has been destroyed three times before. Legends of this tribe say that the First World, or epoch, was destroyed by fire. In particular this may have been an asteroid accompanied by volcanism. The Second World was terminated by ice—possibly a pole shift leading to an Ice Age.

The Third World was decimated by a flood, mythological variations of which exist in most cultures around the globe. The few virtuous Hopis who still clung to the ways of the Creator escaped the rising waters by crawling up through a bamboo reed that extended to the sky and stuck up into the next world like a kiva ladder.

In the progression from the Third to our current Fourth World, three birds were present: a swallow (or swift), a white dove, and a hawk. Each one in turn flew up through the hole in the sky in an attempt to reach the upper world, but each one failed. Finally a catbird (or shrike) flew through this hole (called a *sipapu*). While flying around, the catbird saw Masau'u, god of both the earth and the Underworld, and asked permission for the people to live there.

Left: A Hopi bride carries a reed mat that contains her wedding blanket. She wears this blanket at the next katsina farewell ceremony in July and also at the naming of her first child. In the end it becomes her shroud.
[*www.gutenberg.org/files/ 15888/15888-h/15888-h.htm*]
Below: Atlantes (Toltec warrior statues) at Tula, Hidalgo, known as "The Place of the Reeds."
[*http://en.wikipedia.org/wiki/ Tula,_Mexico*]

Then the humble chipmunk planted a sunflower seed, a spruce seed, a pine seed, and finally a bamboo seed in the ground. The growth of one of these would to serve as a ladder to the upper world. It is only the bamboo reed, however, that was tall and straight enough to pierce the sky. The people ascended through the tunnel of the great reed to the upper world and emerged upon the Colorado Plateau, where they still live.

No native bamboo grows on the Colorado Plateau, but a species reaching a height of fifteen to twenty feet is found in southwestern Arizona. The Hopi word for bamboo reed is *paaqavi*. The first Hopi village was established on Second Mesa in northern Arizona about 1100 AD. It was called Songòopavi, or literally "the place by the spring where the tall reeds grow." Another village established much later was called Bacavi, or "place of the jointed reed." The Hopi also have a Bamboo Clan called Wukopaqavi, meaning "large reed." The word for reed flute is *paqaplena*.

Incredible as it may seem, the Hopi, those inveterate denizens of the desert, were once a seafaring people—or at least another of their clans was. In an alternate version of the legend described above, the Water Clan escaped the deluge by sailing on reed boats eastward across the Pacific Ocean to dry land. The Hopi name for this clan is Patkinyamu, literally "Houseboat Clan."

Drifting toward the rising sun, the people landed on one "steppingstone" after another. They wanted to stay but were told by Spider Woman that these islands were too pleasant and that they must keep moving. (A common theme in Hopi migrations is that places of ease naturally lead to sloth and corruption.) Still they sailed onward, going "uphill" (upstream?), "...traveling, still east and a little north." It is possible that after crossing the sea they floated into the Gulf of California and paddled up the Colorado River.

One steppingstone on this monumental journey may have been the remote South Pacific islands of Fiji. Here the highly secretive Baki ceremony was once held. This was essentially a youth initiation and fertility ritual. Because the Hopi language usually does not recognize the sound of the letter 'b', the word *paki* sounds nearly the same. This Hopi word means "entered" or "started being initiated," similar in meaning to the Fiji word. The kiva used during the Snake Dance is called a *pakit*.

Where the Hopi originated is a great mystery. The Hopi word for the Milky Way is *songwuka*, literally "the big reed." The cognate *so'ngwamiq* means "towards the end" or "towards the source." The related term *songowu* refers to the smaller reeds used to make a storage case for a woman's wedding robe woven of white cotton that will be buried with her after her death. (See photo on the top of p. 128.) This tradition reminds us of the mythological significance of the hollow reed in the Hopi migration from the previous Third World to the present Fourth World, and the fact that reed boats were used to navigate to the west coast of North America.

Breaking down the word *songwuka*, we find that *soo-* is the prefix of the word "star" and *ngwuvi* is a root that means "climb." From this we can deduce that *songwuka* is the galactic tunnel through which the ancient star people journeyed in order to descend to their terrestrial home.

Again, the first village settled on the Hopi Mesa was called Songòopavi, literally "place of the reed." Perhaps this name not only describes the moist area of settlement where an abundance of reeds once grew but more importantly it commemorates the Ancient Ones' crossing over to Earth through the metonymic reed known as the Milky Way. In addition, the Reed Clan is associated with Sótuknang, who is the Hopi "Heart of the Sky" god. (See drawing on p. 99.)

Mesoamerica also has a number of locations designated by the reed. The ancestral home of the Aztecs was known not only as "place of the heron" but also the "place of the reeds." The Aztecs initially assumed that Hernando Cortés was the feathered serpent Quetzalcoatl making his prophesied return. Cortés and his conquistadores arrived on the Atlantic coast on Easter 1519, which was the Aztec year Ce Acatl, or One Reed. This year marked the end of a fifty-two year cycle when the world would either be renewed or destroyed. Sadly for the Aztec leader Moctezuma of Tenochtitlán (now Mexico City), the latter occurred.

The apotheosized chieftain of the Toltecs was called Mixcoatl, or "Cloud Serpent." About 900 AD his son, who was named Ce Acatl Topiltzin (a.k.a. Quetzalcoatl), founded the city of Tula, or Tollan. This means the "Place of Reeds." (See photo on the bottom of p. 128.)

The late Linda Schele, a Maya archeologist, speculated that the original "place of the reeds" was the Gulf Coast swamps of the Olmec heartland. This is apparently where civilization, writing, the arts, and organized warfare for this whole region began. Later the name was applied to the major Toltec center of Teotihuacán as well. Mayan cities with this same identification include Uxmal, Copan, Tikal, and Utatlán.

The pre-Incan Uros people along with the Aymara living around Lake Titicaca in Peru claim to be descendants of the builders of the Tiahuanaco. Some archaeologists estimate this grand city to be an astounding 15,000 to 20,000 years old. The Uros still reside on floating islands made of totora reeds. As the bottoms of the islands rot away, they add more reeds to the tops. This quintessential reed culture lives in reed houses, sails on reed boats, and weaves reed handicrafts.

North and South America are not the only places where the reed gained cultural significance.

The ancient Egyptian afterlife similar to the Greek Elysian Fields was called the Field of Reeds. An oasis called the Faiyum was probably the naturalistic origin of this concept.

Some of the vignettes in *The Book of the Dead* depict the Heron of Plenty perched upon a small pyramid. It is interesting to note that the hieroglyph of a heron upon a pyramid corresponds to the word *bah*, meaning "to flood, to inundate." This, of course, is just the environment where reeds grow. Other vignettes show a celestial bark containing a staircase, which looks like half a stepped pyramid cut vertically. These stairs represent transcendence and rebirth.

Commenting on Egyptian funerary literature, Zecharia Sitchin writes in his book *The Stairway to Heaven*:

> "The pictorial depictions which accompanied the hiero-glyphic texts surprisingly showed the Stream of Osiris as meandering its way from an agricultural area, through a chain of mountains, to where the stream divides into trib-utaries. There, watched over by the legendary Phoenix birds, the Stairway to Heaven was situated; there, the Celestial Boat of Ra was depicted as sitting atop a moun-tain, or rising heavenward upon streams of fire."

In papyrus illustrations of The Field of Rushes we also find either the falcon or a small, human-headed bird represent-ing the *ba*, sounding the same as the word *bah* previously men-tioned. The *ba*, or "soul," perches atop a pylon, which is a mas-sive rectangular gateway to a temple or hypostyle hall. Thus, the pylon is a perfect symbol for the stargate. In addition, the walls of the Field of Rushes are made of iron, presumably meteoric iron, which further stresses its celestial meaning.

The more mundane usage of the reed was connected to writing. The reed's cultural significance is emphasized by its use as both an instrument for writing and the material for making papyrus.

Music is also an earmark of culture. Reeds of different lengths are put together to form the panpipe, or syrinx. The Greek nymph Syrnix was lasciviously pursued by Pan and changed into a reed to escape violence.

The Babylonian creation myth called the *Enuma elish* envi-sions a primeval time before reeds grew. Used for building houses and boats, the reed would become an essential cultural artifact for the ancient marshland dwellers of southern Iraq. One version of the creation describes the dragon slayer Merodach laying a reed upon the surface of the water and pouring dust upon it to create humankind.

***Vignette from* The Egyptian Book of the Dead.
On second level: heron (phoenix) on pyramid.
Lower level: "The Boat of Millions of Years."**

The Egyptian **ba** *represented the "soul."
This bird with a human head
raises its hands in prayer or praise.*

The Japanese creation myth says that the first object to arise out of the ocean of chaos was a reed named Kunitokotachi, the eternal ruler of land. In Philippine mythology the first man and woman named Sikalak and Sikabay came out of a split bamboo reed. In China the bamboo was a symbol of longevity and was one of the Four Noble Plants. Its fiber was also used to make paper.

Given the variety of geographical locations across the globe for the "place of the reeds," we may conclude that it is much more than a reference to flora. For the Hopi Indians of Arizona the reed certainly represents migration, a vast journey across either an ocean of salt water or an ocean of stars.

Ultimately the reed or bamboo designates a place of high culture and ancient wisdom—the sort of location where astronomer-priests would normally scan the heavens for door-ways through which the soul could make its passage to the Otherworld.

Whether used for houses, boats, ropes, writing implements, paper, musical instruments, or passageways to higher dimensions, the reed resonates through the winds of time, playing upon our imagination.

Is the figure on the right an Egyptian hedjet *crown (front toward bottom)? Cottonwood Creek Ruin, Arizona. (See bottom of next page.)*

*Petroglyphs, left to right: round face (the Hopi god Masau'u),
ritual artifact connected to a human figure in the "prayer stance,"
heron stabbling a human (or frog?) in same stance.
Below bird is an inverted pyramid
and possibly thirteen dots formed in a circle.
The heron is frequently associated with "place of the reeds."
Newspaper Rock at Petrified Forest National Park, Arizona.*

*The Narmer Palette, reverse side,
c. 3100 BC (Age of Taurus). King
Narmer (possibly Menes) wears the
White Crown of Upper Egypt. A falcon (representing Horus) perches
on six papyrus reeds. Some suggest that Narmer is identified with
Orion (Osiris), while the two figures
below are the Gemini twins. Behind
Narmer is a bright star (Sirius?);
in front are the fanning reed stalks
(perhaps the six main stars of the
V-shaped Hyades cluster in
Taurus). Note bull-heads at top. The
Tau symbol between them contains
the ruler's name. (See Chapter 14.
Also read Greg Taylor's fine essay
at: www.dailygrail.com/node/297.)*

135

Chapter 12: The Nagas—Origin of the Hopi Snake Clan?

The Snake Dance has both attracted and repulsed non-Indian spectators since the late nineteenth century. During this infamous ritual performed every other August on the Hopi Mesas of Arizona, participants handle a mass of venomous and non-venomous snakes. Some even put necks and bodies into their mouths.

Unlike ophiolatry (serpent worship), the Snake Dance is a plea for agricultural fertility and rain in a beautiful but harsh desert landscape. Many spectators would be surprised to learn, however, that this bizarre rite came from India, the traditional land of snake charmers.

An ancient Hopi myth describes a migration from the flooded Third World (or era) to the Fourth World. The ancestral Hopi escaped on reed rafts and made their way to the mouth of the Colorado River, up which they traveled to seek their final destination upon the Colorado Plateau.

In the last chapter we mentioned Fiji as a possible "steppingstone" in this migration to the New World. A *naga* or *nanaga* was one of many walled sites where Fiji boys entered manhood. Explorer David Hatcher Childress writes in his book *Ancient Tonga & the Lost City of Mu'a* that "...one of the ancient races of Southeast Asia is the Nagas, a seafaring race of people who traded in their 'Serpent Boats' similar to the Dragon ships of the Vikings."

Originating in India, the Nagas established religious centers throughout the country, including the Kingdom of Kashi on the Ganges, Kashmir to the north, and Nagpur in central India. The Nagas also inhabited the great metropolitan centers of Mohenjo-Daro and Harrappa in the Indus River Valley. They founded a port city on the Arabian Sea and exchanged goods globally, using a universal currency of cowries.

**Hopi Snake Priests
with snake in mouth,
circa 1930.
The Snake Dance
is still performed
in Hopiland.
[*www.gutenberg.org/files/
15888/15888-h/15888-h.htm*]**

**Snake charmer
in Jaipur, India—
original country
of the Nagas.**

137

As masters of arcane wisdom, the Nagas bequeathed to Mesoamerica the concept of *nagual*—too complex to explain here but thoroughly delineated in the books by Carlos Castaneda about his tutelage with the Yaqui sorcerer Don Juan Matus.

The Nagas may also have been the Snake People whom the Hopi culture hero Tiyo met on his epic voyage across the ocean. In the underworld he enters a room where people wear snake skins. He is initiated into strange ceremonials, in which he learns rain prayers. After the young man is given a pair of maidens who sing to help corn grow, he carries them home to the earth's surface. The Snake Woman becomes his wife, while the other becomes the bride of Flute youth. Finally his wife gives birth to reptiles, which causes Tiyo to leave his family and migrate to another country.

Like Homer's *Odyssey*, the story involves a subterranean visit. Paradoxically, the Hopi conceptualize this as a realm of both water and stars. Nanga Sohu is the Chasing Star *katsina*, who wears a Plains-style eagle feather headdress and a large four-pointed star painted on his mask. (*Katsinam,* we recall, are spirits in the form of any object, creature, or phenomenon.)

Nanga means "to pursue" and *sohu* means "star." The snake-like headdress somewhat resembles a meteor trail.

Related to Naga, the Hopi word *nga'at* means "medicine root" with magical healing properties. A root is both chthonic and morphologically snake-like. The term *nakwa* refers to headdress feathers worn during a sacred ceremony. This plumage suggests the feathered serpent. Another related word, *naqvu'at*, means "ear," and *naaqa* refers to "ear pendant," frequently made of abalone.

**Hopi drawing of Nanga Sohu, Chasing Star katsina.
[Fewkes, Hopi Katcinas, Dover Publications, Inc.]**

This jewelry was worn in respectful imitation rather than mere adornment. Childress, in the same book cited above, describes the so-called Long Ears:

"As tall, bearded navigators of the world, they were probably a combination of Egyptian, Libyan, Phoenician, Ethiopian, Greek and Celtic sailors in combination with Indo-Europeans from the Indian subcontinent. According to Polynesian legend, these sailors also have the famous 'long ears' that are well known on both Rapa Nui [Easter Island] and Rarotonga."

According to the mariner/scholar Thor Heyerdahl, ruling families of the Incas artificially lengthened their earlobes to distinguish themselves vis-à-vis their subjects. (An earmark indeed! Perhaps Buddha with his long earlobes is no coincidence either.)

Author James Bailey believes that these rulers of Peru and some Pacific islands were Aryan and Semitic peoples originating from the Indus River Valley. He writes in his book *The God-King & the Titans*:

"[Heyerdahl] showed that there lived on Easter Island the survivors of two distinct populations; the long-ears, a fair or red-headed European people who used to stretch their ear-lobes with wooden plugs so that they reached down to their shoulders and a Polynesian group of conventional Polynesian type, with natural ears. The first people had been known on the island as 'long ears', the second people as 'short-ears'."

The former group attained an average height of six-and-a-half feet, and had white skin with red hair. It may be more than coincidence that members of the Hopi Fire Clan were known as the "redheads." These war-like people lived with the Snake Clan at Betatakin, a late thirteenth century Arizona cliff dwelling (now in Navajo National Monument).

Easter Island statue.

Easter Island may have been another steppingstone in the ancient Hopi migration. Some of the tall, long-eared statues called Moai were carved with red top-knots. That Easter Island lies on the same meridian as does the current home of the Hopi may be just another "coincidence."

Noting the earplugs worn by tribes in Tanzania, Bailey comments on the ubiquity of this artifact: "The ear-plug is itself symptomatic of contact with sea-people and I believe has a common origin all over the world, wherever it is found."

As noted before, one example of this ring-type earplug carved from schist was found in ancient ruins near Phoenix, Arizona. Here we see artifacts common to both desert and maritime people.

Mythological themes common to disparate cultures also exist. Scholar Cyrus H. Gordon relates a narrative from the early second millennium BC. An Egyptian captain is shipwrecked on the "island of Ka," possibly located near Somalia in the Indian Ocean. (The Hopi *ka-* in *katsina* is foreign and may be related to the Egyptian *Ka*, or *doppelgänger*. See Chapter 16.) This paradise abounds in gorgeous birds as well as huge fish, delicious fruits, and vegetables. There's only one catch. A serpent thirty cubits (forty-five feet) long rules it. This giant snake has gold plated skin, lapis lazuli eyebrows, and a beard extending two cubits (three feet).

After the sovereign serpent threatens to incinerate him for remaining silent, the captain relates how he and his crew were driven there by a fierce storm. In turn, the king describes his brethren and children, who once totaled seventy-two. He continues: "Then a star fell and these (serpents) went forth in the flame it produced. It chanced I was not with them when they were burned. I was not among them (but) I just about died for them, when I found them as one corpse."

The captain's boat is then loaded with fine spices including myrrh, elephant tusks, giraffe tails, and monkeys. Before allowing him to leave, the king makes this curious remark: "It will happen that when you depart from this place, this island will never be seen again, for it will become water." [Gordon, *Before Columbus*]

Whether or not he had long ears, the tale does not say. However, we may be witnessing one of the legendary Nagas. Beside the serpentine motif, this fabulous story contains a theme redolent of Atlantis or Mu. An Edenic island suddenly disappears beneath the waves in a celestial cataclysm destroying many lives.

Do the Hopi myth of Tiyo's journey to the Island of Snakes and the Egyptian myth of the anonymous captain's journey to the Island of Ka have a common source? We will never know for certain.

Likewise, we can only speculate on the seventy-two serpents encoded in the latter myth. This might refer to an astronomical movement of which astute mariners were undoubtedly aware.

Due to the precession of the equinoxes, zodiac stars rising on the first day of spring and autumn shift backwards (currently from Pisces to Aquarius) one degree every seventy-two years. This is caused by the wobble of the Earth's axis (its precession) like a spinning top. In the Egyptian tale the king's seventy-two relatives were killed by a falling sidereal event. Hence, the "skyscape" known for a lifetime or more was overturned, only to be replaced by a slightly altered one.

An isolationist would say that ancient people lacked the sophisticated observational skills to recognize a single degree of difference, or that early civilizations were technologically incapable of crossing oceans. In fact, many myths contradicting this seem to have been conceived by diffusionists. (See Appendix 2.)

I am not suggesting that an elite corps of Old World Whites came to "save" the scattered bands of "savage" Native Americans, thereby allowing the latter to flourish. (The cultural genocide in the New World during 16th through the 19th centuries makes that scenario particularly ironic.) This view denigrates both cultures, assigning a monolithic imperialism to the former and an evolutionary inferiority to the latter. In short, this is racism at its worst.

I *am* saying that the collective ingenuity of the peoples of North and South America together with the peoples of Oceania allowed them to sail to distant lands very early on. Likewise, the peoples of Europe and Asia used the same ingenuity to land on equally distant shores. The navigational knowledge of seafarers from all over the globe must have been a common currency.

This may be how a serpent cult from India made it to the high desert of Arizona.

***Hopi Snake Dance, late 19th or early 20th century.
(Courtesy of The U.S. National Archives
and Records Administration.)***

Chapter 13: Thunderclouds Over Palatki—
A Sanskrit OM Symbol In Arizona

*—dedicated to Shree. T. L. Subash Chandira Bose,
brother, friend, colleague.*

"The goal which all Vedas proclaim, which all austerities
aim at, and which humans desire when they live a life of
continence and service, I will tell it to thee briefly—it is
OM."

Katha Upanishad

Palatki must have been an incredibly gorgeous place to
live. Located in Loy Canyon in the Sedona red rock country of
Arizona, impressive blood-hued buttes and blazing orange cliffs
rise to dizzying heights. Even the casual tourist is not immune
from the peaceful waves of bliss washing across this magical
landscape. Deer skitter between agave cacti and juniper bushes,
while turkey vultures drift on spiral updrafts. Thunderclaps
crack against canyon walls, and resplendent ribbons of water
cascade down each cliff face, producing cool rivulets of rebirth.
Here the mystery of OM is manifested in nature herself.

Palatki in the Hopi language simply means "red house."
The two-story pueblo ruin of stacked masonry was just one hundred and twenty feet long and contained at least seven ground
floor rooms in a single row. The bow-shaped front wall of the
structure stands at the base of towering cliffs made of brilliant
red Supai sandstone. The cliff dwelling was inhabited from
about 1150 through 1300 AD.

This pueblo was built by the ancestral Hopi who were
called the Hisatsinom, meaning "ancient people." Archaeologists
label this group the Southern Sinagua, a Spanish term that
means "without water." As we shall see, this term is a misnomer.

Curving wall of Palatki Ruin near Sedona.
Note window blocked with masonry.
Did the inhabitants hope to return one day?

Pictographs at Palatki Ruin. Top humanoid figure done in red
Barrier Canyon style. Rock cleft portal faces summer solstice
sunrise on the horizon. Reading rock art is always risky:
Is the central helix a DNA strand with 24 pairs of chromosomes
instead of the normal 23? Note the faint crescent atop the axis.

About one-half mile west of the ruin, the largest group of pictographs (painted rock art) in the Verde Valley is located. It spans six thousand years of human habitation, with many of the pictographs being made long before the cliff dwelling was constructed. This rock art ranges from the Archaic Period (4000 BC – 300 BC), through the Basketmaker Period (300 BC – 750 AD) and the Pueblo Period (750 AD – 1300 AD), to historic times (1550 – the 1800's AD).

The pictographs arranged in a number of shallow alcoves or grottoes were executed in a variety of colors, including red (hematite), white (kaolin), black (charcoal), and occasionally yellow (limonite). Many of the charcoal figures, especially those showing mounted horsemen, are the work of the Yavapai and Apache cultures, which arrived in the area about 1300 and 1500 AD respectively. The iconography done in red or white is much older.

The imagery includes sun shields, squiggles, grids, rakes, star symbols, a star chart showing the Milky Way, circles, diamond shapes, patterns of dots, concentric circles or spirals, helixes, and snakes as well as human and animal figures. In addition, a few tall, ghostly humanoid figures similar to those found in southern Utah's Barrier Canyon loom in red on the canyon walls. One Kokopelli figure, also known as the humpbacked flute player, raises his instrument in eternal silence.

There are also many examples of petroglyphs (pecked or incised rock art). These consist of mostly vertically scratched or abraded lines and may even have been created in a time preceding the Archaic Period.

Now let's take a closer look at the word Palatki, or "red house." Archaeologist Jesse Walter Fewkes named this picturesque site in 1895. The Hopi word *palat* means "red" and *ki* means "residence."

This name, however, may be related to Palatkwapi, the "mythical" red-walled city in the south mentioned in Hopi migration legends. The settlement was once destroyed due to human corruption by a great flood, from which its inhabitants were forced to flee. Many versions of the legend include the presence of a giant horned water serpent that came up from the shadowy depths. This creature named Palulukang also surprisingly had breasts as well as feathers. Hence, the hybrid united the three planes of subterranean, terrestrial, and celestial by its corresponding characteristics of reptile, mammal, and bird. (See drawing on p. 283.)

The Hopi word *pa* means "water" but it also means "awe" or "wonder." Water is always an amazing thing in the desert because of its scarcity there. The people who settled at Palatki were mainly from the Patki (Water) Clan. Sometimes they might be called either the Dwelling-on-Water Clan (Houseboat) or the Rain-cloud Clan. From the south they brought many sacred ceremonies still performed today by the Hopi. Alexander M. Stephen, an early ethnographer of the Hopi, quotes a member of this clan:

> "The Patki clan came from Pala'tkwabi [Palatkwapi]. No one knows just where that Red land is, but it is somewhere in the far southwest. Our people, the Water people, carried all these things you see at the altar on their backs. Men, women, and youths carried them. The Water people brought the Kwa'kwantü [the One Horn ritual, part of the New Fire ceremony performed in early November], the La'lakontü [the Basket Dance, a women's corn harvest ceremony performed in October], and the Shoiya'luña [the Soyal, or winter solstice ceremony] with them." [*Hopi Journal*]

During the course of land migrations that lasted centuries, the Patki Clan traveled to this place from a "red city" located perhaps either in Mexico or the American Southwest. One possible origin is the Mayan city of Palenque in Chiapis in southern Mexico. In about 700 AD the stucco walls of this city were painted a brilliant crimson color. Another possible location for Palatkwapi is the site known as Paquimé (also called Casas Grandes) located in Chihuahua in northern Mexico. West of this large adobe village is a red rock canyon much like the area around Sedona. (Note the *pa-* prefixes in the names of these two sites.)

Still another candidate for the mythical red city is the Hohokam pueblo that archaeologists have named Snaketown. Located a few miles south of the modern metropolis of Phoenix, Arizona, this adobe village also had exterior red stucco walls. The Hohokam culture lived in the Phoenix Basin from about 300 BC – 1450 AD and built the largest system of irrigation canals in North America. We don't know what the Hohokam actually called Snaketown, but it probably had something to do with water. This is because in all the indigenous cultures of the American Southwest, snakes symbolize flowing water in either rivers or underground streams.

Extensive copper deposits both to the east of Snaketown near the modern town of Globe and to the southwest near the smaller town of Ajo reinforce the association of the color red. We should also relate here that in the late 19th century the United Verde Copper Company operated a profitable mine and smelter less than twelve miles south of Palatki, near the large Sinagua ruin named Tuzigoot. The Hopi word for copper is *palásiva*. The prefix *pa-* seems to be cropping up all over the place.

At any rate, the Patki Clan may have journeyed in ancient times from the red city of the south to settle at this red rock area now famously known the world over as Sedona.

A person known as the sun chief (in Hopi, *tawa-mongwi*) is also selected from the Patki Clan. He calibrates the position of the sun on the horizon at the summer and winter solstices. The importance of this fact will become apparent when we discuss the OM symbol directly.

Despite its politically incorrect tone, another piece of evidence adds to the overall enigma: "One thing you hear from the Patki people is that in ancient times they were white, not Indian color. They say, 'My ancestors had white skins, but because of evil things that happened, we lost all that.' They also say, 'The Patki people are the ones who are supposed to teach the Hopis good moral values, how to lead good lives.'" [Albert Yava, *Big Snow Falling*] The significance of this too will be dealt with toward the end of this chapter.

As briefly described above, many intriguing rock paintings can be found at Palatki. One of the most interesting figures, however, was discovered in 2001 by Jack Andrews. He initially published his findings in an article titled "Ancient Sanskrit Pictograph near Sedona, Arizona?"
[Find it in *Ancient American*, Vol. 7 No. 44, and online at Viewzone, www.viewzone.com/ancientsanskrit.htm]

The OM symbol is painted inside an alcove in hematite (iron oxide pigment perhaps mixed with blood) about seven feet above the floor. It is about eight inches wide and eight inches high. Curiously, it is rotated counter-clockwise 90° from the usual orientation of the OM symbol. As we shall see, this has a particular significance in regard to the Hopi. To the left of the curved figure are three vertical lines. The line closest to the curved figure has two short perpendicular lines at its top. Below the main symbol are a number of short vertical dashes.

OM symbol at Palatki Ruin.

It is very difficult to sum up the ancient meaning of OM in a few words. This venerable utterance of Hindu antiquity is omnipotent, omnipresent, and omniscient. It is the sound of the incomprehensible Brahman, the impersonal Absolute. It is the essence of all Vedic texts, prayers, and rituals. OM encompasses the light of the farthest star, yet it is as close as each breath we take. Westerners can glimpse its significance in one of the gospels:

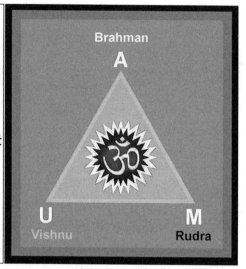

Gayatri Mantra

Om bhoor bhuva suvah
tat savitur varenyam
bhargo devasya dheemahi
dahiyo yo nah prachodayaat

**"May we attain that excellent
glory of Satvitr [solar deity],
So may he stimulate
our prayers."**
***Rigveda*, 3.62.10**
(Thanks to Adam Burke of Phoenix
for his knowledge on the subject.)

"In the beginning was the Word, and the Word was with God, and the Word was God." It is the timeless vibration of the primordial Logos.

This monosyllable is itself a Trinity comprised of three elements: A–U–M. The first part corresponds to Brahma the Creator (golden), the second to Vishnu the Preserver (blue), and the third to Rudra, or Magesh, the Destroyer (red). AUM also relates to the three states of consciousness: waking, dreaming, and deep sleep. These combined form the super-conscious reality of the Unknowable. AUM is the realization of peace, harmony, and bliss. It is infinite and eternal, yet it contains our entire past, present, and future. Both existence and nonexistence are consumed in the black hole of its Oneness.

So what is this hyper-sacred symbol from India doing in the hinterlands of the American Southwest?

In his article cited above Jack Andrews beautifully and succinctly asks the question that many traditional archaeologists are simply afraid to delve into.

> "Palatki has many strange mystical symbols painted on the rocks over the centuries by visitors and inhabitants of the area. Certain Native American tribes still use the loca-

tion for spiritual ceremonies. Did ancient travelers from India visit Palatki and meet with native inhabitants, experiencing the sacred nature of this special location, becoming so enthralled that they left this potent and powerful eastern spiritual symbol in red iron oxide pigment as a remembrance to the future, or a gift of spiritual awareness to the site in pictographic form?"

Historian and comparative linguistics scholar Gene D. Matlock suggests that Palatki may be related to the Sanskrit word *Palayat*, which means "divine protection" + *G*, which refers to a mystical syllable or utterance. More specifically he offers the following from the Sanskrit dictionary:

> *PAla* – a guard, protector of the earth; a king or prince
> *aT* – to roam or wander about zealously or habitually, especially as a religious mendicant
> *gir* – addressing, invoking, praising; a kind of mystical syllable; an outcry, shout

Gene writes: "In my estimation, Palatki fits the description perfectly. The man who painted [the OM symbol] was a mendicant Hindu monk." [personal communication with the author] Thus, the OM symbol was probably a visual representation of the sacred sound designed to guard or protect the people who lived there.

We said before that the Hopi word for water is *pa*. Is it merely a coincidence, then, that the Sanskrit word denoting "the act of drinking" is also *pa*? Perhaps it is instead what some would call synchronicity, or a "meaningful coincidence."

The site of Palatki had been inhabited since at least 4000 BC. It is possible that the Hindu rishis, or wandering sages, journeyed to the American Southwest long before the birth of Christ. This diffusionist theory is, of course, derided by traditional academics. According to them, the North American continent was isolated from foreign contact until Columbus reached the shores of the New World. Even this watertight theory is beginning to spring leaks, though, especially after the discovery of the ruins of Viking settlements in Newfoundland dating from about 1000 AD.

Matlock observes that the Phoenicians were a maritime-trader caste long recognized in India. As ship builders, merchants, and sailors, their influence was global. They apparently transported huge numbers of people to America in pre-Christian times. Their name, by the way, was Pani—another *pa* root word. Among their passengers may have been travelers from India. [See Gene's archive: www.mondovista.com/hinduturk.html]

We will not settle this highly contentious, diffusionist-versus-isolationist debate in one short chapter. (See Appendix 2.) So let's put aside the "how" of the early migrations across the oceans in order to take a closer look at the OM symbol at Palatki and the way it relates to the ancestral Hopi.

The holy men of India might have tried to convey the deep meaning of OM to the Hopi Patki Clan. As we have seen, the symbol at Palatki is rotated anticlockwise 90°. That is, the two semicircles are curving upward instead of to the right. Why was it painted on the surface of the stone in this direction?

The Hopi have a similar icon that refers to clouds. It is usually drawn with two semicircles side by side or sometimes with another semicircle on top of the lower two. From the bottom horizon line, a number of short parallel lines extend vertically to represent rainfall. Usually one or two zigzag lines extend diagonally from the semicircles to represent lightning.

Hopi cosmology is quite distinct from our modern paradigm of scientific materialism. The Hopi do not conceptualize clouds as merely a meteorological phenomenon. Instead clouds are actually the embodiment of ancestor spirits who have come to the village to offer life-giving water. The spirits of the dead ascend from the underworld in vaporous forms as cloud people to bring rain to the high desert. The chief of the clouds is known as Muy'ingwa, the underworld god of germination. He directs these personal spirits who arrive bearing moisture and fertility, thereby assisting the agricultural cycle.

Hopi cloud symbols, from *Rock Art Symbols Of the Greater Southwest*, Alex Patterson

On the left in top row, the first symbol is turned 90° clockwise—
like the OM symbol. The third symbol from the left in bottom row
shows corn sprouting from a cloud and a star overhead.

In Sanskrit the Patala is the name of the seven regions under the earth that are the abode of demons or Nagas (serpent people—see previous chapter). In this context it is probably more correct to use the word "daimon," or manifestation of divine power, than to use "demon" with its negative connotation. Serpents or snakes are natural denizens of the subterranean realms and are usually associated with water.

The Hopi word *patala* means "gleaming or shining with water, as after a rain." The Hopi consider Grand Canyon as the shimmering entrance to the underworld. In the American Southwest there is also a legend of Chicomostoc, the Seven Caves from which the Aztecs emerged.

Perhaps one of the most stunning revelations of this whole subject, however, is the Hopi name for clouds: *Omau*.

Did Hindu wanderers impart both the sound of OM and the visual symbol of OM to the Patki Clan in a manner its members could understand? The complex interrelationship between the cloud spirits (*Omau*), agricultural growth, and the life of the people was apparently bound together by this mystical icon.

The scenario might have gone something like this: Hindu monk: "In my homeland we have a very sacred symbol called OM." (He chants OM.) Hopi chief: "Oh, you mean Omau?" Hindu: "Yes, that's it!" (Nodding his head and smiling.) Hopi: "Omau is our word for cloud." (Points to the sky.) Hindu: "This is what it looks like." (Draws OM symbol in the red dust.) Hopi: "Here is what Omau looks like." (Draws Patki [Water Clan] cloud symbol in the dust next to the OM symbol.) Hindu: "They look very much alike." (Points to one drawing, then to the other and clasps his hands together.) Hopi: "In very ancient times our ancestors must have been brothers!" (They both smile.)

One independent researcher named Sudheer Birodkar has shown that the origin of the OM symbol in India looks surprisingly like the Hopi cloud symbol. "This is believed to be the original depiction of the syllable OM." (See facing page below.)

The OM symbol at Palatki is also oriented in a very specific direction. It is directly aligned with the winter solstice sunrise, which at this latitude is 120° azimuth. (Azimuth is the number of degrees measured clockwise on the horizon from true north. For instance, north is 0°, east is 90°, south is 180°, and west is 270°.) The sun rises at 120° on the horizon (roughly southeast) on the first day of winter. The Hopi call this the winter "sun house," or *tawaki*.

The winter solstice ceremony known as Soyal is performed at this time, in part to assist Tawa, the sun, on his journey northward from his southernmost position on the horizon. This is a period of fasting, purification, and meditative silence. As we previously mentioned, members of the Patki Clan who lived at Palatki brought this ceremony there from far to the south where the sun goes in the winter. In addition, they in particular are designated as the sun-watchers, or those who help to regulate the agricultural calendar by keeping track of the solstices and equinoxes. During the Soyal the many prayer-sticks or prayer-feathers called *pahos* are also made in the Patki Clan house.

We mentioned before that this clan was thought to have lighter skin color than the rest of the Hopi. They furthermore are considered to be teachers of purity and morality. Did people from northern India come to Arizona, perhaps to even mate with the ancient Hopi, eventually giving this particular clan its lighter shade of skin? In that case something more than goods, cultural values, ceremonies, and philosophies may have been exchanged.

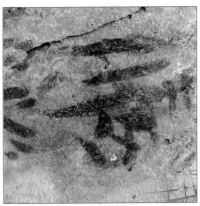
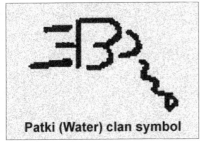

Patki (Water) clan symbol

Left-above: Hindu Omkar.
Right-above: Palatki symbol
rotated clockwise 90°.
Left: This representation of
the symbol for the Patki Clan
of the Hopi especially
resembles the OM symbol.

Original OM symbol.
[www.hindubooks.org/
sudheer_birodkar/
hindu_history/omkar.html.]

155

Though difficult to prove, this theory is certainly an interesting possibility. The OM pictograph at Palatki also resembles the early Sharada script from Kashmir in northern India where people typically have a fairer skin color.
[http://en.wikipedia.org/wiki/Sharada_script]

One more *pa*-term needs to be discussed: Pahana. The Hopi word *pahana* currently refers to "white person." However, Pahana is also the "mythical" Elder White Brother who was there when the ancient Hopi migrations commenced.

At the beginning of the present Fourth World (or era) just after the emergence from the subterranean Third World, Pahana broke off a corner of a small stone tablet owned by the Fire Clan and walked eastward toward the rising sun. At the same time the Younger Red Brother stayed back, traveling the spiral road of migrations. This latter figure representing the Hopi them-selves started to construct pueblos throughout the American Southwest. They gradually settled in the villages much as we see them today. Every year thousands visit their ruins, like those at Palatki.

Similar to the Mayan figure of Kukulkan or the Aztec Quetzalcoatl (the plumed serpent of Mesoamerican myths), Pahana would return at the End Times to match up with the other part of the Fire Clan tablet the corner that he carried. In this way the people would know him. He would then save the righteous Hopi from foreign forces bent on destroying the land. (Read about the Hopi stone tablets in Chapter 17.)

Like most ancient cultures, the Hopi were attuned to wordplay and may have noticed this pun: as stated, *pa* means "water" but *hana* means "to bring down." If you put these two words together, they form *pa-hana*—to bring down water, or rain. So Pahana may have had something to do with precipita-tion as well. Incidentally, the related Sanskrit noun *pAyana* means "causing or giving to drink."
[http://webapps.uni-koeln.de/tamil]

Is Pahana somehow connected to the Hindu mystics who came to to Arizona in the millennia before Christ and created the OM symbol on the wall of a red sandstone cliff? Is *Omau*, the

OM - The Dhirga Pranava Mantra

Om Symbol South Africa found by Rob Milne

Om Parvat in Himalaya, India

Om Symbol Palatki, Arizona U.S.A. found by Jack Andrews

"OM, AUM, UM, HUM, AMAN and AMEEN", all are one and the same, but varies due to pronunciation. It is combination of three letters A, U, and M.

We are all from the One. And we shall return to that One". - T.L.Subash Chandira Bose, Gary A. David, Jack Andrews, Rob Milne

Hopi word for cloud, related to the divine OM? Is this pictograph at Palatki a cross-cultural relic from an ancient time when Hindus walked the Americas?

These questions recede into the mist of the sacred syllable whose peace passes our understanding.

Note: The upper right-hand corner of the graphic on p. 157 refers to an OM symbol in South Africa. Read more about Rob Milne's fantasic discoveries in Appendix 1, p. 268.

**Jack Andrews, who lives near Tucson, Arizona,
discovered the OM symbol at Palatki.
See his Website: www.mysteriousarizona.com.**

**T. L. Subash Chandira Bose of Tamil Nadu, India,
at Palatki site in Arizona—Omkar behind him.
Visit his Website: www.geocities.com/tlscbose/Pazankasu.**

Chapter 14: The Tau (or T-shaped) Cross— Hopi-Maya-Egyptian Connections

*—dedicated in memory of my friend and colleague,
the Arizona scholar Todd Greaves (1952 – 2008).*

The Tau is an icon that carries a universal significance across the globe. In the New World the T-shaped doorway or window appears as a common architectural motif in stone masonry villages all across the Anasazi (ancient Hopi) Southwest. It is found, for instance, at Chaco Canyon in northern New Mexico and Mesa Verde in southwestern Colorado.

The Greek letter T is called the *tau* cross, which echoes the name of the Hopi sun god Tawa. Every day the sun emerges from the Underworld through a T-shaped doorway, the horizontal bar serving as the horizon. At some point in the past the form of the Hopi kiva (subterranean prayer chamber) changed from round, like the one at Chaco Canyon, to rectangular, located on an east-west axis. The floor plan was sometimes widened at one end to reflect the T-shape. Hopis say that this form also represents the traditional male hairstyle of bangs falling down over the ears.

Masau'u is the name of the Hopi god of the Underworld, fire, and death. His head is sometimes carved in rock art as a modified rectangle to suggest a stylized skull. (See photo in the middle of the facing page.)

We also find the T-shaped cross far to the south at the Mayan city of Palenque in Chiapas, Mexico. Specifically, a number of T-shaped windows were incorporated into the building called the Palace.

Steps leading through a T-shaped doorway down into Casa Rinconada, the Great Kiva at Chaco Canyon, New Mexico.

Petroglyph of two humanoids, Perry Mesa Ruins north of Phoenix, Arizona. The figure on the left with the T-shaped head may represent Masau'u.

T-shaped windows, Palenque Palace. (Photo © courtesy of George DeLange, www.delange.org.)

The Mayan daykeeper, artist, and historian Hunbatz Men explains the meaning of this motif in his book *Secrets of Mayan Science/Religion*:

> "A transcendental synthesis of human religious experience is inherent in the word *te*, Sacred Tree, which emerged from the words *teol* and *teotl* the names of God the Creator in Mayan and Nahuatl. These most revered and sacred words of the ancient people, symbolized by the Sacred Tree, were represented in the Mayan hieroglyphs as the symbol 'T.' Additionally, this symbol represented the air, the wind, the divine breath of God."

In other words, the T-shaped doorway/window symbolizes the Sacred Tree at the Center of the World (*axis mundi*) upon which the shaman's spirit may climb. It also functions as the portal leading to the Great Spirit, through which the breath of life may pass.

In numerous cultures *tau* was connected to abundant water or rain-deities. For instance, Augustus Le Plongeon, one of the first archaeologists of the Maya, writes in his book *Sacred Mysteries Among the Mayas And the Quiches* that the T-shape corresponds to Crux, or the Southern Cross. This constellation appears shortly before the beginning of the rainy season in southern Mexico.

> "The ancient Maya astronomers had observed that at a certain period of the year, at the beginning of our month of May, that owes its name to the goddess MAYA, *the good dame, mother of the gods*, the *"Southern Cross,"* appears perfectly perpendicular above the line of the horizon. This is why the Catholic church celebrates the feast of the *exaltation of the holy cross* on the third day of that month, which it has consecrated particularly to the *Mother of God*, the *Good Lady*, the virgin *Ma-R-ia*, or the goddess Isis anthropomorphized by Bishop Cyril of Alexandria."

Is it more than a coincidence that the name of this Mesoamerican tribe should be the same as the Sanskrit word for the veil of illusion? The Mother Goddess Shakti, otherwise known as the Divine Mother Devi, gives birth to all phenomenal forms that we mistakenly perceive as being real. Queen Maya was impregnated by a white elephant entering her side and subsequently gave birth to Siddhartha Gautama the Buddha.

tau CROSS

from Sacred Mysteries Among the Mayas and the Quiches by Augustus LePiongeon

Mexican MS. in British Museum.

Breast-like fruit growing from the trunk of the sacred yaxche tree. Bird as spirit messenger on top.

Furthermore, Maia was the Greek goddess of spring and the Roman goddess of the earth or growth. Her fertility celebration is either the 1st or the 15th of May. She was also the eldest sister and the brightest star of the Pleiades. In the land of the Maya tribe, the sun in conjunction with the Pleiades passes through the zenith during the month of May.

In Egypt the *ankh*, or ansate cross, was the "key to the Nile" by which Osiris, husband of Isis, accomplished his annual riparian inundations. The upper loop represents the womb, and the lower straight portion represents either the birth canal or the phallus.

It is interesting to note that when Moses entered the Sinai desert, he found the Midianite tribe (also called the Kenites) wearing the T-shape on their foreheads. This sign, which represented their

Ankh between two pairs of a scepter called the Was, carved on temple wall, Egypt.

163

god of storms (bringing water) and war (thunder), later became known as the "Yahweh Mark."

Much later Jesus may well have been crucified on a Tau or St. Anthony's cross instead of on the Latin cross we think of today, though this will probably be forever debated.

In his classic book *Atlantis: the Antediluvian World*, Ignatius Donnelly states that *tau* was an important icon signifying "hidden wisdom" for Mexicans as well as for Peruvians, Egyptians, Phoenicians, and Chaldeans. In general, it was emblematic of rejuvenation, freedom from physical suffering, hope, immortality, and divine unity.

Thus we have seen how many cultures associate the T-shape with burgeoning new life, the rising sun, psycho-spiritual journeying, and ultimate resurrection.

Sometimes the simplest symbols contain the deepest meanings.

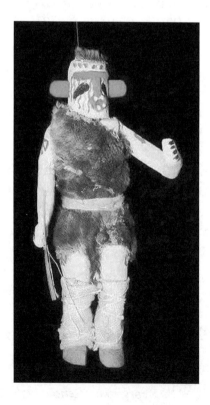

Hopi Heyeya katsina doll with Tau on forehead. At times clouds symbols (like those seen on p. 153) instead of vertical zigzags are painted on the masks of these messengers of the rain gods.

Dotting the I's and Crossing the Tau's

In this chapter I have merely touched upon the potency of this symbol. The late iconographer Todd Greaves, on the other hand, has made an intensive study of its various meanings for well over a decade.

He identifies a number of principal meanings. These include the association with rain or water, cardinal directions or sacred mountains (when the Tau is used in the four-fold), gateways or doors, and eternal life or regeneration. In the context of the American Southwest, he writes the following:

"The U.S. Southwest's Pueblo III period (A.D. 1100 – 1330) of Ancestral Puebloan culture corresponds in time to Europe's Middle Ages. T-shaped doorways are so characteristic of Pueblo III Anasazi architecture that many believe that they were a unique invention of that culture. For decades, these portals were presumed to be utilitarian, although no one could demonstrate what useful purpose they served. The idea that Pueblo doorways were sometimes made wider above to allow easy access for those carrying bundles of sticks for the fireplace is refuted by the fact that two of the most impressive T doors in the Southwest (at Casa Rinconada in Chaco Canyon, New Mexico) are nearly four meters (13 ft.) high. [See photo on the top of p. 161.] There can be no doubt that these doorways were symbolic and religious in nature. They were among the earliest datable of such entryways in Puebloan contexts. Beyond this, the Greater Southwest abounds in non-architectural kinds of T symbolism, the shape being found on Zuni altars, Mesa Verdean Anasazi mugs, and other pottery, and as a petroglyph motif." [Greaves]

The dynamics of this icon will undoubtably resonate for years to come from Four Corners, U.S.A., to the four corners of the globe.

Chapter 15: The Maltese Cross—Hopi Version of a Knights Templar Symbol

The Templar Cross

Columbus and his crew sailed across the Atlantic and into the history books in three rather puny ships. Each of the main-sails, however, brandished a powerful icon—the blood-red Maltese Cross. It is less well known that his wife Filipa Perestrello, daughter of a wealthy Portuguese, was also related to the famous Sinclair (or St. Clair) family of Roslyn, Scotland. Besides a son, their union may have yielded maps, sea charts, and navigational knowledge.

*An artist's conception of Columbus' Santa Maria
and a solar sail for interstellar spacecraft.
(Courtesy NASA/JPL-Caltech.)*

Some historians believe that Prince Henry Sinclair, Earl of Orkney, made a voyage to the New World nearly a century before Columbus, stopping in Nova Scotia and on the eastern seaboard of the United States. Sinclair may have also built the

Newport Tower in Rhode Island, a round structure of stone similar to the baptisteries that the Knights Templar erected in Europe. (See photo on p. 120.)

This fraternal organization was formed during the Crusades to ostensibly protect pilgrims in the Holy Land. Its members customarily wore Maltese Cross insignias on their capes. The huge fleet of Knights Templar ships mysteriously disappeared in 1307, just before King Philippe IV of France conspired with Pope Clement V to disband and ultimately destroy the order. Scholars believe that the fleet sailed to Scotland, but at least part of the fleet may instead have crossed the Atlantic headed for America.

Did they make earlier voyages to the New World as well? If so, they certainly would have brought their characteristic cross. The Knights Templar may have even influenced the Hopi tribe living in stone villages atop high desert mesas of the American Southwest.

The Universal Cross

The Maltese Cross is found in virtually all corners of the world. It is basically an eight-pointed, equilateral cross with each arm gradually expanding in width at the outer edge. The octagonal shape, by the way, was incorporated into Christian baptismal fonts, perhaps because the Arabic numeral **8** turned on its side represents infinity. This cross looks like a grouping of four arrowheads with their apexes converging at a central point. It symbolizes either the four cardinal directions or the four points on the horizon corresponding to the sunrises and sunsets of the summer and winter solstices. The latter context represents the sun.

Maltese Cross

Variations of the cross go by different names according to different uses. The slightly flared cross formée, for instance, is used today by one of Arizona's managed health care providers. The cross pattée, on the other hand, looks like the Iron Cross (or Prussian Cross) that bikers or motorcycle gangs are fond of putting on their clothing. This cross is actually the emblem of the *Bundeswehr*, the German armed forces. They used this symbol during World War I, which is perhaps the reason for its negative connotation.

The Rosicrucian (or Rose Cross) represents the redemptive power of the blood of Christ. (See facing page.) The letters on the four rays combine to form INRI, meaning not only "King of the Jews" but also the Latin motto *Igne Natura renovatur integra.* ("Nature is entirely renovated by fire.") At the center of the cross is a multi-colored rose with twenty-two petals, corresponding to the letters of the Hebrew alphabet. The Rosicrucian Order (AMORC) survives to this day. The 18th degree of Scottish Freemasonry is called the Knight of the Rose Croix. Its symbol is the Maltese Cross.

The Alisee pattée is the technical term for the Templar

Cross. Its arms are curved at the perimeter, which indicates a cruciform enclosed within a circle. This represents the spirit containing the body rather than the reverse. It is thought that a brotherhood known as the Children of Solomon constructed a number of Gothic cathedrals, including Chartes. Their signature was the chrisme à l' epée, the Celtic Cross inside a circle.

The Celtic Cross of Ireland was widely known in antiquity. (See facing page.) Crichton EM Miller claims that this cross was actually both an architectural tool for construction of megalithic structures, such as pyramids, and a navigational instrument that allowed mariners to sail the world in very ancient times. [www.crichtonmiller.com] The crosses we still find in some churchyards are merely the symbolic remnant of a sophisticated apparatus that allowed for a system of global contact and commerce.

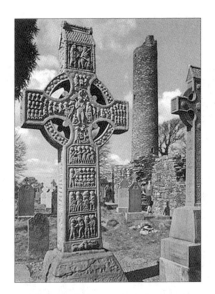

Upper left: Celtic Cross and round tower at Monasterboice monastery in Ireland.
Upper right:
King Shamshi-Ada V, ruler of Nimrud, Iraq, 9th century BC.
Lower left : Rosicrucian cross.

Lower right: Cross at Sri Ranganathaswamy Temple, Tamil Nadu, India. Note "orb" upper right-hand corner. (Courtesy of T. L. Subash Chandira Bose.)

The Maltese Cross is also a badge of honor and a common symbol of protection for fire fighters everywhere. Its origin again goes back to the Crusades when the Knights of St. John were fighting the Saracens in the Holy Land. The latter would hurl glass globes filled with naphtha at their enemy and then ignite the fluid, forcing the Knights to attempt a rescue of their comrades from an excruciating death.

The adjective "Maltese" refers to the island of Malta in the Mediterranean where Knights of St. John lived for over three centuries. Some the world's oldest megalithic round temples dedicated to the mother goddess are also located there.

The Maltese Cross and the star were the primary emblems of the Babylonian sky god Anu. One of his sons, Vilkan, was god of fire, metals, and weapons. The British Museum contains a stele with a large Maltese Cross hanging around the neck of King Shamshi-Adad V, ruler of Nimrud in northern Iraq about 824 to 811 BC. (See photo on p. 169.) Maltese crosses were also painted on pottery found at the fourth millennium site of Susa in western Iran—the biblical Shushan.

In his book *Lost Cities of Atlantis, Ancient Europe & the Mediterranean*, David Hatcher Childress notes the large numbers of "sun-wheels" (a Maltese Cross within a circle) inscribed on Linear A tablets from the 15th century BC in Crete. On the island of Philae in Upper Egypt, one temple was engraved with a Maltese Cross beside a traditional crux ansata, or *ankh*.

The Ashanti tribe of Ghana crafted gold weights carved with the Maltese Cross, while the Wagogo tribe of Tanzania wore earplugs inscribed with the same cross. Duffusionist James Bailey claims that this distinctive jewelry is the classic "earmark" of seafarers.

Researcher George Erikson in his book *Atlantis In America* (co-authored by Ivar Zapp) calls the Maltese Cross the quintessential symbol of navigation. During early transoceanic voyages Phoenician traders or even the serpent cult of the Nagas from India may have first introduced this cross to America.

India was certainly the country of origin for many Maltese Crosses. The symbols in the photo at the bottom of p.

169 are engraved on a massive stone slab on top of the southern gate of Sri Ranganathaswamy Temple in the city of Tiruchirapalli, Tamil Nadu. This unusual variation of the Maltese Cross is a stylized lotus plant with four leaves representing the cardinal directions and four petals representing the intercardinal directions. Also note the Star of David at the upper left.

The New World Cross

New World evidence of this unique cross also abounds. At Tiahuanaco in Bolivia a bronze breastplate or altarpiece was inscribed with a number of Maltese Crosses. One Garcilasco de Vega, the mid-sixteenth century son of a Spanish soldier and an Incan woman, wrote that the Maltese cross was kept in a sacred precinct of Cuzco, Peru.

An obsidian eagle carved with a Maltese Cross as one of its eyes was unearthed at La Venta, the Olmec area of southeastern Mexico. The fifteenth century Codex Fejervary-Mayer of the Aztec depicts a T-shaped Cross within each of the four directions of a larger Maltese Cross. (See drawing on the top of p. 172.) The sixteenth century Codex Florentine of the Aztecs shows a figure atop a temple altar with a Maltese Cross-shield in one hand and a snake in the other. The list goes on.

Navajo (or Diné) sand paintings, which are similar to Tibetan mandalas and used in healing rituals in the American Southwest, sometimes display the Maltese Cross. Apache medicine men living in Arizona and New Mexico drew this image on their shirts in order to make themselves invisible. (See photo on p. 172.) The Chumash Indians of California also painted many examples of this cross inside caves. (See bottom of same page.)

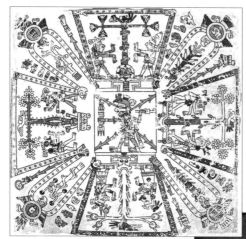

Left:
Aztec Maltese Cross.

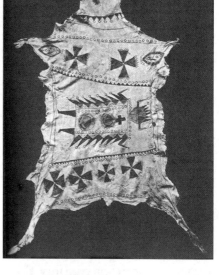

Right:
Apache medicine shirt.

Left:
Chumash cave
paintings near
Santa Barbara,
California.

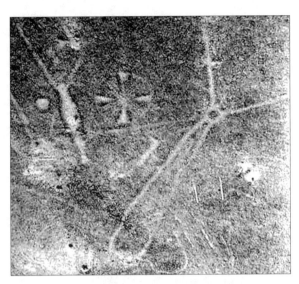

**Aerial photo of geoglyph complex
near lower Colorado River.**

The Maltese Cross appears as a huge icon in the deserts of the Southwest. On both sides of the lower Colorado River along the California/Arizona border we find many geoglyphs (geo-, "earth" + glyph, "carving"). Also called intaglios, these earth figures were constructed on river terraces by removing darker cobbles to reveal a lighter subsurface. Like the famous Nazca lines of Peru, the human-made geomorphs are sometimes hundreds of feet in length. They were laid out to variously represent humans, animals, snakes, spirals, stars, circles or other geometric shapes. Although either the ancestral Hopi or the ancient Quechan and Mohave Indians may have constructed them, many different tribes visited these sites to perform ceremonies as early as 3,000 years ago. And like the Nazca lines, geoglyphs are best appreciated from the air, so they probably were intended as homage to sky gods. (See description on p. 89.)

The Ripley geoglyph complex is located about a dozen miles south of Blythe, California. One site on the Arizona side of the Colorado River contains a Maltese Cross nearly ten feet in diameter located adjacent to two humanoid figures whose heads are roughly pointing southeast. The larger figure appears to be holding the cross in its right hand. The smaller figure to its left

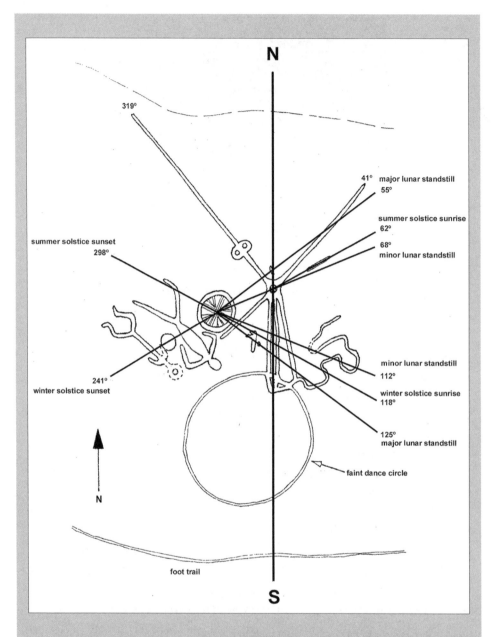

Geoglyph (or intaglio) designs in the desert.
On the left, two humanoids with circle and Maltese Cross.
Various alignments show all the solstice sunrise and
sunset points plus the extremes of the moonrise points.
(Original graphic courtesy of Boma Johnson,
Earth Figures of the Lower Colorado and Gila River Deserts.)

is apparently missing its head and seems to be holding a circle, also in its right hand. This circle may represent either the sun or the moon.

A double line approximately twenty feet long is located on an exact north/south axis. From a central point at the north end of this double line, two dance paths head to the northwest and northeast, perhaps pointing toward sacred mountains in the distance. A faint dance circle is located at the south end of this geoglyph, which in its entirety is about ninety feet wide by one hundred and twenty feet long.

Preliminary investigations suggest that the offset Maltese cross contains a number of archaeo-astronomical alignments. (See previous page.) It is oriented on an axis of the winter solstice sunrise point in the southeast and the summer solstice sunset point in the northwest. Moreover, alignments seem to incorporate all the summer and winter sunrise and sunset points on the horizon as well as the moonrise points at their maximum and minimum limits (technically called "lunar standstills"). Clearly the people who constructed this geoglyph were concerned with the celestial realm ruled by both the solar (masculine) and the lunar (feminine).

Boma Johnson's book describes a Yavapai Indian healing ritual (similar to the Navajo sanding paintings previously mentioned) that uses a red Maltese Cross at the center.

Archaeologist Emil Haury compares Hohokam (ancestral Tohono O'odham) shell pendants and pottery designs discovered at the village of Snaketown near modern-day Phoenix, Arizona, with the Mexican "Cross of Quetzalcoatl"—again, the Maltese Cross. Quetzalcoatl, of course, is the Aztec name for the "feathered serpent."

The Three Rivers Petroglyphs site, located on the western base of New Mexico's Sacramento Mountains, is one of the largest rock art sites in the Southwest. The park contains over 20,000 petroglyphs carved atop a ridge by the Jornada Mogollon culture (possible ancestors of the Hopi) between 900 and 1400 A.D. One geometric design located there is a Maltese Cross within a circle surrounded by a ring of seventeen dots.

Incidentally, this site is located at the same latitude as both Phoenix and the geoglyphs: the sacred Masonic number of 33 degrees. (Again, see Chaper 6.)

**Three Rivers Petroglyph site
in south-central New Mexico.**

The Hopi Cross

The Hopi Indians of Arizona also claim the Maltese Cross as part of their cultural heritage. The *nögla*, meaning literally "butterfly whorl," is a women's hair disk three to four inches in diameter. It was traditionally worn by virgins on both sides of the head above the ears, especially during the Bean Germination Ceremony. Two of these hair disks laid perpendicular to each other resemble the Maltese Cross.

The butterfly is a symbol of fertility, both human and agricultural. The Butterfly *katsina* maiden (in Hopi, Poli Mana) wears a two-dimensional headdress known as a *tablita*. It is sometimes painted with Maltese Crosses and terraced rain clouds. *Katsinam* are spirit messengers that the Hopi petition for rain and general health. These colorful figures are impersonated in dances held during the spring and early summer in pueblo village plazas.

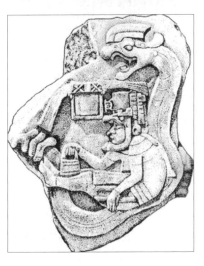

**Upper left: Drawing
of Butterfly katsina.
[Dover Publications, Inc.]
Upper right: Hopi maiden
with "butterfly whorls."
Middle right: Two small
St. Andrew's Crosses
above Olmec figure
in the belly of serpent.**

**Lower left:
Drawing of Hopi
ceramic box,
northern Arizona.
[Dover
Publications, Inc.]**

Many instances of Maltese Crosses have been found painted on ancient Hopi pottery as well. Among ruins of Sikyatki at the base of the Hopi First Mesa, an unusual rectangular "medicine box" has been discovered. On one side was painted a white Maltese Cross, inside of which is a star formed by four triangles whose apexes point outward from a small circle at its center. (See bottom of previous page.)

Incidentally, the very same image of a four-pointed star within a Maltese Cross was sculpted at the Garway Church in Herefordshire in Britain. (See Illustration 9 of *The Temple and the Lodge* by Michael Baigent and Richard Leigh.)

Commenting on ancestral Hopi pottery, Jesse Walter Fewkes writes in his book *Prehistoric Pottery Designs*:

> "There are several specimens of figures of the Maltese Cross, and one closely approximating the Saint Andrew's Cross. It is scarcely necessary to say that the presence of the various kinds of crosses do not necessarily indicate the influence of Semitic or Aryan races, for I have already shown that even cross-shape prayer-sticks were in use among the Pueblos when Coronado first visited them."

This archaeologist of late 19th century illustrates his isolationist or anti-diffusionist bias here. Like many academics today, he would have found it difficult to accept the possibility of a Knights Templar visitation to the New World at least a century before Coronado but perhaps as much as three centuries before that first Spanish foray through the Southwest.

St. Andrew is the patron saint of Scotland. The St. Andrew's Cross is a simple, X-shaped cross found, for instance, at the pre-Incan site of Tiahuanaco, at the Mayan site of Uxmal, and at the Olmec center of La Venta. (See drawing on p. 177.) This cross also appears on Hopi sand altars during the Snake Dance ceremony.

During this strange ritual performed every other August on the three Hopi Mesas, participants handle a mass of poisonous snakes. Some even put necks and bodies into their mouths. As noted in Chapter 12, the Snake Dance is performed to enhance rainfall and agricultural fertility on the Arizona high desert. In this case the St. Andrew's Cross was apparently inspired by the diamond pattern on the backs of rattlesnakes.

Mayan St. Andrew's Cross.

In other Hopi rituals this variation of the cross represents a star or generally the sky. Hence, we see it associated with both the serpent and ascension. This again evokes Quetzalcoatl, which the Hopi call Palulukang. This latter term literally means "Water Serpent." (See drawing on p. 283.)

In 1881 James Bourke discovered a Maltese Cross carved into a ritual pipe used in the Snake Dance ceremony. The Nagas of the Indus River Valley, we remember, also utilized the spiritual healing power of the snake.

The Apocalyptic Cross

The Maltese Cross plays a key role in Hopi prophecies of the apocalyptic End Times. The Creator will decide when Pahana will return to Hopiland. This venerable figure wears either a red hat or a red cape. Modern day Shriners wear a red fez, and some contemporary Knights Templar orders don a red pillbox hat. The "red cape" might refer to the Templar red cross upon a white mantle. In this context the Red Hat sect of Tibetan Buddhism also comes to mind.

At any rate, Pahana will prove his identity by providing a stone piece that matches the broken section of an ancient tablet. (See Chapter 17.) He will be accompanied by two helpers, one of which carries a masculine swastika –itself a sort of hooked cross– that signifies the four directions. The first helper also transports a Maltese Cross. The lines between the arms of

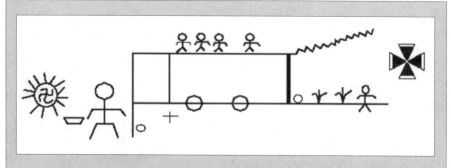

**Drawing of Prophecy Rock, a petroglyph near Oraibi, Arizona.
The upper horizontal line followed by a zigzag represents
the rootless, materialistic culture of modern society.
The two circles on the lower horizontal line signify
the two world wars, while the corn plants and human figure
at the right represent harmony with nature.**

**The Maltese Cross is ruler of this latter realm. As stated, both the
swastika and the cross that one of the helpers of Pahana carries
are key elements in the Hopi prophecy of End Times.**

this cross represent in particular the blood of menstruation. The second helper conveys merely a sun symbol. The combined forces of these three icons will begin the cataclysmic process of global purification. (See Chapter 18 and Afterword.) The two human figures of the Ripley geoglyph discussed above perhaps correspond to these two helpers.

The Blood Cross

A number of themes seem to occur again and again in our discussion of the Maltese Cross: (1) the sun or fire, (2) the moon or stars, (3) serpents or snakes, and (4) blood. Dan Brown's immensely popular novel *The Da Vinci Code* suggests that the Knights Templar were guarding a secret they discovered in artifacts or documents uncovered at Solomon's Temple in Jerusalem during the Crusades. Brown implies that the Holy Grail was not a physical cup but instead the womb of Mary Magdalene—a notion heretical to many devout Christians. Nonetheless, the Knights Templar organization may indeed have been formed to serve as guardians of the bloodline of Christ.

The Hopi Indians conceive (no pun intended) of the Maltese Cross as directly related to fertility and menstrual blood. Is this the intended meaning of the cross that the Knights Templar wore on their clothing and shields? Perhaps their fixation on round temple architecture reflects the circular form of the womb. The ancestors of the Hopi also built round towers, which for some reason they refer to as "snake houses." (See Chapter 10.)

By the way, if we shift the previously mentioned St. Andrew's cross forty-five degrees, we get the Red Cross—the international philanthropic organization to which people frequently donate their blood.

Maurice Chatelain, a former NASA scientist who worked on the Apollo moon mission, writes in his book *Our Cosmic Ancestors*:

"The Maltese cross presents a very curious characteristic. When the eight outer points are set in a circle, the eight radii divide it in sections of 3/28 and of 4/28 of the circle. That could have been just a whim of the creators of this geometric figure, but a closer look reveals some hidden meaning... as far as we know nobody in classical antiquity divided a full circle in 28 sectors."

However, this number corresponds to the number of spokes in the Bighorn Medicine Wheel in Wyoming. It is also the number of niches in the Casa Rinconada, or the round Great Kiva—a subterranean prayer chamber that the ancestors of the Hopi used at Chaco Canyon in New Mexico. Incidentally, the Bighorn Medicine Wheel and Chaco Canyon are on the exact same longitude line (107 degrees west), even though they are separated by nearly six hundred miles. The number twenty-eight is, of course, the duration of both the lunar cycle and the menstrual cycle.

Copy right to T.L.Subash Chandira Bose 2006

Graphic courtesy of T. L. Subash Chandira Bose.

The Bighorn Medicine Wheel in Wyoming has twenty-eight spokes and is aligned with the summer solstice sunrise and sunset.

Twenty-eight niches in Great Kiva, Chaco Canyon. Window faces summer solstice sunrise.

Why are serpents associated all over the world with Maltese Crosses? If the latter were somehow connected to the blood of Christ, one would think the snake and this type of cross would be mutually exclusive. The Bible is entirely ambiguous in this regard. The Lord sends "fiery serpents" to bite sinful people, who are then healed by simply gazing upon the "serpent of brass" on the pole that Moses holds. (Numbers 21: 6-9.)

This may be the origin of the *caduceus* carried by the Greek god Hermes, or the Roman god Mercury—itself a sort of cross whose horizontal stave is formed by a pair of wings.

During medieval times the alchemical image of the "crucified snake" (seen to the right) symbolized the concoction of

mercury, an elixir that removed poisonous or volatile elements. This was probably inspired by the biblical verses of John 3:14-15: "And as Moses lifted up the serpent in the wilderness, even so must the Son of Man be lifted up: That whosoever believeth in him should not perish, but have everlasting life." The Son/Sun homonym was an obvious proselytizing tool for early English Christians. Lifted up to the stars, perhaps?

The Maltese Cross is associated in particular with what grandmaster Freemason Albert Pike calls the "Blazing Star," or Sirius. This emblem for the brightest sidereal fire in the sky is found at the entrances of Masonic lodges worldwide. In Egypt the star symbolized Isis, the Eternal Female. The Hopi call Sirius *Ponotsona*, "The One That Sucks From the Belly," emphasizing its lactational or mammalian aspect.

After the Crucifixion, so the legend goes, Mary Magdalene fearing persecution fled to southern France to live out her days with her daughter Sarah, the holy offspring of Jesus. This region eventually known as Languedoc became the stronghold of the Knights Templar after the Crusades. Toward the end of its historical influence this group became ardently antithetical to the patriarchal Catholic Church. In fact, at the

Eye of the Phoenix

beginning of the fourteenth century some members were even burned at the stake for their beliefs. Before the organization's demise, however, they may have spread the Maltese Cross worldwide, even as far as the isolated deserts of Arizona. (See drawing on the facing page.)

Some of the Knights Templar may have sailed to America after the 1307 purge of their order or perhaps even before that.

We find it as easily in the hinterlands of the New World as in the Place du Capitole of Toulouse, the ancient center of the Rosicrucian international conclave. This twelve-pointed type of "Cross of Languedoc" reflects either the zodiac or Jesus' twelve disciples.

The French phrase *langue d'oc* literally means the "language of yes," what we've come to see as an unequivocal positive: $+$. This is also the symbol for the masculine principle—half of the alchemical *coniunctio*, or Sacred Marriage. For the Hopi the Maltese Cross represents the other half, the feminine principle. The Hopi word *taq* sounds similar to *doc*, since there is no "d" in Hopi language. Surprisingly this word means "male."

Or, considering what has come before, perhaps it is no surprise at all but just a part of the creative resonance of this universal symbol.

184

**Drawing of Hopi pottery bowl,
Sikyatki Ruin, northern Arizona,
about 1375 AD.
[Dover Publications, Inc.]**

**The Cross of Moretti,
Place du Capitole, Toulouse, France.
[*www.toulouse.fr*]**

Chapter 16: Who Put the Ka-
In the Hopi Katsina?

The Colorful Spirit Beings of Arizona

At dawn the *katsinam* rise from an underground prayer chamber called a kiva and stream into the sunlit plaza of the old village. (*Katsinam* is the plural of *katsina*, sometimes spelled *kachina*.) In a single file procession they step as one entity to the steady pulse of a lone cottonwood drum. A circle of spirit dancers soon forms inside the negative space made by clusters of low, masonry houses. It becomes one grand *katsina* wheel turning in perfect synchronization to the rhythms of the seasons around the communal heart of Oraibi. This stone village built in northern Arizona by the Hopi around 1100 AD is the oldest continuously inhabited village on the North American continent.

The *katsina* cult, as it is sometimes called, remains a crucial force in Hopi cosmology and religion in the American Southwest. But as we shall see, its etymology and conceptual significance stretch back to antiquity and go far beyond this region to encompass the globe.

Katsinam are essentially spirit-messengers who act as intermediaries between the realm of humans and the realm of the gods. Their presence assures rainfall, fertility, and the well being of the people. The Hopi carve dolls (*tihuta*) that look like the various types of *katsinam*. One purpose of these dolls is to teach the children about the various types of otherworldly entities. In addition, sacred dances are held from about April until July in the village plazas to honor these spiritual beings by imitating them. The dances are more than simply imitation, however. In the process of the ritual, the dancers actually become the *katsinam*.

Amid this desert landscape of muted earth tones and pale sandstone, the stately yet primal presence of the *katsinam* strikes the eye with the startling brilliance of their primary colors.

Sashes and clan kilts, eagles plumes and bandoleers, fox fur and turkey feathers, willow bows and yucca whips, blue spruce or pinyon ruffs, turquoise pendants on painted chests, gourd rattles and knee bells, tortoise shell leg tinklers and moccasins—

Ladders protruding from kivas in Oraibi. [www.gutenberg.org/files/ 15888/15888-h/15888-h.htm]

the variation is endless. A dizzying array of multi-colored masks, costumes, and accouterments clad and equip these spirit messengers as they dance for rain or the overall well being of the Hopi people.

The masks originally made from buckskin are now stitched from rawhide or stretched cloth that extends entirely around the head. They come in a multitude of forms: circular, ovoid, dome-shaped, cylindrical, square, etc. Some are adorned with horns, feathers, or dark hair; others have brightly painted *tablitas* rising from the tops of their heads like clouds stylized in stepped formation. Some appear bug-eyed, others merely have painted slits for eyes, while still others have no eyes at all. Several *katsina* masks display tube-shaped or squash-shaped snouts, while some reveal sharp fangs or extended tongues. A few masks have ears but many lack noses. Unless they clearly represent animal or bird spirits, some *katsinam* even project the uncanny appearance of wearing helmets of an alien origin rather than masks.

Unlike the Plains Indians' sun dance songs that seem to aggressively pierce the sky like rays of sunlight, these Hopi songs project a more reserved or moderate character. This is because their voices are muffled by these extraordinary masks, which sometimes even resonate with a soft buzzing.

Katsina *dolls: Ahöla,*
(the germination god,
on left) and Sowi'ingw
(deer) katsina.
(Museum of Northern
Arizona.)

Oraibi village on Third Mesa, Arizona.
[*http://en.wikipedia.org/wiki/Oraibi*]

Moreover, the attention of the sedentary Hopi people is primarily focused downward to the earth, urging the forces of fertility to rise. From daybreak to nightfall with only brief intervals of rest, the singers' intoned prayers are pressed into the ground by a continous series of dance steps, thereby assisting the cycle of agricultural growth in an extremely harsh land. At last the sun slips beyond the western rim of the horizon and is gone, making its daily descent to the underworld.

The etymology of the term *katsina* may be derived from the word *kátci*, "spread out," "horizontal," or "surface of the earth" and *náa*, "father," thus giving to the term a literal meaning of "surface of the land father." In this sense the *katsinam* are perhaps related to Masau'u, the Hopi god of the earth. Author Frederick J. Dockstader believes that *kachi* refers to "life father" or "spirit father," but the horizontal sense of reclining can be interpreted as "...a 'sitter.' i.e., one who sits with the people (and among other things, listens to their petitions for rain and other spiritual and material blessings)." [*The Kachina and the White Man*]

This description parallels that of the angelic entities discussed in the apocryphal *Book of Enoch*, who are deemed "the Watchers." One of the kivas on the First Mesa ancient stone village of Waalpi (Walpi) is, in fact, called Wikwa'lobi, "Place of the Watchers." This kiva holds the esoteric rituals pertaining to the outward form of the Snake Dance Ceremony. (See Chapter 12.) In addition, Sótuknang, the Hopi Heart of the Sky god, is also known as "the Watcher." (See drawing on p. 99.)

In the pseudo-epigraphal *Book of Jubilees* composed in the second century BC from earlier sources, we encounter a figure named Kainam, the grandson of Noah.

"And the son grew, and his father [Arpachshad] taught him writing, and he went to seek for himself a place where he might seize for himself a city. And he found a writing which former generations had carved on the rock, and he read what was thereon, and he transcribed it and sinned owing to it; for it contained the teaching of the Watchers in accordance with which they used to observe the omens of the sun and moon and stars in all the signs of heaven. And he wrote it down and said nothing regarding it; for he was afraid to speak to Noah about it lest he should be angry with him on account of it." [http://wesley.nnu.edu/biblical_studies/noncanon/ot/pseudo/jubilee.htm, Chapter 8: 2-5]

Here we see that the teachings of the Watchers regarding astronomical lore are transmitted in much the same manner as the Hopi might have received information, specifically, through petroglyphs. The name Kainam more importantly bears a striking resemblance to the plural form of the name for the Hopi spiritual benefactors, the *katsinam*. Was the name of this antediluvian patriarch who held knowledge so secret that he was afraid to tell his grandfather somehow transferred across the sea to the land of the Hopi as a description of the Watchers?

The word *katsina* is interesting in light of the fact that it is an apparent import to the American Southwest. According to archaeologist Charles E. Adams, "There is no translation for *katsina*. It is certainly a borrowed word.... Foremost, there is no initial syllable *ka-* in Hopi. Evidence to suggest it is a borrowed term from outside the Pueblo area, rather than being indigenous, lies in the similarity of its pronunciation in the Zuni language and in Keresan spoken in Acoma." [*The Origin and Development of the Pueblo Katsina Cult*]

From this evidence we can deduce that the *katsinam* and their correlates in other pueblo groups were derived from a single, monolithic source. We ultimately have a case where spirit beings of foreign origin wearing trans-mundane helmets and bizarre regalia once sat with the people and listened to their pleas for succor. These spirit-messengers once apparently walked among the ancient Hopi to provide physical aid and spiritual guidance.

Surveying words beginning with *ka-* in the Hopi dictionary, we find many words with meanings such as sheep, goat, horse, wagon, watermelon, cassava melon, etc. These were all non-indigenous items imported to Arizona in historic times. Was the word *ka* imported as well? The Hopi *kavati*, for instance, means purple. The Phoencians, which we will discuss shortly, were world renowned for Tyrian purple dye made from murex shellfish.

So where did the *katsinam* come from, and why?

The Worldwide Reach of *Ka*

We have noted that the syllable *ka-* was of foreign origin. In other words, the initial syllable *ka-* is not native to the languages of the Pueblo people of the American Southwest.

Tribes in the vicinity of the Hopi, however, also have a relationship to *ka*. For instance, the Zuni, a tribe culturally though not linguistically related to the Hopi, were led on their ancient migrations to find the center of the earth by a chief named Kawimosa. He is responsible for instituting a sacred dance or drama called *Kaka*. On their journey they came to a great divided mountain with water in between called Káyemäshi, possibly a reference to Grand Canyon. In the Zuni creation story a water-skate named K'yan asdebi determined the six directions (the four solstice sunrise and sunset points in summer and winter plus the zenith and nadir) by stretching out its six legs. This figure is in actuality the Sun-father.

In the Tohono O'odham (Papago) tradition of southern Arizona, the word *Ka* means "clearing for a field," and *Ka-ka* is the plural. *Kaka* is the name of one of the four main Tohono O'odham settlements.

The Chumash of the southern California coast once performed a winter solstice ceremony called *Kakunupmawa*. An astronomer-priest and his twelve helpers ushered the sun back north by the use of "sunsticks."

Ka refers to the number "two" in the Mayan language. The Mayan word *kah* means village. In Yukatek Maya, *k'ah* means "to know," "to make known," or "to commemorate."

*Palace of the Chac
Masks, Kabah.
Chac is the Mayan
god of water/rain.
(Photo © courtesy of
George DeLange,
www.delange.org.)*

*Ka/ankh on djed pillar
holds the sun.
It is flanked by Isis
and Nephthy plus baboons
with upraised hands,
from The Book of the Dead.*

One Mayan temple complex in Yucatan, Mexico, is known as Kabah. On a highly ornate façade of the Palace of Masks, what appear to be elephant trunks are sculpted in great number. (See photo on preceding page.) "Between each set of eyes is a greater or lesser trunk going out, down, around, and back." [Ferguson, *Mayan Ruins of Mexico*] Each one of these 260 *Codz Pop* (literally, "rolled mats" — reed? see Chapter 11) corresponds to a specific day in the Mayan calendar. How did representations of a species found only in African or India get to the New World in pre-Columbian times? We will have more to say about the Maya in a later section of this chapter.

Hindu mythology refers to *Ka* (or *Kha*) as the Unknown God, or "Who," an indefinable Absolute. Book X, Hymn 121 of the *Rigveda* is dedicated to him. He is earth's begetter and heaven's creator. In the beginning he was the Golden Seed rising from the waters of chaos to bestow vital breath, power, and vigor to all living things. He is both the transcendent God ruling by law and the immanent spirit pervading all life. *Ka* is lord of men and lord of cattle. He is also known as Prajapati, master of created beings. Prajapati is essentially the protective father of those with progeny.

The Hindu Devanagari glyph for *ka* has its origin in the Brahmi glyph with the shape of an equilateral cross. The ancient people in the American Southwest saw this type of cross as representing a star, many examples of which are found in the rock art of the region. Comparative linguistics scholar Gene D. Matlock says that the Sanskrit word *Ka* means "sun" or "king." [www.mondovista.com/kokopeli.html]

A charming story about *Ka* comes from friend and colleague T. L. Subash Chandira Bose, who grew up in Tamil Nadu, India.

"In childhood, my parents told me to go to the roof of our house carrying the banana leaf with food, to offer 'food' to the birds particularly to the 'crow'. They also said to call the birds with the words 'Ka, Kha' and I did so. I was surprised to observe that the crow and other birds came to our roof flying from all the directions. Once I kept away from the food, the birds came down and consumed the food. I was in surprise and my parents asked me whether the birds came and consumed the food or not. I relayed, yes. Then they said, it is fine; you come down now to have our food.

"One day I asked my parents: Why we should offer food to the birds? And what is the significance of calling the birds with words 'Ka, Kha'? My parents smiled and looked at each other, then my mother said, 'My dear son, you will know it by yourself.' She continued, 'My son, this is the knowledge each and every body has to search independently in their birth; knowing about Ka, Kha is one among the sacred knowledge.' She blessed me, 'Dear child, you will know much sacred knowledge and share with others.'"

Sri Jagannatha Swami, M.A., M.Phil., Ph.D., also of Tamil Nadu, India, provides the subtext of this anecdote: "In Sanskrit the letter Ka is the first consonant and it means Brahma the creator and creation. Kha is the second letter in that varga [class] and it means Sun. But when we write the name of the bird (crow) in Sanskrit we use "ka ka" only. It denotes the creation and destruction. Hindus believe that the food offered to crows is equivalent to that offered to the ancestors." [www.spiritualmindpower.com] The very same tradition occurs in both the ancient Egyptian culture and the Hopi culture.

In the Egyptian ontology, *Ka* refers to the etheric double, or *doppelgänger*. This reinforces the Mayan meaning of *Ka* as "two" or "twin." An Egyptian tomb statuette resembling the deceased at the height of his or her physical power and beauty was frequently constructed for the *Ka* to inhabit. In addition, food offerings were often made to the *Ka*. A similar custom still exists on the Hopi reservation during the early November Wuwtsim (New Fire Ceremony). At this time spirits of the dead return to the villages and feast on the food offerings left on the western edge of the village. In Egypt the direction of west is universally associated with the land of the dead.

The *Ka* symbolizes the transmission of vital essence from gods to men. *Ka* may be conceptualized as something akin to our notion of the guardian angel or perhaps the alter ego. The *Ka* is also associated with the ancestors, and to die is to go back to the protective embrace of one's *Ka*.

Joseph Campbell states that the "maid servants of the *kas*" form a constellation of fourteen qualities, namely: might, radiance, prosperity, victory, wealth, plenty, augustness, readiness, creative action, intelligence, adornment, stability, obedience, and taste. It is interesting to note that the Egyptians loved anagrams. Thus *ka* represents power but *ak* represents weakness, sorrow, pain, or destruction. As another example of this type of wordplay, *ab* means "heart" and *ba* means "soul." [*The Masks of God*]

"Bull-god" is another Egyptian connotation of *Ka*, thereby stressing male potency. *Ka* also known as "the grandfather of all the gods." To procreate reinforces the link with one's ancestral past.

The *Ka* sound is also astronomically connected to the second brightest star in the heavens after Sirius, which is located in Canis Major. Canopus (in Greek, literally "eye of the dog") in the constellation Carina, the Keel, is known as the southern polar star. The name Canopus maybe derived from the Egyptian or Coptic *kahi nub*, meaning "golden earth." (Note all the *ka-* sounds in the preceding proper nouns. We are also reminded here of canopic jars.)

The hieroglyph for *Ka* is two uplifted arms whose elbows form right angles. The open palms are held forward and the shoulders are fused together, thus forming a U shape. (See drawing on p. 192.) The same characteristic "prayer stance" is found in great numbers among the petroglyphs of the ancient Hopi all over the Southwest. The human figure is shown with both arms raised to the sky and both feet on the ground. (See photo on p. 28.) In this stance the knees somtimes form right angles like the elbows. The position of the arms is, incidentally, the same as in the "Grand Hailing Sign of Distress" in Freemasonry.

Incredible as it may seem, the non-indigenous *ka-* of the Arizona's *katsinam* may have somehow been affected by the Egyptian conception of *Ka*. Its influence, however, appears to be global.

The Sumerian word *ka* means either "gate" or "mouth." The former is the passageway between worlds; the latter allows life to continue through the ingestion of food and serves as the shaper of sounds and language.

The Kabbalah (**ka**-ba-la) is the ancient system of Jewish esoteric knowledge and practice. The Ka'ba (in Egyptian *ka*, "spirit-double" and *ba*, "soul") is a sacred cube located at the holiest spot in Islam: the center of the Muslim world at Mecca.

A *Kaddish* is a Jewish prayer for the dead chanted en masse by mourners at a funeral or recited by children of the deceased. A *kalif* is a religious and civil leader in a Muslim state. On the other hand, *kafir* is Arabic for "infidel " or "nonbeliever," perhaps one who instead believes in the paganistic aspects of *ka*.

The Merkabah (mer-**ka**-ba) is the throne-chariot of God, the biblical four-wheeled vehicle found in Ezekiel 1:4-26. In New Age metaphysics the MerKaBa refers to two interlocking, counterrotating tetrahedra of equal size pointed in opposite directions. This interdimensional vehicle is known as a Star Tetrahedron, or a three-dimensional Star of David. It is basically a meditation device used simultaneously with breath control and certain eye and hand movements to activate a saucer-shaped energy field capable of transporting consciousness to a higher dimension.

The initial *ka-* sound is found globally in certain words. *Kahuna*, for instance, is the Polynesian name for medicine man or priest. In Japanese *ka* (oringally *oka*) means "the people." In addition, the Japanese word *kami* means "deity" or "deified hero." The Old English word *kaser*, or *kaiser*, refers to "emperor." In Iran Kai Ka'us was a legendary shah. *Kala* is the theosophical term for Infinite Time. *Khan* refers to "prince," "king," "chief," or "govenor" of Mongolian or Turkish regions, as in, for example, Gengis Khan.

The Indians that Christopher Columbus encountered on the island of Española had spears, the tops of which were made from a metal later determined to be an alloy of gold, silver, and copper. The Indians claimed they had received this metal they called *gua-nin* from black traders. The Vei tribe of West Africa call this same metal *ka-ni*.

The *Kan* form will be discussed in the other sections of this chapter. The following words of a Lakota (Sioux) from South Dakota illustrate its long reach: "*Kan* means anything that is old or that has existed for a long time or that should be accepted because it has been so in former times, or it may mean a strange or wonderful thing or that which can not be comprehended, or that which should not be questioned or it may mean a sacred or supernatural thing." [Walker, *Lakota Belief and Ritual*]

The Diverse Deities of *Ka*

A surprising number of primary gods and goddesses around the world have names that begin with *ka-*. These are mostly known either as the creator or as part of the celestial realm, in particular the sun.

Kalliphos is one of the many names of the Greek sun god used to invoke spirits or to conjure. (The prefix *kalli-* means "bright, good" and the suffix *phos* means "light.") The Celtic god of sky and war is named Camalus (prounced with a hard "C").

Kari is the Norse leader of the storm giants. Kalma is the goddess of death in Finland and is perhaps related to the Hindu Kali, the black goddess of destruction, dissolution, and time. In the *Rigveda*, Kavya Ushanas is seen as a special friend of Indra, who received his thunderbolt from the former.

Katonda is the creator god and supreme being of the Baganda tribe of Uganda. From the same country the Kiga tribe see Kazoba as their remote but benevolent creator god who is also associated with the sun, moon, and stars. Kanu is the supreme god of the Safroko Limba of Sierra Leon, while in the Numba Mountains of Sudan, Kando is the sky god.

For the Pomo Indians of California, Ka'a djaj is the god of the east or "daylight man." The Salish Indians of the Pacific Northwest know Kals as their highest god and "great transformer." Karakwa is the sun god of the Iroquois Indians from the eastern U.S., while Kamantowit is the great god of the Algonquins who created humankind.

Ka'k'och is the creator and prime mover for the Lacandon Maya from Chiapis, Mexico, while Kankin is the sun god of the Maya in the Corozal District of Belize. For the Warrau of Venezuela, Kanobo is the benevolent supreme being propitiated during floods.

Karai Kasang is the omnipresent, omnipotent, and omniscient supreme being invoked to testify to the truth for the Katchins of Burma. (Note that the spelling of this tribe is similar to the Hopi *katsina*, sometimes spelled *katchina*.) For the Altaians of Siberia, Kaira Kan is the benevolent high god invoked by shamans at the start of their ecstatic journeys.

Kaleya Ngungu is the supreme being of the Sunday Islanders of Australia, while Kasiwa is the omniscient supreme god of the Nukumanu tribe of Micronesia. Kambel is the sky god and father of the moon for the Keraki-Papuans of New Guinea. Kayai is the sky god, supreme being, and punishing god of thunderstorms for the Aeta (Negritos) of Luzon in the Philippines.

Kane is the Hawaiian creator of the universe and humankind. He is also the god of light and bringer of culture. Also in Hawaii, Ka-onohi-o-ka-la is the "eyeball of the sun," who escorts the souls of heroes to heaven.
[An extensive list of gods beginning with *Ka-* is found at: www.angelfire.com/journal/cathbodua/Gods/Gods2.html.]

Thus, *Ka* is apparently either a creator of the world or a creature of the sky.

The Ka'nas *Katsinam* of the Sacred Peaks

Returning to the Hopi realm of northern Arizona, let's now discuss a specific *katsina* called the Ka'nas *katsina*. This group supposedly lived in the ice caves near Sunset Crater, a volcano near the San Francisco Peaks that erupted in the autumn of 1064 AD and ceased in about 1250 AD.

Volcanic cone of Sunset Crater formed in the mid-11th century.
(Aerial photo by Wendell Duffield, courtesy of U.S. Geological Survey.)

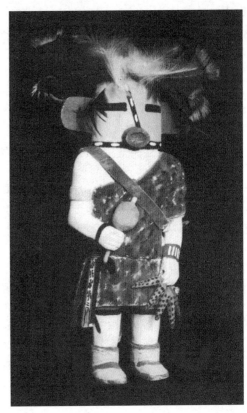

Above:
Angwusnasomtaka,
Crow Mother katsina.
[Dover Publications, Inc.]
Right:
Ka'nas katsina *doll.*

Traditional academics speculate that "Ka'nas" is actually the native name for the tribal group called the Sinagua, which migrated from far to the south. (*Sinagua* is a Spanish term mean ing "without water.") A special type of pottery called Kana-a black-on-white found in the area of the San Francisco Peaks is dated from between 800 and 1000 AD.

The Ka'nas *katsina* wears a case mask that is half white and half yellow, the colors divided by a diagonal line. He has horizontal slit eyes and a tube moth. He also wears a bobcat or rabbit skin robe and red moccasins. (See photo on p. 199.)

Another way to spell this name is Ka-naas. As noted above, *náa* is the Hopi word for "father," which reinforces many of the masculine meanings of *Ka* from Egypt and India.

The Ka'nas is one of the few *katsinam* to which a folktale is attributed. One long and complex myth in particular reveals the eerily alien nature of this *katsina*. After a series of ordeals (paralleling the Greek myth of Eros and Psyche) on the sacred San Francisco Peaks (Arizona's highest mountains), a young bride accompanies her handsome Ka'nas *katsina* husband back to her village of Musungnuvi (Mishongnovi) on Second Mesa.

Meanwhile a group of sorcerers decides that one of them should impersonate the *katsina* while he is absent from the village. In this guise the chosen sorcerer seduces the *katsina*'s wife and sleeps with her.

Despite this act of unavoidable adultery caused by trickery, the Ka'nas nonetheless jealously ignites a fire near the San Francisco Peaks, which somehow gets out of control and burns into the ground. As a result, the volcanic eruption occurs, which threatens to destroy Musungnuvi. At the last moment the *katsina* takes pity on the people and summons the wind god Yopontsa living at the base of Palotsmo (Sunset Crater) to help him blow back the flames from the path of the Hopi village.

On the west side of the mesa below the village of Musungnuvi is a rectangular rock that acts as shrine called the "Ka'nas *katsina* house." Many members of the darker skinned Crow Clan migrated from the San Francisco Peak area to Musungnuvi. The Crow Mother *katsina* is considered the mother of all the *katsinam*. (See drawing on p. 199.) We recall the above discussion of the association in Hindu lore of the cawing crow with the ancestors. Perhaps the Crow Clan was intimately connected with the Ka'nas *katsinam* as well.

Incidentally, the customary modes of transportation for this Ka'nas *katsina* are either a rainbow-road or a "flying shield"—in Hopi, *paatuwvota*. (See Chapter 7.) Thus, in this case we are clearly talking about a supernatural entity rather than an ordinary tribal person.

We can conclude that the Ka'nas *katsinam* were an outside force that irrevocably altered the character of the ancient Pueblo culture. Initially they were perceived not as abstract ethereal spirits but as benevolent physical entities that had come into the land of the ancestral Hopi from some distant place. As the Hopi and nearby language groups all attest, the very name of this cult is not native to the region.

So where exactly did the miraculous Ka'nas *katsinam* originate?

The Phoenician *Kan*

An interesting linguistic "coincidence" is presented in the word *Kana'ana*. This refers to the Ka-naanites, or Canaanites. This people lived in the lowlands west of the Lebanon Mountains in modern day Lebanon and Syria. (A geographic "coincidence" is manifested by the fact that the land of the Canaanites and the land of the Hopi are at the exact same latitude.) Known by the Greeks as the Phoenicians, the Canaanites were the quintessential sailors, ship builders, merchants, and traders of the Mediterranean region during the two millennia before the Common Era. They spoke a dialect of Aramaic and were the first in the world to use an alphabetic system.

In order to write, one sometimes used a reed pen. The Hebrew word for "reed" is *Kanah*. The reed is universally symbolic of the refinements of civilization and culture. (See Chapter 11.) In a New Testament context we recall that Jesus performed his first miracle of turning water into wine at Cana (hard "C") in Galilee.

The complex pantheistic religion of the Phoneicians was based upon the natural world, especially the celestial realm. Biblical scholar William Smith grudgingly comments on the power of their belief system:

> "In its popular form, [the Phoenician religion] was especially a worship of the sun, moon, and five planets, or as it might have been expressed according to ancient notions, of the seven planets—*the most beautiful and perhaps the most natural form of idolatry ever presented to the human imagination.* [emphasis added] These planets, however, were not regarded as lifeless globes of matter, obedient to physical laws, but as intelligent animated powers, influencing the human will, and controlling human destinies." [*Smith's Bible Dictionary*]

The word *ana* in *Kana'ana* is similar to the Anak or Anakim, which referred to either the progenitor of the family or the tribe of giant people in Canaan. The word *anak* actually means "neck" or "long neck" and may be associated with the biblical Nephilim or the "giants in the earth." These were the progeny of the "sons of god" (or the Watchers previously mentioned) and the "daughters of men."

Sumerian scholar Zecharia Sitchin believes that the figure of Ka'in from Mesopotamian mythology was actually Cain in the Book of Genesis. Paralleling the biblical story, Ka'in was originally a tiller of the soil who was then cursed to roam.

In light of all this, we must ask: Were the *Kana'ana* (Phoenicians) also initially a failure at farming only to become one of the world's greatest maritime and mercantile success stories? Their intimate knowledge of the stars and planets certainly would have greatly assisted their navigational skills across vast stretches of ocean.

The Hawaiian god of the ocean was named Kanaloa. He was also one of gods who created the heaven and the earth. He is furthermore known as the ruler of Po, the Dark realm, and leader of the rebellious spirits, much like Cain. In this context it is interesting to note the *Oxford English Dictionary* definition of the Hawaiian word *Kanaka*: "A native of the South Sea Islands."

The Phoenicians may not have merely sailed to Britain or hugged the coastlines of Africa, as some claim. They may have also ventured into the Indian Ocean, veering northeast past Sumatra, Java, and Borneo in order to catch a ride eastward on that trans-Pacific conveyor belt called the Equatorial Counter Currents. If so, they finally

Clay bust with beard, pointed hat, and earplugs, Tres Zapotes, Mexico.

would have landed at the Isthmus of Panama or the Isthmus of Tehuantepec in southern Mexico. These two narrow strips of land are about seventy-five miles and one hundred and twenty-five miles wide respectively from the Pacific to the Atlantic coast.

Many Phoenician artifacts have been discovered from the ancient cities of La Venta and Tres Zapotes founded about 800 BC in the Olmec region of Veracruz, Mexico. These include a life-like clay head with earplugs (the classic "earmark" of sailors), a very non-Indian mustache and pointed beard, and a peaked hat called a *hennin*.

Sometimes referred to as a Phrygian cap, the particular type of hat worn by the Phoenician depicted in the sculpture somewhat resembles the curved headdress worn by the Hopi "heart of the sky" god, Sótuknang. (His name literally means "star-thunderhead-heart." See drawing on p. 99.) In addition, the Mayan "heart of the sky" god was named Huracán (Hu-ra-*kan*), from which we derive the word "hurricane." His alternate name is K'awil. (More on the Mayan *Kan* in a subsequent section of this chapter.)

Admittedly, it is a long stretch in time between 800 BC and 1000 AD, when the Ka'nas *katsinam* inhabited northern Arizona.

Suppose for a moment, though, that the Phoenician colonists settled in Mexico. Over the centuries their ancestors would have traded with local Olmec and Mayan groups and may have finally traveled north to interact with the indigenous people of the American Southwest. These pioneering Phoenicians gradually lost some of their Old World influences and customs to become part of the North American continent in much the same way that Americans are now distinct from the British. Certainly Phoenicians and native peoples of the "New World" would have shared linguistic concepts.

The Confusionist *Kan* (Con) of the Ivory Tower

The notion of Canaanites (or Phoenicians) in America is anathema to academia. Put simply, cultural diffusionism proposes that ancient people got around on foot or by boat a lot more than commonly assumed—around the world, in fact. This theory posits that a free flow of trade goods and cultural motifs existed globally, perhaps as early as the Neolithic period.

During the 20th century anthropologists and archaeologists, many of them tenured or supported by universities, had suggested that the diffusionist theory, which prevailed in the last part of the previous century, is inherently racist. The theory, they said, implies that Caucasians had bestowed the benefits of civilization on the "darker" races in order to bring them toward the light.

Proposing an alternative isolationist theory, this Columbus-was-first crowd described a scenario of scattered, provincial tribes of Native Americans going it alone the best way they could on a sparsely populated continent. In our current age when racial equality is at least an ideal, the notion of a group of white, patriarchal benefactors influencing the "benighted" aboriginal cultures is indeed repugnant and retrograde—if it were true.

But in some ways the isolationist theory is the racist one because it assumes that the native peoples of North and South America were not intelligent or skilled enough to accomplish long distance travel by land or sea—other than the initial push from Siberia to Alaska and Canada via the Bering Straits.

On the contrary, the cultural interaction between continents, which began in pre-Christian times, was most likely a two-way street. In other words, Semitic, Egyptian, Hindu, and European cultures may have benefited as much or more from interaction with Native Americans than the reverse.
(For more on diffusionism, see Appendix 2, p. 275.)

The following section provides more evidence from the Maya realm of Mesoamerica, pointing to the idea that a global culture once existed in an age far earlier than our own.

The Mayan *Kan*

A constellation of Mayan words and concepts is relevant here. *Kan* means "snake," but it also means "sky." (In the univer-

sal word-reversal game, the Mayan *nak* means "ascension.") Thus, we see the elegant rationale for the Mayan god Kukulkan, the feathered snake or plumed serpent. Corresponding to the Aztecan god Quetzalcoatl, this benefactor once lived in Mexico and imparted knowledge of agriculture (particularly the growth of maize), the calendar, books, and astronomy. He then sailed to the east on a raft made of snakes, promising to return at the end of the age.

Rising "Vision Serpent."

In addition, the word *kan* refers to "rope" but also to the number "four," as in the four directions. Similar to the Egyptian anagrams previously noted, the Mayan anagram *nak* significantly designates "throne" as well.

Kanal means "on high" or "heaven." In Yukatek Maya,

kanul is a supernatural guardian or protector that usually takes the form of a wild animal. *Kanan* refers to "overflow" or "abundance." The related word *qaanab* means "of the sea." *K'an* is the Cakchiquel Maya word for the iguana or tree lizard.

As we shall see shortly, a similar reptile is also significant in the American Southwest.

Kan also means "precious," "yellow," or "ripe" and refers to either corn or the Maize God, also known as First Father. In some Mayan friezes this deity carries what is called a *Kan* cross as he emerges from the cracked carapace of a turtle. The cross, which looks somewhat like a Maltese cross (see Chapter 15), is also found on the cake-shaped headpiece of another sculpture with a Semitic pointed beard found in the Olmec area of Veracruz. The icon is additionally found at Palenque in the Temple of the Foliated Cross, which represents a cosmic corn plant. The emergence of the Maize God symbolizes his resurrection and the simultaneous recreation of the world.

In Mayan iconography the turtle represents Orion. This constellation lies close to the ecliptic (the apparent path of the planets and zodiac constellations) between Taurus and Gemini. Linda Schele, the late epigrapher of the Maya, has determined that the *Kan* cross signifies the place near the zenith where the ecliptic crosses the center of the Milky Way at a nearly perpendicular angle. "The K'an cross is a kind of 'X marks the spot' symbol of rebirth and Creation." [*Maya Cosmos*] The *kan* denotation of "rope" corresponds to the cosmic umbilical cord that connects to the Heart of Sky, which the Quiché Maya call *cah*. Incidentally, the Mayan word for turtle is *ak*, an anagram of *ka*. The Mayan *ek* means star.

According to archaeologist Sylvanus G. Morley, the Maize God is the primary Mayan deity characterized by an elongation of the skull. "Of all the gods represented in the codices this youthful deity shows the greatest amount of head deformation. Notice his markedly retreating forehead. His name-glyph [the *Kan* cross] is his own head, which merges at the top into a highly conventional ear of corn, surmounted by leaves." [*The Ancient Maya*]

Right: Turtle carrying three hearth stones of creation: Alnitak, Saiph, and Rigel in Orion. Cords represent the ecliptic. (Madrid Codex) The stones' position mirrors Hopi cloud icon. (See p. 153.)

Mayan glyph for east.

Ek Chuah, Mayan merchant god. Holding a thunder ax, he was also patron of warriors.

"Paddler" with non-Mayan face, female with long forehead. (Dresden Codex)

This type of skull deformation called dolichocephalous was known not only among the upper classes of the Maya but also among the Inca of Peru and the ancient Egyptians (both pre-dynastic and during the Armarnian dynasty of Akhenaton). It has even been found on the island of Malta not far from the Phoenician port city of Carthage. The Phrygian cap previously mentioned may have been an attempt to mimic this odd skull shape. [www.andrewcollins.com/page/articles/maltaskulls.htm]

The Bacabs (*ba-ka-b*) of Mayan cosmology are also relevant here. These are four brothers who support the sky with upraised arms (much like the "prayer stance" mentioned above) and represent the four cardinal directions. Columns at the Castillo in Chichén Itzá in Yucatan show the Bacabs as bearded and one of them has a turtle shell (Orion) on his back. The Dresden Codex shows a Bacab disguised as an opossum carrying in the Maize God as the ruler of the incoming year.

Each Bacal is also assigned a color. The Bacab of the east is associated with the color red and is patron of the *Kan* years. It is interesting to note that the Phoenicians were known as the "red people." The clairvoyant Edgar Cayce says that one of the five races on the Earth was the red race, inhabiting both Atlantis and America. The Olmecs and the Mayans used to grind up hematite into a glittering purple-red powder for body adornment or use in burials.

The Mayan glyph for the direction of east shows a figure with a tube mouth and a vertical stripe down the forehead, much like the Ka'nas *katsina* of the Hopi. (See photo on p. 199.)

The term *Bacab* means either "around the world" or "around the hive." The latter term emphasizes the Bacabs' additional duty as the god of honey and apiaries. Perhaps it is more than a coincidence that the island of Malta, which was colonized very early by the Phoenicians, may have derived its name from Melita. In Latin the name means "land of honey." The island of Malta is still world-renowned for the superior quality of its honey. Exodus 3:8 refers to "...the land flowing with milk and honey, the country of the Canaanites [Phoenicians] ..." Traditionally thought to be Palestine, this land might refer to Malta as well.

The Mayan merchant god (sometimes referred to as God M) is known as Ek Chuah, literally "black star" in Yucatec. (See drawing on p. 207.) The related name Ah Chuah is the Yucatec term for certain wild bees. The merchant god has a long nose and a protruding lower lip, both uncharacteristic of the native Mayans. He also carries a bundle of merchandise on his back and is patron of cacao beans, which were used in Mesoamerica as a form of currency. A mural from Santa Rita, British Honduras (Belize), clearly shows him with a long beard. Another depiction portrays him with the head of Xaman (pronounced "shaman") Ek, or the North Star, which is the "guide of merchants."

Our discussion of *Kan* and related Mayan words clearly shows that the accompanying concepts were not restricted to Mesoamerica but were well known to the east and possibly to the west as well.

A Few Cross-cultural Artifacts

All of this is highly speculative, especially if we remain merely in the realm of comparative linguistics—in other words, the *Kana'ana* of the Old World and either the *kan* root words of the Maya or the Ka'nas *katsinam* of the Arizona Hopi.

A couple artifacts from these respective continents bear scrutiny. (See next page.) The first is a stele discovered at Dougga in Tunis, not far from the ancient Phoenician colony of Carthage (in Phoenician, **K**art-hadasht, or "new town") in North Africa. The top of the stele is triangular or pyramid-shaped, under which are three concentric circles (sun) and a crescent moon. At the bottom right is a female figure with upraised arms and a triangular-shaped dress. At the bottom left are two vertical circles linked together with a curved line and a spear-shaped figure on top. The female represents Tanit (Ashtar or Astarte), goddess of love and fertility—both procreative and vegetative.

*Right: Phoenician stele,
Tunis, 4th century BC.
Sun, crescent moon,
navigational instrument (?),
and female figure wearing
a triangular-shaped dress
and assuming
a prayer stance.*

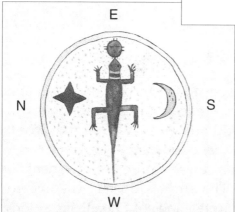

*Left: Ritual sand painting,
Acoma Pueblo, New Mexico.
Sun, lizard with wedge-
shaped head, star,
and crescent moon.*

Note: On p. 197 of his book Sailing to Paradise, *Jim Bailey provides a sketch of a sculpture at Byblos depicting the Phoenician sky god Baal Shamin (Zeus Hypsistos). A monitor lizard similar to this Native American version hovers over his right shoulder. Bailey claims that this reptile is the "Creator's vicar on earth." He also believes that it may be the origin of the Cross of Lorraine (‡), which was carried to the Crusades by the Knights Templar. During the Renaissance this cross signified the risen Christ ruling over the world, and also the alchemical maxim: "As above, so below." The cross furthermore looks like the* vajra *that the Hindu god Indra wields, as well as the double trident resembling both the staff of Jupiter and the staff of Odin.*

Another artifact comes from Acoma pueblo in northwestern New Mexico. Like the Zuni, the Acoma people are culturally but not linguistically related to the Hopi. The sand painting depicts a lizard with both arms stylistically spread in a fashion akin to the upraised arms found in both the previous artifact mentioned and the Egyptian *Ka*. For the Pueblo people the lizard generally represents dreaming, good luck, and conservation. This lizard has a triangular-shaped head and a body that is positioned on an east-west axis. A Zia sun symbol is balanced on the apex of the lizard's head, showing it is dawn. To the right (or south) is a crescent moon, and to the left (north) is a star icon, perhaps representing either Polaris or Venus.

In his book *When Time Began*, Zecharia Sitchin describes both a Sumerian and a Phoenician astronomical, navigational, and calendrical instrument that contains all the elements we have been discussing here. Something like the modern-day theodolite used in measuring horizontal and vertical angles, this instrument had short vertical posts on a horizontal bar mounted atop a triangular base. His depiction of a so-called votive tablet found in the ruins of a Phoenician colony in Sicily also includes the doubled-ringed icon shown on the Carthaginian stele.

Sitchin claims that the Egyptians symbolized this instrument by the fusion of the hieroglyph of upraised arms of *Ka* with the hieroglyph that means horizon, or the sun between two mountains. "That the origin of *Ka* was, to begin with, an astronomical instrument is suggested by an archaic Egyptian depiction of a viewing device in front of a temple." [*When Time Began*] At any rate, physical biremes once traversed star-sparkling oceans assisted by such instruments in the same way that the *Ka* ultimately made the journey to the Afterlife, or the "planet of millions of years."

The historian Gene Matlock, whom we cited above, opines that the **Kha**iberi (Cabeiri), which literally means "connected," was basically the conjoined group of Phoenicians and Jews, the Gemini twins of the Old World (who also wore the Phrygian cap). [www.viewzone.com/phoenician.html]

**The Los Lunas Decalogue Stone. [Photo by Dan Raber,
www.econ.ohio-state.edu/jhm/arch/loslunas.html.]
Estimates of its age vary from 500 to 2,000 or more years old.**

This jibes too with the Mayan meaning of *Ka* as "twins." In
Greek, **Ka**stor (Castor) means "he who excels," while Polydeuces
(Pollux) means "very sweet."

In this context I want to mention one more curious artifact,
which is located not far from the Rio Grande, a major passageway
into the region. A little over thirty miles east of Acoma pueblo and
just over fifteen miles west of Los Lunas, New Mexico, is the Los
Lunas Decalogue Stone. (See photo above.) This eighty-ton boulder
of volcanic basalt about eight meters long rests on the north side of
Hidden Mountain. Incised on its rock face are nine rows of 216
characters of mixed paleo-Hebrew and Phoenician scripts with a
few additional Greek letters. In essence it is a slightly abbreviated
version of the Decalogue, or the Ten Commandments.

One of the letters in the inscription is a Phoenician *Kaph*,
which looks like a reversed letter "K." This character means
"open palm." This is the same icon of the "prayer stance" we have
seen in both the rock art of the American Southwest and the
hieroglyphs of the Egyptians as well as in the vignettes accom-

panying their ancient texts, especially *The Book of the Dead*.

Also, the Mayan words *k'a*, *k'al*, and *k'ab* all refer to "hand," while the Mayan *k'alah* means "hand with extended fingers."

Was some sort of hand-held instrument used by the Phoenicians for navigation taken to the American Southwest and shown to the indigenous people, who incorporated it into their ritual artwork and artifacts? The evidence for a pre-Columbian global exchange of goods, customs, and concepts keeps mounting.

The *Ka* of Apocalypse

K'a is also a Cholti Maya word that means "to end" or "to terminate." Many Hopi elders believe that we are living in the last days of the present Fourth World, though they give no exact date for its end. One of the many signs of the End Times is that fewer and fewer *katsina* dances are being held. The ones being performed today are, sadly, not done with the vitality and ritual precision of previous periods. One interesting pair of related Hopi words is the following: *sootu* (with an extended long "o" sound), which means "stars," and *sòoti*, which means "end."

According to the Mayan calendar, the date named 4 Ahau 3 Kankin concludes 5,126-year cycle of the world epoch that began on August 13, 3114 BC. *Ahau* means "lord" and *Kankin* means "snake-sun." This date is, of course, December 21, 2012.

On this rapidly approaching day, the *Kan* cross, or cosmic crossroads, will appear in the heart of the sky. Specifically, the ecliptic will cross the center of the Milky Way at about a 60° angle between the constellation Sagittarius to the east and Scorpius to the west. This direction points to the very hub of our spiral galaxy, where astrophysicists say a black hole lies. This ecliptic-galactic axis crossing is not at all unusual though.

A very rare astronomical phenomenon does, however, occur in 2012. At 11:11 GMT the December solstice sun will rest directly upon the *Kan* cross at the galactic equator or the center of our Milky Way. Because of the precession of the equinoxes (or the slow wobble of the Earth on its axis like a spinning top), this happens only once every 25,920 years. Also on 12.21.12, Pluto (the planet of death, radical transformation, and rebirth) will be conjunct with the sun.

This is the moment when the Mayan calendar apparently ends. During this period Hopi elders, as they have for thousands of years, will be performing the winter solstice ceremony down in their kivas. It is carried out in part to marshal the reborn sun northward on the horizon. At the same time the *katsinam* are performing their summer solstice ceremony down in the underworld.

The *Ka* of Creation has always pervaded the entire universe with its diverse hallowed guises such as solar deity, celestial spirit, earth fertility figure, ruler, leader, or primordial essence. Even the end of our temporal cycle, if it does indeed arrive, will not stop this omnipotent force.

Mayan Day of Destruction. Dragon and clawed creature pour torrents of water on dark figure. (End of Dresden Codex.)

Chapter 17: The Hopi Stone Tablets of *Tutskwa I'qatsi*

The Hopi phrase *tutskwa i'qatsi* (also spelled *techqua ikachi*) literally means "land and life." These two concepts are inseparable in the Hopi mind. Simply stated, the land cannot be abstractly divorced from the human, animal, and plant life that depends on it for survival. This might seem obvious in our contemporary ecological age, but the Hopi have maintained a lifestyle in accordance with this philosophy for thousands of years.

Like the Jewish people led by Moses, this tribe living in northern Arizona was apparently guided by a set of stone tablets. These artifacts led the Hopi not only in the literal sense of direction but also through divine principles. In essence, the carved stones taught them how to live in a sacred manner upon the land.

The god of the earth and the Underworld named Masau'u along with a figure known as Kokyangwuti, or Spider Woman, gave them these tablets called *owatutuveni*. This occurred at the beginning of the current age just before the Hopi left on their migrations that lasted centuries. Together the two deities breathed on them and etched into stone what was apparently a map of the Hopi territory.

These tablets are crucial to both the history and the destiny of the Hopi. In his 1972 monograph the spiritual leader Dan Katchongva emphasized their cultural significance:

> "Before the first people had begun their migrations the people named Hopi were given a set of stone tablets. Into these tablets the Great Spirit inscribed the laws by which the Hopi were to travel and live the good way of life, the peaceful way. They also contain a warning that the Hopi must beware, for in time they would be influenced by wicked people to forsake the life plan of Maasau'u."
> [www.crystalinks.com/hopimyths.html]

215

In 1993 the spiritual elder Martin Gashweseoma addressed the General Assembly of United Nations: "We still have the sacred stone tablets given to us by the Spider Woman. This is our title and deed to this world, and it was given to us with the life plan to follow, and with strong instructions and serious warnings." [www.hopiland.net/prophecy/gash-un1.htm]

Hopi prophecy foresaw tribal representatives knocking on the door of this "House of Mica" four times. If the world rejects the Hopi plan for peace each time, the current world will soon come to an end. This, sadly, is what has happened. (See Chapter 18.)

The four stone tablets are identified as the following: the First, Second, and Third Bear Clan Tablets plus the Fire Clan Tablet. The Bear Clan, which is the primary Hopi clan comprised of spiritual leaders, was originally given the first three tablets weighing about eight pounds each. The tablets are inscribed with a number of symbols, including star, sun, snake, cloud, corn, bear paw, lightning, swastika, humanoid, and friendship (called a *nakwatsveni*).

Although nearly all Hopi informants and mythological sources mention them at one time or another, only the third Bear Clan tablet was witnessed by just two non-Indians: anthropologist Mischa Titiev sometime between 1932 and 1934, and the author Frank Waters in 1960. The extremely sacred nature of these artifacts probably precluded most incidents of casual exposure.

Waters relied upon the mere description of his informant Oswald White Bear Fredericks for the first two Bear Clan tablets and the Fire Clan tablet, whereas he actually saw both sides of the Third Bear Clan Tablet. (All tablet drawings adapted from Frank Waters, *Book of the Hopi*.)

The front of the **First Bear Clan Tablet** depicts an irregular grid of land plots surrounding a settlement. It is traversed by a track running diagonally from the bottom left corner to the top right corner. The back of the tablet simply shows a pair of bear tracks, which certifies the Bear Clan's initial claim to this territory.

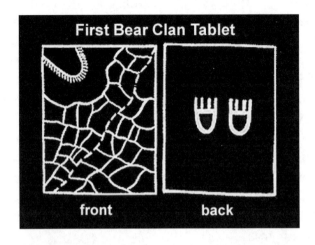

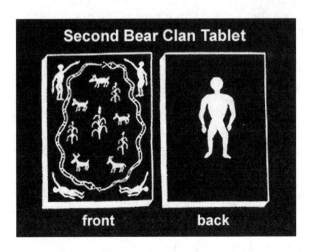

One Robert Nelson claims that this tablet is actually about a one-square-mile map of the Colorado River in Marble Canyon near Tatahatso Point and President Harding Rapids and that the dotted line on the tablet shows the Eminence Break fault line. [www.viewzone.com/thomasomills.html — Scroll to bottom.] This place is near the sacred Sipapuni, the spot where the Hopi emerged from the Third World into the current Fourth world. Although interesting, this is difficult to prove.

However, the ancient Hopi were accustomed to making maps of this sort in stone. On previous page look at the photo of petroglyphs at the V-Bar-V Heritage Site in the Verde Valley of Arizona. The square-shaped spiral in the upper left-hand corner may represent migrations. The grid itself may depict agricutural fields in the area.

The **Second Bear Clan Tablet** could possibly be a map. (Again, see previous page.) On the front of this tablet is a hoop formed by two snakes that Waters says are the Rio Grande and the Colorado River, roughly conforming to the eastern and western boundaries of the ancestral Hopi territory. At the center is a large cornstalk with three other cornstalks within the serpentine circle.

Also depicted are side-view silhouettes of five animals: a deer, a mountain sheep, and possibly three canines. The Hopi totemic correlatives for the intercardinal directions are as follows: a deer for the northwest, a mountain sheep for the southwest, a gray wolf for the southeast, and a wildcat (bobcat) for the northeast. The discrepancy between this symbology and that found on the tablet is plausibly the result of a faulty description of the latter. Again, Waters never saw this tablet.

On the outside of the hoop are four figures, one located in each corner and each figure with an outstretched arm. Waters believes these represent spiritual leaders who are holding and claiming the Hopi land.

On the back of this tablet is simply a large figure standing with knees slightly flexed and arms hanging to each side. If we accept that these double-sided tablets reflect the duality inherent in the Hopi cosmology, then we can easily imagine this figure to

Third Bear Clan Tablet

front   back

be Masau'u in his dark Underworld domain (which paradoxically includes the sky). On the opposite side is the animal and vegetable world shared with humans and drenched with the life-giving sunlight of Tawa, the Hopi sun god.

On the front of the **Third Bear Clan Tablet** is a rectangle with double borders representing the land over which Masau'u presides, surrounded by six naked male figures thought to be either leaders of the most important clans or priests who conduct the Soyal, or winter solstice ceremony. This geometric form is symbolic of Masau'u in particular and land in general.

Titiev describes the physical tablet itself:

> "It is a rectangular block of greyish-white, smooth-grained stone, about 16 inches long, 8 inches wide, and one and a half inches thick, splotched here and there with irregular dots which the chief interprets as points of land.... Along the edge representing the east, there is a line of small scratches, interspersed with occasional circles or crosses, which depict the proper Hopi path that the chiefs are supposed to travel." [*Old Oraibi*]

On the back of the tablet is a variety of iconography, which Titiev enumerates (even though he unfortunately reproduces only the front in his book):

"One surface is covered with miscellaneous symbols, including a row of eight little scratches, said to stand for the eight-day period during which the Soyal is observed; clouds and lightning emblems in a random arrangement; an unidentified Katcina [*katsina*] figure; two or three sets of bear claws; an old age crook; a poorly executed serpent, said to represent the Little Colorado river; and eight circles arranged in parallel rows, which the chief explains as thunder (?) because the sound of a thunder clap is like that of a number of objects being struck in succession." [*Old Oraibi*]

This does indeed sound like a map.

The crook does not appear on Waters' version of the tablet, unless it can be construed as the bending leaves of either of the two corn plants inscribed at the top left and right corners. The "Katcina" figure, which is actually in duplicate, looks more like a Masau'u representation with its white body and round head devoid of facial features. Since the cloud-and-lightning images are located directly above these figures, however, they might conceivably represent the Omau (Cloud) *katsina*. (See Chapter 13.)

Both Titiev and Waters remark that the snake is emblematic of the rivers that mark the boundaries of Hopi territory. If the snake on the back of the tablet is indeed the Little Colorado River, then we can orient some of the other images in relation to it. This snake is located at the bottom of the tablet above the four pairs of "little scratches," which might also depict water signs; therefore, this would represent the west.

Two bear claws are located in the northwest corner of the tablet, signaling the direction from which this clan came to settle the Tuuwanasavi, the Hopi center of the world. The bear is traditionally associated with the intercardinal direction of southwest.

Arranged vertically in the center of the tablet are Titiev's "eight circles," the thunder interpretation of which he seems to doubt. In Waters' version of the tablet, however, there are five *nakwatsveni* (friendship symbols) in a row, which are known to also represent water.

Parallel and to the right (or south) of this row extending vertically from top to bottom are the following: a sun symbol, a star symbol, two concentric circles, another star symbol, and another sun symbol that is near the snake. If we orient these images in relation to the snake/river, the two sun symbols could represent the eastern (sunrise) and western (sunset) houses of Tawa. In between these two solar emblems are three images that might delineate the three Hopi Mesas *and* simultaneously the three stars in the belt of Orion. (For a full discussion of the Orion Correlation in Arizona, see my book *The Orion Zone: Ancient Star Cities of the American Southwest*, Adventures Unlimited Press, 2006.)

If this is the case, the top equilateral cross correlates to Walpi/Alnitak, while the bottom one represents Oraibi/Mintaka. In the middle are the two concentric circles, which correspond to Songòopavi/Alnilam, both the first village established and what is called the "mother village." Concentric circles are also con-ceived of as Masau'u's footprints. (The original name for Old Songòopavi was Masipa—the root word of the god.)

We find represented here the very center of the Center-place, the *sanctum sanctorum*, thereby augmenting its signifi-cance. Even though such discussions as the meaning of aborigi-nal iconography are highly speculative, on the back of this third Bear Clan tablet we seem to have an actual cartographic repre-sentation of *tutskwa i'qatsi*.

A smaller tablet about four inches square with a corner broken off was given to the Fire Clan. The missing corner was given to the Pahana, the Elder White Brother, who was supposed to migrate toward the rising sun and wait there until he heard the cries of distress from the Younger Brother, or the Hopi them-selves. Finally he would return at the End Times, coming to their aid and purifying the land. He would prove his identity by fit-ting the two pieces of the tablet together.

Fire Clan Tablet

front   back

As the contemporary term for "white person," *Pahana* is also archetypally related to the plumed serpent Kukulkan of the Maya and Quetzalcoatl of the Aztecs.

The front of the **Fire Clan Tablet** depicts a swastika (the four directions) in the upper left corner and three dots within a circle that probably represent the face of Masau'u. In the middle of the right-hand side is a sun symbol wedged into a right angle. In the center of the tablet is the river/snake motif. On the left just above the broken bottom corner is a V-shape, although it is impossible to determine its exact meaning because most of the symbol is missing.

The back of the Fire Clan tablet has a rectangle enclosing a headless figure at the center. Also within the rectangle are a *nakwatsveni* in the middle at the left, a flattened S-shape, and another V-shape broken off at the lower right-hand corner. Outside the rectangle at the top are a half moon and another V-shape.

So what can we make of these symbols? The headless figure certainly evokes uncomfortable feelings in our own age. Dan Katchongva, the Hopi spiritual elder who is quoted above, stated that during the End Times the evil people will be beheaded and will speak no more. The Fire Clan is the most warlike of the Hopi clans, and its clan deity is none other than Masau'u, god of death. But who exactly are the evil ones? The Hopi would probably say they are the ones who deviate from the laws of Masau'u and the Creator.

When seen as a whole, the Hopi stone tablets function as a title to the land, a map, and a pictorial example for the life plan of Masau'u. They are moreover an *imago mundi*—a sacred "image" that once allowed the ancient people of Arizona to conceptualize their mysterious and sometimes volatile world. These tablets are even more unfathomable for us today, as we try to make sense of an increasingly chaotic world.

Petroglyph near Homolovi State Park, Arizona

On far left Masau'u as god of earth is on the same plane as the animals at center and far right. Seen below, a pair of snakes with bifurcated tongues rises from the Underworld. Seen above, a pair of Palulukang (plumed serpent) figures flies horizontally through the sky, their bodies jointly forming the glyph for water. At the center a horizontal, undulating line from left to right bisects a cleft (natural?) in the rock (possibly representing Grand Canyon) and ends with a straight line that is crossed by a perpendicular, T-shaped figure (perhaps the Hopi Tuuwanasavi, or "the Center of the World"). Two circles, each with a straight line streaming from it and one with a dot at its center, appear to be either comets or meteors. (See Afterword of this book.)

Chapter 18: The Four Arms of Destiny— Swastikas In the Hopi World of the End Times

When masked *katsinam* dance in the plazas of Hopi villages in northern Arizona during annual ceremonies to pray for

Hopi Aya, or "moisture rattle."

rainfall and fecundity, they usually carry a flat gourd rattle in their right hand. Sometimes these rattles bear the icon of the swastika. Far older than Germany's Nazi regime, this Anasazi (or ancient Hopi) symbol once conveyed a sacred rather than a malevolent meaning. Specifically, it represented the center of ancestral Hopi land.

In *Book of the Hopi,* author Frank Waters explains the swastika in terms of the tribe's prehistoric migrations. "We can now see that the complete pattern formed by the

migrations was a great cross whose center, Túwanasavi [Center of the Universe], lay in what is now the Hopi country in the southwestern part of the United States, and whose arms extended to the four directional *pásos.*"

In early times at the start of the Fourth World (the current epoch), one Hopi clan after another began great migrations to the four directions represented by the venerable symbol of the swastika. Waters believes that the Hopi migrated from the Atlantic coast to the Pacific coast and from the Arctic Circle to Tierra del Fuego, though the range may actually be narrower. Certainly the Anasazi traveled from the Colorado River to the Rio Grande, and from the San Juan River south to the lands of the Toltecs in Mexico and the Maya in Central America. Macaw and parrot feathers or even whole birds have been found in burial sites around the Colorado Plateau. This indicates that the Anasazi had well established trade routes to the south.

Regardless of what the farthest limits of actual migration were, the point where the four arms of the geo-morphic swastika meet is known as the Center of the World, the Tuuwanasavi, supposedly a spot a few miles from the Arizona village of Oraibi on the Hopi Third Mesa. Founded about 1120 AD, Oraibi has been continuously inhabited longer than any community on the North American continent. Oraibi literally means "Round Rock," but the full name of this village is Sip Oraibi, "the place where the earth was made solid" or "the place where the roots solidify." The first syllable of the name is similar to the Hopi word for navel: *sipna'at*. Hence, this tribe considers the spot to be the navel of the world.

Waters also suggests that a counterclockwise-turning swastika represents the earth, whereas a clockwise-turning one represents the sun in its movement across the sky. This indicates the dynamically potent nature of the symbol.

In addition to its importance in the beginning times, the swastika also plays a key role in Hopi prophecy of the End Times. In a period preordained by the Creator, the enigmatic figure of Pahana will return wearing a red cap or a red cape. Some modern Knights Templar orders, incidentally, wear a red pillbox hat. The traditional Shriners' red fez also comes to mind. The red Templar cross on the white mantle might possibly fit the "red cape" description as well.

Pahana will verify his authenticity by bearing a stone piece that will match up with the rest of the sacred tablet the Creator had given the Hopi before they began their migrations. (See Chapter 17.) Two helpers will accompany Pahana, one of which carries a masculine swastika representing purity and the four directions. The first helper also brings a Maltese cross with lines between the arms signifying menstrual blood, while the second helper holds merely a sun symbol. The combined forces of these three icons will "shake the world" and bring about global purification.

These hoary emblems of Hopi prophecy may represent the Central Powers of World War I (the Iron Cross) and the Axis Powers of World War II (the Swastika and the Rising Sun), whereas the final purification of the planet will present itself as World War III. Let's hope this interpretation does not come to pass.

Pahana is probably not a single figure but an anthropo-morphized composite, since it is said that his population will be great. In addition, Pahana supposedly has no religion but his own. This sounds very much like the charge that fundamental-ist opponents make against the Freemasons. This was partially the reason why leaders of the Knights Templar were tortured and executed in the early fourteenth century.

At any rate, if Pahana and his two helpers fail to stop human inequities, an unnamed figure from the west will come "like a big storm." He will unmercifully purge evildoers, though he too is said to be a large number of people. Sun Clan leader Dan Katchongva has said:

> "The Purifier, commanded by the Red symbol [Maltese cross], with the help of the Sun and the Meha [swastika], will weed out the wicked who have disturbed the way of life of the Hopi, the true way of life on Earth. The wicked will be beheaded and will speak no more. This will be the purification for all the righteous people, the Earth, and all living things on the Earth. The ills of the Earth will be cured. Mother Earth will bloom again and all the people will unite into peace and harmony for a long time to come." [www.hopiland.net/prophecy/katch-1.htm]

However, if the Hopi nation disappears totally, the motion of the planet will become eccentric, and a great flood will again engulf the land as it did at the end of the Third World. Eventually, hordes of ants will inherit the Earth. (See discussion of the Ant People, Chapter 9.)

Beyond the Hopi connotations of the swastika, this icon transcends any specific culture by virtue of its global occurrence.

An example of a swastika *petroglyph is found at El Morro National Monument in northwestern New Mexico. Rising two hundred feet above the desert, a massive sandstone mesa shelters the watering hole at its base. Over the course of thousands of years, diverse travelers found respite. These include the ancestral Zuni (a tribe culturally though not linguistically related to the Hopi), conquistadors, emigrants, surveyors, settlers, and cowboys. On the top are the ruins of an 875-room pueblo built by the native people in the late 13th century AD. Along the vertical faces of this bluff are more than 2,000 ancient petroglyphs or more recent signatures carved into the rock.*

The swastika itself (at center-right just above more recent initials) is adjacent to a number of vertical grooves technically called incised abstract petroglyphs. This indicates that they may have been scratched into the stone in the Archaic period as early as 1000 BC. Near the counterclockwise-turning swastika is a curving snake or water petroglyph along with a sun shield or mask traditionally worn during the winter solstice ceremony.

J. E. Cirlot's *Dictionary of Symbols* comments on its universality: "The graphic symbol is to be found in almost every ancient and primitive cult all over the world—in Christian catacombs, in Britain, Ireland, Mycenae and Gascony; among the Etruscans, the Hindus, the Celts and the Germanic peoples; in central Asia as well as in pre-Columbian America."

Despite the negative associations of Fascism in the modern consciousness, swastikas still hold inestimable power and beauty resonating deep within the human soul. It remains to be seen whether or not these four-armed emblems will usher in both the termination of our current age of chaos (the Hopi Fourth World) and the advent of an age of peace.

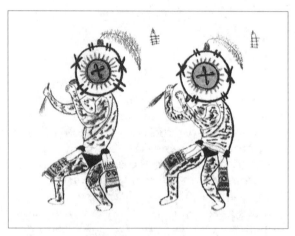

A pair of Aya (Runner) katsinam
with a swastika on each side of their masks.
These beings race with men in the spring.
The rolls above them are the paper-thin
piki bread made from blue corn
that winners of the race receive as a prize.
[Hopi drawing from Fewkes, Hopi Katcinas,
Dover Publications, Inc.]

Chapter 19: Spiral Gate—The Arc of the Covenant

The Galactic Spiral

Gazing into the heart of a spiral galaxy, we sense a familiar path, a journey taken long ago, resonating perhaps from another lifetime. We are awed by the vibrant colors the Hubble Space Telescope beams back. Despite the high-tech clarity of these images, a primordial urgency rises to greet us.

(Courtesy of NASA and the Hubble Heritage Team.)

If we stare long enough, the pinwheel of stars entrances our sensibilities until we enter a golden realm of *déjà vu*, traveling back to the ultimate Source. It is the Tibetan mandala, the Diné (Navajo) sand painting, and Dante's Mystic Rose all rolled into one.

Our own Milky Way drifts through space like a bioluminescent starfish. Technically called a barred spiral galaxy, it measures over 100,000 light-years across and 1,000 light-years thick at the outer edges. The elegant theories of modern astronomers place a mysterious black hole at the center of most galaxies, including our own.

As the ultimate manifestation of the devouring Hindu goddess Kali (Sanskrit for 'black'), this juggernaut's "event horizon," or rim – analogous to Kali's necklace of skulls– lets nothing escape. Suns and planets, comets, galactic dust, gravity, even light—all are subject to its voracious attraction.

Hunab K'u

The Maya knew this dark heart as *Hunab K'u*, the Only Giver of Movement and Measure, represented by the spiral or stepped fret. Located upon the star road of the Milky Way between the constellations of Sagittarius and Scorpius, our Great Mystery beckons.

Merely one among incomprehensibly vast multitudes, the solar system where we live is poised on the inner edge of a sidereal arc, about a dozen of which forms our celestial spiral. This local arc is known as the Orion Arm. In other words, we inhabit an arc of stars that reaches from the heart of the cosmos toward the constellation Orion.

Surprisingly, this and adjacent constellations are brought down to Earth in the American Southwest as a pattern of ancient star cities and sacred canyons or caverns coordinated by a special type of spiral.

The Golden Mean Spiral

This unique spiral is ubiquitously created in nature by what is called the Golden Mean, Golden Section, or Divine Proportion. Also known as phi, this ratio is simply 1:1.6180339....

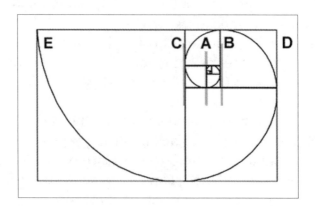

It is derived from Fibonacci's series, or a numerical list whereby each new number is the sum of the previous two numbers: 0, 1, 1, 2, 3, 5, 8, 13, 21, 34, 55, 89, 144... and so on. Regardless of how large the spiral becomes, the ratio of its dimensions remains constant. For instance, the proportion **AB** to **AC** is the same as **BC** to **BD** or **CD** to **CE**. (See graphic on bottom of previous page.)

The map on p. 233 shows how the Golden Mean spiral integrates many of the ancient pueblo sites in northern Arizona with a specific pattern of stars.

The "terrestrial" Orion closely mirrors his celestial counterpart, with prehistoric "cities" corresponding to every major star in the constellation. His belt is represented by the three Hopi Mesas, where the Hisatsinom (ancient Hopi) settled about 1100 AD. (Again, Gary A. David's *The Orion Zone: Ancient Star Cities of the American Southwest* details this correspondence of earth and sky.)

Near the top right of the map, the blue-white supergiant Rigel (Orion's left leg) correlates to Betatakin ruin at Navajo National Monument, while the faint yellow star Saiph (his right leg) is represented by the ruins in Canyon de Chelly National Monument. The red supergiant Betelgeuse (his right shoulder) corresponds to Homolovi Ruins State Park near Winslow, whereas the blue giant Bellatrix (his left shoulder) is equated with the ruins at Wupatki National Monument north of Flagstaff. (This terrestrial Orion is upside down compared to the way people in the northern hemisphere see Orion in the sky.)

Orion's upraised right arm points south toward the ruins of the Hohokam (the ancestors of the Tohono O'odham) near the Phoenix metropolis. His left arm holding a shield or a bow is aimed at the smaller Hisatsinom ruins located throughout Grand Canyon.

Also depicted on this map are Taurus and the Pleiades, corresponding to Grand Canyon Caverns and Nevada's Grapevine Canyon respectively.

Orion's chakra line runs from the belt's middle star (Alnilam, corresponding to Songòopavi, also spelled Shungopovi, first Hopi village settled) to his Third Eye (Meissa, corresponding to the ruins at Walnut Canyon National Monument). It continues southwest across Arizona toward the mouth of the Colorado River (not shown on map). In the opposite direction (northeast) this same line traverses the cliff dwellings at Mesa Verde National Park in southwestern Colorado (also not shown).

The esoteric philosopher Daniel Winter positions the center of the Golden Mean spiral at Orion's heart chakra. [www.zayra.de/soulcom/orion/orionheart.html] It passes through Bellatrix and then arcs across the belt stars of Mintaka, Alnilam, and Alnitak. On our map the center of the spiral, which wells up from Orion's throat chakra, correlates to Grand Falls along the Little Colorado River.

The Hopi word for this site is Söynapi, which means 'sound of rushing water'. Another name for it is Pòosiw, or 'waterfall'—a place where whirlpools naturally abound. However, the related term *poosi'at* means 'eye', while *poosi'ytaqa* refers to a medicine man using a crystal for diagnosis. Grand Falls may be connected to the concept of vision, especially that done in a sacred way—as if one is staring into a spiral portal between dimensions.

The Earth Spiral

Many examples of the spiral are found painted on ancient pottery from the American Southwest. In particular, the whirlpool or double-spiral motif represents the "gate of Masau's house." This portal located at the bottom of Grand Canyon is also called the Sipapuni, actually a travertine dome. Legends say that the Hisatsinom emerged from the past Third World (or era) to the present Fourth World from this place.

Masau'u is the complex Hopi god of war, death, fire, the Underworld, and the earth, but he is also god of transformation. He was present when the Hisatsinom came forth upon the surface of the earth and began to make their migrations; he was there again when they finished them after many centuries.

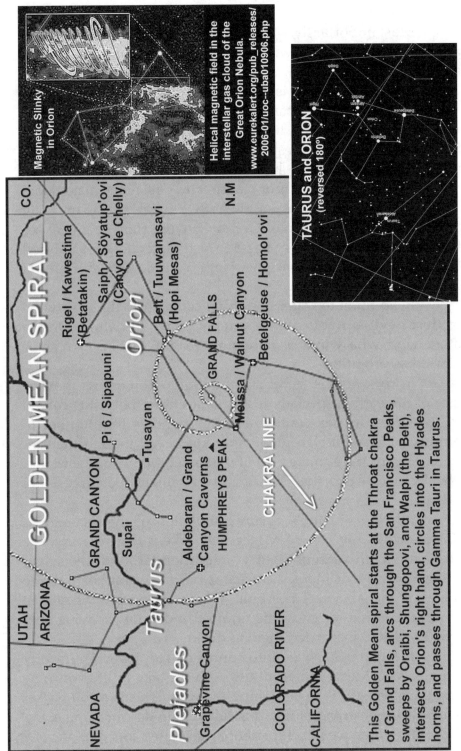

Magnetic Slinky in Orion

Helical magnetic field in the interstellar gas cloud of the Great Orion Nebula.
www.eurekalert.org/pub_releases/2006-01/uoc--uba010906.php

TAURUS and ORION
(reversed 180°)

GOLDEN MEAN SPIRAL

CO.

UTAH
ARIZONA
NEVADA

Rigel / Kawestima (Betatakin)
Saiph / Söyatup'ovi (Canyon de Chelly)
Belt / Tuuwanasavi (Hopi Mesas)
N.M

Orion

Pi 6 / Sipapuni
GRAND CANYON
Supai
GRAND FALLS
Tusayan
Meissa / Walnut Canyon
Betelgeuse / Homol'ovi

Aldebaran / Grand Canyon Caverns
HUMPHREYS PEAK

CHAKRA LINE

Taurus

Pleiades
Grapevine Canyon

COLORADO RIVER

CALIFORNIA

This Golden Mean spiral starts at the Throat chakra of Grand Falls, arcs through the San Francisco Peaks, sweeps by Oraibi, Shungopovi, and Walpi (the Belt), intersects Orion's right hand, circles into the Hyades horns, and passes through Gamma Tauri in Taurus.

Most importantly, Masau'u serves as the humble agrarian deity who lives in balance with his harsh environment. Carrying a dibble stick and a sack of seeds, he provides a paradigm of purity and simplicity. It is Masau with whom the Hopi established their divine Covenant. (See graphic on p. 107.)

On a naturalistic level the spiral represents water, an indispensable element, especially for a desert existence. The presence of a spiral petroglyph (in Hopi known as *potave'yta*) can mean that a water source is or was nearby. One of the major Hopi shrines is called Potavetaka (literally, 'spiral nest'), or Point Sublime on the north rim of Grand Canyon. Here again we see the spiral motif –an icon of passage or transcendence– associated with the canyon that the Hopi consider their Place of Emergence.

In addition to water, the spiral can refer to the whirlwind or dust devil, a frequently destructive force in nature. On the other hand, whirlwinds usually precede rain, so they also can be viewed as propitious.

In rock art the spiral suggests migration across the surface of the earth, especially if it is adjacent to footprints carved in the stone. In this context a spiral signifies the number of rounds, or *pásos*, a clan made as it journeyed though the centuries toward its ultimate goal of the sacred Center of the World. The Hopi call this the Tuuwanasavi, namely the three Hopi Mesas.

While a Muslim's circumambulation of the rectangular Ka'ba in the holy city of Mecca may take a dozen hours, the Hisatsinom circumambulatory migration around their *axis mundi* ('world-axis') took a dozen or more generations. During this time the Ancient Ones built a series of pueblo villages in which they lived for a varying number of decades, moving only when Masau'u instructed them to do so.

The plaques woven into spirals by Hopi women (mostly from Second Mesa) represent the path we take in life's journey and the adversities we face along the way. "This is a coil basket symbolizing the road of life. It is called 'Boo-da', meaning some great test which we will experience during our journey."

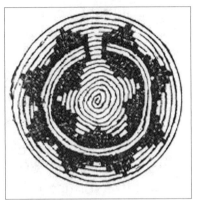

Hopi woven plaque.

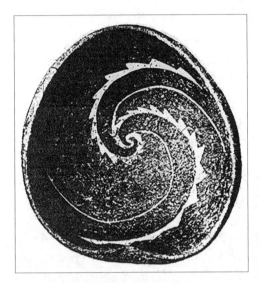

Hopi ceramic bowl.
(Bureau of American Ethnology)

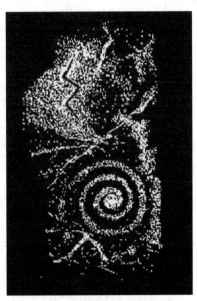

Spiral petroglyph at
V-Bar-V Heritage Site, Arizona.

Petroglyph of lightning
above spiral at
Tsankawi Mesa, New Mexico.
Drawing by Dawn Senior-Trask.
[http://islandhills.tripod.com/
biosenior.htm]

[*Techqua Ikachi* newsletter, Issue 21,
www.jnanadana.org/hopi/issue_21.html]

Is it merely a coincidence that this Hopi term sounds the same as Buddha, the primary figure in one of the world's great religions?

The Dual Spiral

Most of us recognize the *caduceus* as the symbol of the medical profession. Originally carried by the Greek god Hermes, it is formed by a pair of serpents entwined around a central staff surmounted by a pair of wings. This archetypal motif has been found at differing times in diverse parts of the world.

Some Westerners are now familiar with the age-old Tibetan practice of kundalini, a form of Tantric yoga. The word *Kundala* means 'coiled' and refers to the energy of the cosmic serpent asleep at the base of the spine. In addition to the seven chakras, or the energy wheels positioned along the spinal column, two subtle nerves called the *Pingala* and the *Ida* form a double spiral that interlaces it. They in essence channel solar (masculine) and lunar (feminine) energy up and down the backbone.

According to Frank Waters in his groundbreaking *Book of the Hopi*, this North American tribe was also familiar with the chakra system, utilizing five rather than seven psychophysical centers.

In all the excitement about the human genome mapping project and its potential for medical science, we sometimes forget the ineffable beauty of the DNA double helix, that spiral staircase gently uncoiling itself with mathematical precision inside every living thing. Perhaps the ancients intuited even more so than we its spiritual significance beyond esthetics.

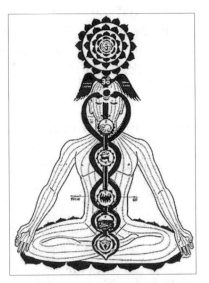

Caduceus and double-spiral
of kundalini chakra system.
[www.celestialhealing.net]

Stylized spiral petroglyph
with "pueblo" icon at center.
(Homolovi Ruins State Park)

Double spiral, clockwise (left)
and counterclockwise (right), with staff.
(Homolovi Ruins State Park, Arizona.)

From his online book *Living In Truth: Archaeology and the Patriarchs*, Charles N. Pope has observed that the double helix is the "fundamental literary structure of the Torah," the body of Jewish religious literature contained in the Old Testament and the Talmud. The name itself is related to the English words tornado and torsion, both meaning 'to twist'.
[www.domainofman.com]

Oddly enough, the Hopi word *tori* means 'twisted spirally', while the word *toriritaqa* means 'whirlwind'. The village at the base of Second Mesa is called Toreva, literally 'twist water', probably referring to a spring.

Why, then, would the Hopi and the Jewish people share both the same etymology and semantics for the spiral? Is this just another coincidence?

The Spirit Spiral

On a more psychospiritual level, the spiral represents a gateway between worlds or dimensions. It is the doorway through which the shaman begins his or her ecstatic quest from the physical to the spiritual plane. The word spiral comes from the Latin *spira*, 'coil', while the term spirit is derived from the Latin *spirare*, 'to breathe'. In a ritualistic trance the shaman's "breath-body" searches the interstices of the spirit world for a specific cure or a personal vision to bring back to the tribe.

The spiral functions as a portal or gateway from the mundane to the eternal realms. The Yaqui sorcerer Don Juan Matus calls these respective states the "*tonal*" and the "*nagual*," although it is much more complex than this simple dichotomy. Anyone well versed in the techniques of non-ordinary reality, however, can gain access to the latter, as the progressive instruction of Carlos Castaneda demonstrates.

The iconography of the spiral is sacred beyond belief. In other words, it goes beyond all belief systems to reach deeply into the processes of astronomy, biology, and human history. The term covenant is derived from the Latin *convenire*, which literally means 'to come together' or 'to unite'.

The spiral unites the firmament and *terra firma*, as illustrated by the template of the Golden Mean spiral linking Orion, Taurus, and the Pleiades to their terrestrial correlations on the Arizona desert.

Is this, then, the deeper significance of the spiral? To provide the Arc (spelled with a "c") of the Covenant by which the realms of earth and sky are bound? If we abide by this Covenant and heed the hermetic maxim "as above, so below," the spiral's numinous path may ultimately reveal the gateway to either resurrection or enlightenment.

Afterword: The Blue Star, Hopi Prophecy, the Phoenix, and 9/11

Comets, Supernovae, and the Coming Catastrophe

1. As Above. . .

Throughout history comets have been the harbingers of doom, civil wars, assassinations, and political unrest. The first century Roman historian and naturalist Pliny the Elder described these celestial phenomena by using the term Crinitae "...as if shaggy with bloody locks, and surrounded by bristles like hair." [*The Natural History of Pliny*, http://books.google.com] They frequently bring "disaster," *dis-* meaning 'apart' or 'asunder' and *aster* meaning 'star'.

Between October 23 and 24, 2007, another "hairy star" named Comet 17P/Holmes literally exploded from a magnitude of 17 to a magnitude of 2.8. In other words, it increased in brightness by a factor of a nearly a million in just a few hours. (The lower the magnitude, the brighter the star.) *Sky and Telescope* magazine has called it "...the weirdest new object to appear in the sky in memory." [www.skyandtelescope.com]

This periodic comet with a revolutionary period of seven years was originally discovered by British amateur astronomer Edwin Holmes on November 6th, 1892, when it also suddenly increased in magnitude, then died down again for the next 115 years.

The comet's core made of rock and ice is only about 3.5 kilometers in diameter, but its coma formed by the gas and dust given off is massive. This greenish-blue ball coldly blazing in an inclined and elliptical solar orbit unexpectedly has become the largest object in our solar system—even bigger than our sun. The mutability of its ion tail makes it look somewhat like a celestial jellyfish. We don't have to worry though, because it always stays between the orbits of Mars and Jupiter. It is actually more of a portent than a threat.

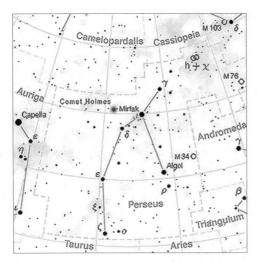

**Sky chart of the constellation Perseus
with Comet Homes and Algol.**

**The Greek hero Perseus carrying
the severed head of Medusa.**

Comet Holmes burst out of the side of the constellation Perseus. (This is, of course, an illusion, since the celestial object is not actually "in" Perseus but in line with the constellation from our perspective on Earth. See top of previous page.) This legendary king of Mycenae is famous for lopping off the head of the Gorgon named Medusa. We recall that this creature with snakes for hair could turn anyone to stone with her gaze.

Perseus carries her head across the night sky, with Algol forming one of her eyes. Richard Hinckley Allen describes this so-called 'Demon Star': "Astrologers of course said that it was the most unfortunate, violent, and dangerous star in the heavens..." [*Star Names*]

This is not merely a Greek connotation. Algol is gruesomely referred to in China as Tseih She, or "Piled-up Corpses." Hebrew apocryphal lore associates Agol with Lilith, Adam's first wife, whom patriarchal sources falsely identify as evil.

The etymology of the Greek mythological hero is also interesting. "Perseus might be from the ancient Greek verb, *perthein*, 'to waste, ravage, sack, destroy', some form of which appears in Homeric epithets.... Cyrus Gordon, known for his daring theories, proposed that Perseus is a Semitic name, from p-r-s, 'to cut.'" [http://en.wikipedia.org/wiki/Perseus]

Comets have long been known as omens of the End Times. The Hopi have a legend of the Blue Star Katsina (Sakwa Sohu). Frank Waters and Hopi informant Oswald White Bear Fredericks in their popular *Book of the Hopi* proclaim: "The end of all Hopi ceremonialism will come when a *kachina* removes his mask during a dance in the plaza before uninitiated." This is rumored to have recently happened on the Hopi Reservation.

The Hopi elder White Feather of the spiritually important Bear Clan describes nine different signs signaling the end of the Fourth World (our current era). The final warning is as follows: "*And this is the Ninth and Last Sign*: You will hear of a dwelling-place in the heavens, above the earth, that shall fall with a great crash. It will appear as a blue star. Very soon after this, the ceremonies of my people will cease."
[www.bibliotecapleyades.net/profecias/esp_profecia01h1.htm]

Waters continues: "World War III will be started by those people who first received the light [the divine wisdom or intelligence] in the other old countries [India, China, Egypt, Palestine, Africa].... That time is not far off. It will come when the Saqusohuh [Sakwa Sohu] Kachina dances in the plaza. He represents a blue star, far off and yet invisible, which will make its appearance soon."

The Hopi word *sakwa* literally means "blue-green," or "turquoise." The photos of Comet Holmes clearly show this particular color. In Hopi cosmology this hue symbolically represents the intercardinal direction of southwest. From the Hopi perspective of their villages, the San Francisco Peaks lie to the southwest. These are the sacred snowy mountains where the *katsinam* live for half of the year. The Hopi term *sakwi*, by the way, means "worn out," "broken down," "ruined" or "destroyed." The Mayan word *sak*, on the other hand, means "white."

It is interesting to note that for the Maya of southern Mexico and Central America, blue symbolized sacrifice. In the later, more corrupt stages of the Classic Maya culture, the bodies of those humans who were to be sacrificed to the gods were painted blue. Director Mel Gibson graphically portrays this in the 2006 film *Apocalypto*.

In an attempt to present a parable for our own time, the movie also shows an old Mayan storyteller who conveys the legend of a man who is "drenched deep in sadness." All the animals respond by giving the man their particular virtues. He receives keen eyesight from the vulture, strength from the jaguar, and the secrets of the earth from the serpent. The deer remarks that this will finally make the man happy because he has all that he needs. But the owl replies: "No, I saw a hole in the Man, deep like a hunger he will never fill. It is what makes him sad and what makes him want. He will go on taking and taking, until one day the World will say, 'I am no more and I have nothing left to give.'"

The late Robert Ghost Wolf, of mixed Hopi, Iroquois, and Lakota descent, speaks about star prophecy in relation to the conclusion of Gaia's current cycle:

"The story of the Blue Kachina is an old story, very old. I have been aware of the story of the Blue Kachina since I was very young. I was told this story by grandfathers who are now between 80 and 108 years of age.... It was told to me that the first Blue Kachina would be seen at the dances, and would make his appearance known to the children in the plaza during the night dance. The event would tell us that the end times are very near. The Blue Star Kachina would physically appear in our heavens which would mean that we are in the end times." [www.wolflodge.org/bluestar/bluestar.htm]

According to Dr. Ghost Wolf, this *katsina* is also known as Nanga Sohu, or Chasing Star Katsina. The Hopi word *nanga* means "to pursue" and *sohu* means "star." Sometimes the *katsina* refers to Venus because its morning and evening appearances seem to chase each other.

Ethnographer Jesse Walter Fewkes conversely says that Nanga Sohu comes in two distinct versions depending on the village in which he dances. The *katsina* of Oraibi has a single four-pointed star in the middle of his mask and trailing eagle feathers similar to that of a Plains Indian war bonnet. (See drawing on p. 138.)

In the village of Walpi, however, the most prominent feature of this spirit being is the three four-pointed stars arranged horizontally in a row across the top of his head. In this case he is referred to as simply Sohu

Sohu Katsina (embroidery applique).

Katsina. These stars bring to mind the most important constellation in Hopi cosmology, Orion, in particular his belt. The prominent sidereal triad is significantly composed of *blue* or *blue-white* stars.

As previously stated, the Hopi word *sootu* means "stars," while *sòoti* means "end."

In August of 2007, a few months before Holmes erupted, headlines also referred to a "bizarre star" named Mira (as in "miraculous") located in the constellation Cetus, the Whale. This ferocious leviathan was, by the way, turned to stone by Medusa's severed head brandished by Perseus.

Actually Mira is a binary star 418 light-years away. (Because vast distances act as a sort of time machine, the starlight we currently see –as of 2007– left its sidereal point in 1589 AD, the year the ill-fated city of Hiroshima was founded.) "Mira A is also an oscillating variable star and was the first non-supernova variable star discovered, with the possible exception of Algol." We recall that Algol in Perseus was known as the "eye of the demon." [http://en.wikipedia.org/wiki/Mira]

Mira, at any rate, is a completely unique astronomical object because of its glowing blue, comet-like tail that extends over a distance of 13 light-years. The Hopi also predicted that soon after the arrival of the Blue Star Katsina, the Red Star Katsina (Paha Sohu) would come and act as the Purifier. It may be significant that Mira is a large red giant star with a long blue tail.

On March 25th of 1996, Comet Hyakutake came within 9.3 million miles of Earth. It was distinctly bluish-turquoise in color and had the longest tail ever seen. It is also a long-period comet, making its previous appearance about 15,000 years ago.

In the following year Comet Hale-Bopp dazzled spectators with its double blue-yellow tail. It was more luminous than any star except the brightest one, Sirius, and was visible to the naked eye for a record eighteen months. It last came around about 4,200 years ago.

Hale-Bopp also fueled the Heaven's Gate mass suicide pact at Rancho Santa Fe, California. Leader Marshall Applewhite and his thirty-eight cult members believed that an alien spacecraft carrying Jesus was hidden behind the comet. By that time millennial fever had clearly set in.

It may be more than a coincidence though, that both Hyakutake and Hale-Bopp passed right between the eyes of Medusa's head in Perseus (though along perpendicular paths) on April 11th—exactly one year apart! [www.eaglestation.com/medusa.html]

Many speculated that either Comet Hyakutake or Comet Hale-Bopp with their long blue tails streaking across the sky was the Blue Star Katsina. A decade later Comet Holmes is being considered for the same prophetic role. During these final days, various signs in the sky are rife.

Astrophysicist Paul A. LaViolette, Ph.D., claims that the Blue Star may instead be a cosmic volley from the center of our galaxy that long ago imprinted itself on the mythological tableaux of many cultures around the world and is likely to recur. The blast would have manifested as a blue-white star a thousand times brighter than Sirius.

> "As the cores of distant exploding galaxies are observed to have a bright blue, star-like appearance, it is reasonable to expect that the core of our own Galaxy would have a similar appearance during its explosive phase, so the legendary appearance of the Blue Star could be referring to an explosion of our Galaxy's core.... This frightening spectacle may have appeared to ancient inhabitants as a gigantic punishing 'Eye' in the sky, the entire form occupying about a 16-degree field of view, or about 32 solar diameters. The 'iris' would have a diameter of about 4 degrees with a brilliant light emanating from its central pupil—the Blue Star." [*Earth Under Fire*]

Back-illuminated amorphous nebulae and dust clouds along with a network of cobweb-like filaments would have surrounded the luminous blue oval in the vicinity of Sagittarius A. Dr. LaViolette says that a superwave of cosmic rays, gravity, electromagnetic energy, and synchrotron radiation accompanied the Blue Star, making it more than a merely visual event.

"Perhaps the most frightening phenomenon to occur in this early stage would be the prompt arrival of the electromagnetic pulse and, some days later, the onslaught of the gravity wave, with its ensuing crustal torque, which would have caused earthquakes and volcanic eruptions." Thus, the eye of our galactic heart may have once been blue.

Just over twenty years ago, Supernova 1987A burst into our consciousness as one of the initial recent candidates for the Hopi Blue Star. Issuing from the Large Megellanic Cloud (a dwarf galaxy located between the southern constellations of Dorado and Mensa), the light from the explosion of this blue supergiant left its surface about 160,000 years ago and finally reached Earth on February 23rd, 1987. By May it reached its maximum magnitude of 3, becoming the brightest supernova since the invention of the telescope.

In her excellent book *Beyond Prophecies and Predictions*, Moira Timms describes its effects:

> "Within the first ten minutes of going supernova, an intense blast of neutrinos –one hundred times more than the sun will radiate in its entire ten billion year lifetime– raced ahead of the shockwave. These subatomic, massless, chargeless particles silently zoomed directly through the Earth, south to north, along the corridor of Earth's magnetic force lines. The neutrino salvo preceded a flash volume of ultraviolet and infrared radiation, X-rays, and gamma rays. Reports said the radiation released in the first few seconds was as much as that from all the stars and galaxies in the visible universe combined."

These neutrinos, or "ghost particles," may have caused subtle mutations in both the DNA of our physical bodies and the vital essence of our etheric bodies, thereby rebooting our individual psyches. It may have also effected the electromagnetic matrix of our entire planetary grid system.

Moreover, the catalytic cosmic particles, radiation, and antimatter streamed from south to north, surging past our own galactic center near Sagittarius and targeting the south pole of the Earth's ecliptic. This transformative star-stuff then shot beyond Ophiuchus, the Serpent Holder, traveled across the thigh of Hercules, and continued northward toward Draco, the Dragon, which is coiled around the north pole crowned by Polaris.

In Hopi cosmology it is significant to note that a hero twin sits at each pole of the world axis. Palöngawhoya commands the serpent spiraling around the south pole and is charged with overseeing the Earth's vibratory centers, or vortexes, as well as vibrations in the air. Pöqánghoya controls the serpent wrapped around the north pole, keeping the earth stable and solid. Together they keep the Earth rotating properly.

The shock wave of cosmic energy from the supernova, however, may have altered this delicate balance. Hence, in the last few decades we have seen an increase in seismic activity (temblors and plate tectonics), volcanoes, magnetic pole shifts, and crustal displacements.

SN1987A arrived, by the way, just six months before the Harmonic Convergence, the New Age event that supposedly heralded the global shift to a new era of peace and started the final quarter-century countdown to the end of the Mayan Calendar on the December solstice in 2012. Timms eloquently describes the impact of the supernova's visitation:

> "With impeccable timing, the Blue Star Supernova appeared in synchronicity with the unfolding of the Mayan calendar and the Hopi revelation. In an instant, quicker than the eye could blink or the phosphene flare in the inner dimensions of the mind, the consciousness of the planet was encoded and imprinted. A superluminal transfer of extragalactic frequencies from deep space impregnated the Earth with the starseeds of neutrinos and radiation. Penetrating to the heart of the Earth's magnetic core, this jump-start of cosmic energy served to accelerate the vibrational frequency of the life force, preparing us for an unprecedented evolutionary leap."

We marvel at sophistocated instruments such as the Chandra X-Ray Telscope or the Hubble Space Telescope and their hauntingly beautiful images of deep space. Recent photos from the latter, for instance, show Supernova 1987A as an expanding orange circle coalescing into radiant pearls of light around a cloudy, bluish-purple center. And this is twenty years after the fact!

2. . . .*So Below*

Instead of entering a ring of enlightenment, however, we may first have to go through a ring of fire. As previously stated, the Blue Star foreshadows an Armageddon-like scenario. Hopi prophesy as recorded in Waters' book bluntly states that atomic weapons and radioactive fallout will ultimately destroy most of America's "land and life" (in Hopi, *tutskwa i'qatsi*).

The Hopi Mesas, however, will be an oasis to which refugees will flee. This will essentially be a war between spiritual and material forces, however. Those who do not participate in the killing and destruction will be the ones who transition to the new Fifth World.

Dakota (Sioux) musician, actor, and activist Floyd Red Crow Westerman has said: "It's the Hopi belief, it's our belief, that if you're not spiritually connected to the Earth and understand the spiritual reality of how to live on Earth, it's likely you will not make it." ["Indigenous Native American Prophecy," video, www.youtube.com]

During the 20th century Hopi elders had continued their longstanding tradition of prophecy. In July of 1955, for instance, the Bureau of Indian Affairs met with Hopi leaders at Keams Canyon, Arizona. The purpose was to hear about problems such as grazing rights, livestock management, forced attendance of boarding schools, dunking of Hopis into sheep-dipping vats, the introduction of alcohol on the reservation, and other such mundane though important matters.

Interspersed in these comments delivered in the Hopi language, however, were legends of the earliest times as well as prophecies of the End Times. [This and subsequent quotations are from *Hopi Hearings, July 15–30, 1955* (Phoenix, Arizona: United States Bureau of Indian Affairs, Hopi Agency: Bureau of Indian Affairs, Phoenix Area Office, 1955.]

For instance, Julius Doopkema remarks directly on Hopi prophecy:

> "It is because I have foresight and can see what there is in store for the Hopi people and because we have received much knowledge and wisdom from our forefathers who taught us in the past and prophesized that such conditions would exist, that there would be many conflicts, that there would be great strife between the people… I might say, too, here that it was told to us by our elders in the tribe that there in time would be a road in the sky, and they also had predicted that there would be many types of vehicles traveling these roads and there would be broad roads graded upon the land. By observing these things, it seems to me it is a fulfillment of the prophecies of our people."

Mr. Doopkema also discusses the conclusion of the Hopi ceremonial cycle:

> "Now here is another theory taught to us by our people: that the time will come that all these ceremonies of our people will cease to function and then again it has been told to us that the Katchina [*katsina*] ceremonies will be toward the last end of the Hopi life."

Lewis Numkena describes the coming world wars:

> "[My grandfather] …also told us that there will be four wars, but he said this would not be taking place until many roads are to be built upon the earth and there will be roads in the air and in the water. And then after these things are completed there will be wars upon the earth, in the air and upon the water and all through the earth,

but not until the fourth time for the people who are known as the 'Reds' will be the last, and the time will come when there will be a rain of bombs and a rain of bullets as he described as hail stones. And then he said there will be a stream of blood as if a river were running on earth, and then the earth will be burned."

Remember that Mr. Numkena is speaking in the mid-twentieth century about precognitive visions his grandfather had seen. Whether or not his mention of "Reds" reflects merely the current preoccupation with Communism is difficult to determine. This might, on the other hand, refer to Tibetan Buddhists with their red robes, or the Red Hat sect of the same religion.

Dan Katchongva talks about the Purification:

"But there will be a purification day where all those who have done wrong or committed great sins will be punished at that time. The Hopi only knows of these great wars to take place. The third war will be the one to take place at purification time upon this land."

Ralph Salina discusses the White Brother named Pahana, who established the Hopi life-pattern at the beginning of the Fourth World, and who will return to make sure that his Red Brother (the Hopi tribe) is still abiding by his original religious teachings. If not, punishment will follow:

"...this is the duty of the Hopi, and so we are not going to let go of this life[-pattern] because we are all fully aware of this White Brother who will come and either destroy us or give us everlasting life."

Andrew Hermquaftewa refers to a "tool" the Purifier will use—perhaps some sort of cosmic weapon of mass destruction. It will not be used, however, if the Hopi continue to follow the initial life-pattern. There is some confusion as to whether Pahana and the Purifier are the same figure:

> "We were instructed that we are all moving towards the day of purification when the Purifier himself will come. He will have the tool, but if we continue to follow this pattern that he has set up for us, the tool will not be able to be used. He will not have any use for it."

In a time when beheadings by jihadist groups are routinely posted on the Internet, one statement by David Monongye is particularly disturbing:

> "These figures up here [on a petroglyph] represent a man without a head. These are the wicked people because wicked people cause other people hardship and do all manner of wickedness in this life, and if we follow them up to the purification time which we all know from our tradition, all wicked people will be beheaded. Everyone knows of these teachings so many of our own Hopi people are holding fast to this life. Let us look back to our own teachings and see that we do not destroy this life and hold fast to it."

Chief Katchongva also comments on the immediate future:

> "Now we are awaiting our brother who has been commissioned at the time we came here to do this duty which was placed upon him. It is he, who, when he comes upon our land, will purify this land. This is his duty…. Now this is the only thing that is left in the future: that is the coming of the Purifier. We have already passed through a great many troubles, and that has been fulfilled. Now we go on to the future."

Either the Purifier is Pahana and the Red Star is the agent of purification or the Purifier is the Red Star Katsina himself. Prophecy is not always crystal-clear. This much, however, is clear: he is coming soon. One Hopi elder also states that the Purifier is commanded by the "Red symbol," or Maltese Cross. (See p. 226, and read more about this cross in Chapter 15.)

Many Hopis believe that the only salvation for humanity will be to act in accordance with Mother Earth and in balance with the natural rhythms of life. The concept mentioned above of *tutskwa i'qatsi* ("land and life") is, they say, the key to our future survival. Peter Nuvamsa spoke about this at the 1955 hearings, years before the ecological movement:

> "The Land and its Purpose—The Hopi Tutsquat (Land) is our love and will always be, and it is our land upon which our leader fixes and tells the dates for our religious life. Our land, our religion and our life are one, and our leader, with humbleness, understanding, and determination, performs his duty to us by keeping them as one and thus insuring prosperity and security for the people."

3. Not In Our Stars, But In Ourselves

As my book *The Orion Zone: Ancient Star Cities of the American Southwest* has shown, the Hopi along with other traditional cultures once abided by the hermetic maxim "As above, so below." To some degree, they still do. We can add a correlative: "As without, so within."

In the time before incandescent lighting and television drove most of us indoors after sunset, sky watchers by moonlight or starlight made precise observations of celestial mechanics. They knew the farthest reaches of the visible universe as intimately as we know our own neighborhoods. Any disruption of the natural rhythms in the glistening dome above soon became glaringly apparent.

The significance went well beyond patient observation and accumulation of data, however. Anomalies such as comets, supernovae, or meteors were the subject of much discussion and debate by astronomer-priests. Chaos in the heavens augured chaos on the earth.

Pioneering Atlantis researcher Ignatius Donnelly sums up the innate trepidation that comets engender:

"Man, by an inherited instinct, regards the comet as a great terror and a great foe; and the heart of humanity sits uneasily when one blazes in the sky. Even to the scholar and the scientist they are a puzzle and a fear; they are erratic, unusual, anarchical, monstrous—something let loose, like a tiger of the heavens, athwart an orderly, peaceful, and harmonious world. They may be impalpable and harmless attenuations of gas, or they may be loaded with death and ruin; but in any event man can not contemplate them without terror." [*Ragnarok*]

The frightening appearance of a comet usually resulted in various clans and ritual societies (especially among the Hopi) performing sacred ceremonies in order to bring the cosmos back into balance. Many times it worked, simply because these traditional cultures were still living in what poet Charles Olson has termed the "human universe."

We now function under a different paradigm, where science frequently cancels out religion. Although the pendulum is starting to swing the other way, and recent theories of astrophysics frequently resemble the arcane doctrines of metaphysics, the quotidian reality for most of us is decidedly secular and material.

What, then, are we to make of yet another comet blasting into our global awareness? This one named 8P/Tuttle became the most visible from Earth on January 2nd, 2008. It was 0.25 AU away from us, or about 23 million miles. (An Astronomical Unit is the average distance between the Earth and the Sun, about 93 million miles. At its closest point Mars, for instance, is 36 million miles away from Earth.) This had promised to be another dramatic "apparition," not of a ghost but of the sudden cometary display visible through binoculars or even the naked eye.

Comet Tuttle generates the Ursids meteor shower (in Ursa Minor) that achieves its maximum on December 22, while the Hopi are performing their Soyal. This winter solstice ceremony

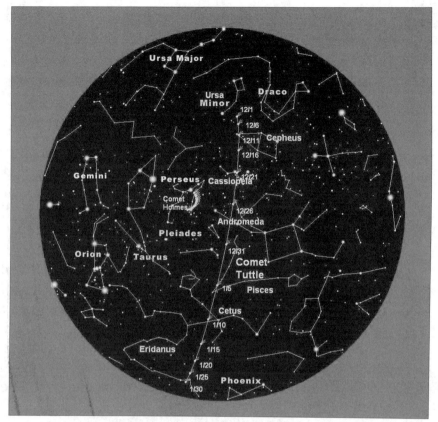

Path of Comet 8P/Tuttle between 12/1/07 and 1/30/08.

marks the end of the non-*katsina* season and the beginning of the *katsina* season in the annual cycle. One of the key figures in this ritual is called "Star Man," who dances in the kiva and wears a headdress made of four white corn leaves representing a four-pointed star, similar to that of the Nanga Sohu previously mentioned.

During this time when the Sun enters the zodiacal sea-goat Capricornus, Comet Tuttle was passing through Cassiopeia. This constellation was named for the vain and haughty queen of Phoenician Ethiopia. (This is not the African country we know today but instead the ancient state whose capital was Joppa, the modern-day port city Jaffa, Israel, where, incidentally, Jonah set off toward Tarshish but encountered along the way a rather big fish.)

Cassiopeia boasted that she was more beautiful than the sea nymphs, which angered Poseidon and caused him to flood her country. (A deluge, the Hopi say, also destroyed their previous Third World.) In order to appease the sea god, she and her husband, King Cepheus, sacrificed their daughter Andromeda by chaining her to the rocks on the Levantine coast for the sea beast Cetus to find and eat. As stated above, Perseus rescued Andromeda by using the Medusa's head to literally petrify Cetus. Perseus was rewarded by gaining Andromeda as his wife.

Is the fact that Comet Tuttle passed through this mythologically rich constellation during the solstice merely fluke? A quirk? The proverbial coincidence? Or is it a more profound case of synchronicity? In this age each of us must pick our individual way through a thicket of conflicting ideologies and worldviews.

We can say with impunity, however, that Comet 17P/Holmes and Comet 8P/Tuttle join the growing list of celestial signals foretelling our potential transition from the current age of dissolution and despair to the pristine world ahead. Whether or not any one of them is actually the Blue Star of Hopi prophecy will depend upon what variable time line the course of history takes.

Because destiny is dynamic rather than fixed, our collective thoughts and actions ultimately influence the outcome. The noosphere of our positive spiritual energy could soften the blows of the coming catastrophe or even avert it altogether. We can look up to the stars for guidance, but the final decision is up to us.

Phoenix Redux

> "That there is a whirlpool in the sky is well known; it is most probably the essential one, and it is precisely placed. It is a group of stars so named (*zalos*) at the foot of Orion, close to Rigel (beta Orionis, Rigel being the Arabic word for 'foot'), the degree of which was called 'death', according to Hermes Trismegistos…"

Thus claims the classic tome *Hamlet's Mill* by Santillana and von Dechend. Whirlpools or spirals, as I stated in Chapter 19, function in a mythological context as interdimensional gateways.

Next to the left foot of Orion is the swirling source of a great starry stream named Eridanus, which flows toward the Phoenix.

One author has called it "the River of the Judge." [Capt] Encompassing the largest area of any constellation, it meanders from the celestial deity the ancient Egyptians identified as Osiris, the judge of the Underworld, toward the southern realms. Hermes Trismegistos, the Greek name for the Egyptian god Thoth, associated this vortex in the sky with death and/or transition.

Eridanus is the place, for instance, where the impetuous Greek youth named Phaeton crashed and burned, after taking the chariot of his father Helios for a joyride.

On the other hand, the name Eridanus may have been derived from the Sumerian city of Eridu. It literally means "mouth (or confluence) of rivers," thus locating the proto-urban center in the marshland near the Persian Gulf. This reputedly was the birthplace of civilization in about 5400 BC (though the settlement of Çatal Höyük in Turkey is actually one-and-a-half millennia older).

Zecharia Sitchen translates ERIDU as "Home in the Faraway" or "Home away from home." [*The Cosmic Code*]. The first home was apparently among the stars. According to a text called the *Sumerian king list*: "After the kingship descended from heaven, the kingship was in Eridu." [www.livius.org/k/kinglist/sumerian.html] This was basically the spot where the gods, specifically the Anunnaki, descended from the heavens to the earth. The names Eridanus and Eridu are perhaps related to the English word for our planet.

Eridu was ruled by the earth/water god Enki. (*En-* means "lord" and *ki* means "earth." The Hopi word *ki*, by the way, means "house.") Enki was also referred to as "Lord of Sweet Waters in the Earth" (fresh water), "Lord of Deep Waters" (salt water?), and "Lord of the Abyss" (the netherworld). His primary symbols included the goat and the fish, which were combined in the zodiacal constellation of Capricornus.

In Sumer there was a custom of human burial called "laying the body in the 'reeds of Enki'," which might refer to placing a corpse in a small boat to float downstream into the canebrakes.

Author Philip Coppens stresses the cultural importance of the reed:

> "Through history, the centre of worship of Enki in Eridu was the reed hut, even though it was surrounded by impressive temples. The reed hut was the original temple and it is important to note that despite technological advances, at the core of the religious belief, a simple hut remained. It shows that the Sumerians never forgot where they came from." [*The Canopus Revelation*]

Coppens also notes that the massive stone blocks of the Egyptian temple at Luxor were carved to give the illusion of being made of reed and papyrus. We furthermore remember that the sacred *djed* pillar was constructed of reeds. This symbol of stability was figuratively referred to as "the backbone of Osiris." (Seeing drawing on p. 118. Also, read more on the Hopi connection to the reed in Chapter 11.)

"Investigative mythologist" William Henry identifies Enki's city of Eridu as another "place of the reeds," which he calls the "Dimension of the Blessed."

> "The metaphor of the reed continues in the afterlife Field or Place of Reeds where it signifies the unfolding of a life in a finer realm, along the heavenly Nile, the Milky Way. Time and again we see paintings of priests and priestesses sailing on the waters of the heavenly Nile in the Blessed Field of Reeds. They are sailing the stars." [*Starwalkers*]

Or in other words, "As here, so hereafter."

Like the marshes of the Nile delta in Egypt, the Euphrates delta in Iraq, and the Colorado delta in Arizona/California, the "end of the river" Eridanus is probably imbued with the spiritual power of the reed as well. Its harbor is the nineth brightest star Achernar with a magnitude of 0.5. (See the bottom of the star chart on p. 255.) "Achernar is a star of the 'Orion' type, a very hot and luminous bluish giant." [Burnham] The star was last visible from the desert basin of Phoenix, Arizona, about 11,000 years ago, and it will again be visible from this point in about 200 years. At both Giza and Eridu, however, it has hovered just above the southern horizon for the last few centuries.

The constellation Phoenix rests where Eridanus empties into the cosmic ocean. As mentioned in Chapter 5, the *bennu* is the Egyptian name for the legendary phoenix. This bird was customarily perched atop either an obelisk or a pyramidion. The latter refers to the capstone of a pyramid known as the *benben*. Sometimes it was made of meteoric iron naturally shaped into a cone or rough pyramid by its fall to earth.

The stars comprising Phoenix, in addition to their aviary connotation, can be conceptualized as a barque. Metaphorically identified in the Egyptian *Book of the Dead* as "The Boat of Millions of Years," thus signifying its journey across the vast reaches of deep space-time, this tiny craft carries the soul to its destiny in the afterlife. (See picture on p. 133.)

The most brilliant star in the constellation is Ankaa, or Al-'Anqa', which literally means "head of the phoenix." But its other Arabic name, Na'ir al Zaurak, denotes "Bright One in the Boat." Located 77 light-years away, this yellow giant is spectral type K with a magnitude of 2.4—not a particularly bright star from our perspective. But in relation to the Sun, it has four times the mass, sixteen times the diameter, and eighty times the luminosity.

A pyramid rises from three major stars in the region. Its base is formed by Fomalhaut (magnitude 1.2) in Piscis Austrinus, the Southern Fish, and Deneb Kaitos (magnitude 2.0) in the tail of the sea monster Cetus. Pointing southward toward the underworld realm of the dead, its apex is formed by Achernar, where the River ends. The constellation of the Sculptor is enclosed within the pyramid near its base, perhaps fashioning or adorning its inner *sanctum sanctorum*.

In the preceding section of the Afterword I said that we ultimately control our fate. This is not to say, however, that the stars do not exert some influence over our earthly existence. For millennia the intuitive science of astrology has studied and catalogued the unique effects of the planets and fixed stars on our lives. Let's take a look at our pyramid of stars.

From Johann Bode's Uranographia

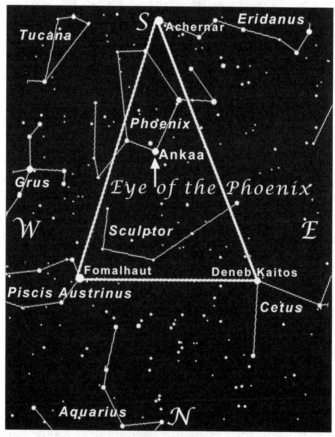

**Eridanus with Achernar at top (south), Aquarius in the zodiac
at bottom (north), Phoenix with Ankaa at center of celestial pyramid.**

Fomalhaut, for instance, is traditionally associated with idealism, mysticism, and lofty visions. Success, immortal fame, and spirituality are the benefits of this star culminating in one's natal chart. It is one of the four Royal Stars of Persia known as the "Watcher of the South." The others are: Regulus in Leo (the "Watcher of the North"), Aldebaran in Taurus (the "Watcher of the East"), and Antares in Scorpius (the "Watcher of the West"). The Watchers, of course, were also known as the Annunaki mentioned above.

The other point forming the pyramid's base, Deneb Kaitos in the whale Cetus, is linked with the devouring aspect of the collective unconscious. It facilitates the unexpected eruption of chaos or mayhem into our lives—the sudden emergence of a juggernaut. In general, the constellation emphasizes the ability to command and make war. [http://users.winshop.com.au/annew/alphabet1.htm]

The apex of the pyramid, Achernar, is connected to natural disasters, including floods and fires. The former makes sense in terms of this turbulent star's position at the end of the Eridanus, the latter by virtue of its location near the conflagration of Phoenix.

Ankaa at the heart of the Phoenix is understandably related to transformation, transfiguration, or transcendence. One personal example has global implications.

> "Joseph Campbell, the famous mythologist and author, has Ankaa culminating with his Sun, indicating that the star was connected to his life work, his career, his mark in the world. Joseph Campbell raised our collective consciousness to a higher level with his understanding, teachings, and writings about the importance of myths." [Brady]

In its manifestation as a barque sailing toward immortality, Ankaa becomes the boatman at the rudder. As the fabulous firebird, Ankaa becomes the all-seeing Eye of the Phoenix. As the temple for both mythological versions, the sidereal pyramid becomes the pyre upon which the Eye of Providence blazes, envisaging the eternal fields of bliss beyond all temporal cycles.

The name Ankaa echoes the Egyptian word *ankh*, the icon of life everlasting. (See photo on p. 163.) The related Egyptian word *anqa* means "cordage, tackle of a boat," thus harkening back to the Phoenix as a vessel used to cross the ocean of time. In addition, Anku is the god that binds the foes of Osiris.

Looking at the Sumerian lexicon, we find that the root *an* refers to "heavenly" and *ka*, as we saw in Chapter 16, means "gateway." Thus, the Sumerians probably knew *an-ka* as a sky portal.

The Hopi word *àngqe*, on the other hand, refers to something distantly perceived or out of sight—similar to the constellation Phoenix, that is, barely perceptible far to the south. Like the ancient Egyptians, the Hopi believe that once a celestial body sets below the horizon it descends to the underworld of spirits.

The Hopi root *an* refers to "ant" and *ka*, as we also saw in Chapter 16, is a word of foreign origin (like the *katsinam* themselves) that has consistent meanings and contexts around the globe. The Hopi word *anki* signifies "anthill." The Ant People, discussed in Chapter 9, played a significant role in Hopi legends of the first two world epochs.

We recall that the beneficent Ant People provided the Hopi with a haven during the destruction of the First World by fire and the Second World by ice. Inexplicably, these crypto-zoomorphs abandoned the Hopi during the previous Third World, which was destroyed by a flood. During these final years of the current Fourth World, however, the Ant People have been seen again. (See, for instance, the drawing on p. 116.) But it remains to be seen whether or not these creatures will assist in our transition to the Fifth World to come.

9/11—Part of the Final Purification?

As I have shown, the Hopi recognize prophecy as a large part of their cultural heritage. Spiritual elders had foreseen many things that have already come to pass. They had envisaged moving houses of iron (trains), horseless wagons traveling on black ribbons (automobiles), people speaking through cobwebs (telegraph and telephone lines), a falling "gourd of ashes" (the atomic bomb), women wearing men's clothing (the Women's Liberation Movement), humans journeying along roads in the sky to live in the heavens (Skylab, MIR, or the International Space Station), and the door of the House of Mica (the United Nations) closing four times on Hopi pleas for peace. These were all foreseen long before they came to pass.

Just after the emergence from the subterranean Third World during the beginning of the present Fourth World, a figure known as Pahana, or Elder White Brother, took with him a corner of the Fire Clan's four-inches-square stone tablet and proceeded eastward toward the rising sun. At the same time the Younger (Red) Brother stayed back, traveling the spiral road of migrations, constructing pueblos throughout the American Southwest, and eventually settling in the Hopi villages much as we see them today. Similar to the Mesoamerican myth of Kukulkan or Quetzalcoatl, it was assumed that Pahana would return at the end of the cycle to save the righteous people from foreign forces destroying the land.

The paragraphs on the next page were originally written as the conclusion of an essay titled "Spiral Gate: the Arc of the Covenant." (See abridged version in the previous chapter.) I researched and wrote this long article in a few weeks in late August of 2001. I was under some inexplicable compulsion to finish it. Then the world changed forever.

Many Hopi elders must surely feel that the world's spirals are wobbling out of control, as the prophesied end of the Fourth World approaches. We need look no further than our ubiquitous TV screens to see that Grandmother Earth is in turmoil.

Environmental degradation on diverse fronts, multiple species extinction, inexplicable genetic mutations, radically shifting weather patterns, more frequent and more devastating hurricanes/tornadoes/floods, global warming with elevated levels of "greenhouse gases," one energy crisis after another triggering "rolling blackouts," increased seismic and volcanic activity, lethal epidemics and pandemics, aberrant human and animal behavior, daily terrorist attacks, oxymoronic "holy wars," the constant threat of chemical and biological warfare, proliferation of nuclear materials, transnational machinations with Machiavellian motives, local political subterfuge resulting in widespread citizen apathy, factional massacres, "ethnic cleansing," mass cult suicides, school shootings, "road rage," increased numbers of paramilitary groups and individual arsenals, addiction to the pornography of media violence or unseemly trivialities, rising prison populations, social chaos and anomie, mental and emotional exhaustion, increased psychosomatic illnesses, religious disorientation and uncertainty, disregard for humanistic or humanitarian principles, widening schisms between social classes causing increased inequities, dire poverty and famine on one hand and conspicuous consumption and opulent wealth on the other, unrestrained avarice and power mongering justified by glib cynicism within a moral vacuum, an almost total disregard for the Golden Rule—the dismal litany goes on and on, all of it symptomatic of the End Times.

Hopi elders did not need technology, however, to envision what is now upon us. They foresaw it long ago in their humble kivas, and have been preparing for the final Purification.

The Hopi have a word for our current condition: *Koyaanisqatsi*, n. 1. crazy life. 2. life in turmoil. 3. life out of balance. 4. life disintegrating. 5. a state of life that calls for another way of living.

The 1982 movie of the same name evokes the disturbing social environment in which we all swim (or sometimes drown). Directed by Godfrey Reggio, with music by Philip Glass and cinematography by Ron Fricke, the film leads us on a mesmerizing and mind-bending journey without the familiar dramatic elements of characters, dialogue, or plot.

Beginning with natural scenes of silent beauty from the majestic landscapes of the American Southwest, a relentless flow of rapid-fire imagery gradually brings us into a milieu dominated by our contemporary technological nightmare. Both time-lapse and slow motion photography are used to show the whirr and blur of urban anonymity. Hot dogs and Twinkies shoot down conveyors belts in the same way that masses of pedestrians scurry up escalators. The assembly line becomes the major paradigm of our time.

The impersonal, all-seeing eye of the camera pans upward as circuit boards morph into city grids. Electric fireflies inside skyscrapers of steel and glass blink on and off, while headlights and taillights surge down highways like white and red blood cells through clogged arteries.

While watching this, I actually experienced a nauseating vertigo. It also reminded me of one of the Hopi prophecies of ants inheriting the earth after the destruction of the Fourth World. The film's portrayal of the frenetic bristling of daily existence suggests this may already be happening.

Even more depressing is the sense of alienation and dissociation the movie conveys. How utterly lonely, fragile, and helpless is our modern human condition! The desolation of abandoned housing projects proclaims the failed attempt to find meaning and dignity in our lives. Watching this, we all feel homeless.

The movie becomes almost prescient, however, when it presents dizzying aerial shots of the Twin Towers along with the controlled demolitions of tall buildings, reminding us of the more recent uncontrolled horror. In what was actually a scene from the riot following the New York City blackout of 1977, a lone fireman trudges through the thick smoke of flooded streets.

The motion picture –a truly apt term for this film– concludes with what looks like the space shuttle *Challenger* engulfed in flames and wildy spinning out of control. (In reality, it was an exploded Atlas rocket from the earlier Project Mercury.) The final image returns to the Southwest with an ancient rock art panel of Fremont pictographs. We are left with a group of tall, ghostly Watchers staring back in disapproving judgment.

Even the traditional leaders from the village of Hotevilla have reacted to the movie after its screening on the reservation. Using the voice of the Great Creator and his Assistants, they deliver this warning:

> "We saw the conflict of Nations against Nations, evil people against the people who saw the consequences fast approaching. We saw the mystic fog covering the planet. We see the world leaders with tongues that deceive you into following them and in believing that they will bring peace with weapons and mighty armies. You are abusing the earth with your powerful tools. You are abusing the natural order of the soil for your own profit from the crops it produces. In many ways have you violated the earth. Above all the powerful weapons are in your hands which will doom the world to a likeness of the moon. We too have weapons that no man on earth will tame. We leave you now to the hour of your decision and judgment."
> [*Techqua Ikachi* newsletter, Issue 24,
> www.jnanadana.org/hopi/issue_24.html]

The world indeed seems to be increasingly out of balance as we race at breakneck speed toward some undefined future cataclysm. And if any one word sums up Hopi cosmology and spiritual philosophy, it would have to be the word "balance."

Was 9/11 just one among many signs that point to the

ending of our current global cycle, which the Hopi call the Fourth World? In the late 50's the elders of the Hopi village of Moencopi (Mùnqapi) may have heralded 9/11 in a specific prophecy. A Hopi man named Ros, who prefers that his surname not be given, remembers what they said to him as a child: "An event will happen when America is sleeping, and we will awaken to a Thunderous Eruption of War (in Hopi, *Pòok-wak-ni*) from another Nation."

Predicting disaster, of course, occurs throughout history and into the present day. The media now bombard us 24/7 with imagery of mass catastrophe and death. Fundamentalist Bible-thumpers preach with perverse glee that the Apocalypse is at hand. Jihadist suicide bombers unconditionally demand a worldwide Islamic theocracy. New Age gurus blissfully predict a new era of peace and enlightenment after 2012.

Who's right? Did the Hopi foresee our ultimate destiny, only to bide their time while patiently tending their corn out on the isolated mesas of the high desert?

*

At sunset one tiny cloud drifts across the limitless blue sky over Arizona. Inside it the voices of the Ancestors faintly whisper. They say they are waiting on the other side of the doorway leading to the Fifth World. They tell us not to hurry, though, because all time there melts away like an early spring snowfall. If the Hopi are right, we will smile as we begin to walk in balance and beauty toward our new life.

"Stellar Rock Observatory" boulder near Lydenburg, South Africa.

This "gateway" at the Boomplaas rock art site has a north-south axis. The boulders are engraved with numerous petro-glyphs, especially concentric circles.

Appendix 1

Boomplaas Petroglyph Site: The "OM" Symbol
Rob Milne, South Africa
www.robmilne.com

The "OM" symbol is engraved on the western aspect of a huge polished boulder on the farm Boomplaas ("Tree Farm") near Lydenburg, Mpumalanga Province, in the Republic of South Africa. There are thousands of petroglyphs carved into hundreds of granite boulders of varying sizes at this archaeological site, which extends for many square kilometers. There is ample evidence of human occupation and visits to the site from Early Stone Age times (about 1.4 million years ago) to the Iron Age (which started about 1,600 years ago), and then Historic times. No scientific attempts have been made to date the rock engravings, but the earliest appear to be cupules hammered out many thousands of years ago. Some of the petroglyphs were undoubtedly engraved by hunter-gatherers during the Late Stone Age, about 25,000 to 1,000 years ago, followed by herder and agrarian immigrants who started arriving from the north about 1,600 years ago. These were the Khoi and then the Bantu, who gradually displaced the last of the Late Stone Age people (the San, or Bushmen) by about 140 years ago. The majority of the petroglyphs appear to originate from the San-Khoi contact period, and to have been continued by the Bantu Iron Age settlers from their arrival to recent times.

An interesting pattern emerged during site mapping: two distinct arrangements of engraved boulders that mirror the position of the stars in Orion's Belt. (See map on p. 273.) One depicts Orion's Belt as it appears in the night sky at the summer solstice, and the other as it appears at the winter solstice. Confirmation that the placement of engraved boulders was no accident is found at a giant split boulder which mirrors the position of

Mintaka in the winter Orion's Belt alignment, which I call "Gary A. David Gateway" in honour of the author of this book. A narrow flat shelf is engraved with three concentric circles (Orion's Belt) and another concentric circle some distance away (Sirius). (See photo and sketch, facing page.)

The petroglyphs at the site include cupules, concentric circles, saurian figures (lizard or crocodile), a rock hydrax, snakes, therianthropes, star maps, agrarian calendars, and records of comets. Apart from the numerous saurian engravings, snakes, and a single rock hydrax, the absence of the usual San petroglyph subjects (such as eland, ostrich and other game animals) is notable. The nearest engraved bucks (two sable antelope) are found over 4 kilometers away from the main Boomplaas engraving site.

One of the most unusual petroglyphs found to date is that of an "OM" symbol. (See bottom of p. 272.) This is a pecked engraving on a solid granite boulder, smoothed and polished over thousands of years, which I call "Stellar Observatory". The proliferation of concentric circle petroglyphs (mostly joined by pecked lines) gives one the unmistakable impression of star maps. Also, the natural depressions in the boulder fill with rainwater in summer, providing the engraver with a convenient mirror that reflects the stars above. The boulder (which is 1.2 meters high, 4 meters long on its east-west axis, and 3.9 meters wide on its north-south axis) is not part of the two Orion's Belt alignments, and stands well apart from other boulders in the southern sector of the engraving site. It has good examples of deep cupule engravings, possibly the earliest executed at the whole site, and the rough granite surface has been polished smooth (possibly with animal hides) over many thousands of years. According to a Shaman this was done to release the energy and power of the engravings. There are also many pecked lines connecting the engraved concentric circles on the top of the boulder to the ground below: "As above, so below"? Another unusual feature of this boulder is its extremely high magnetism—a compass placed on it is deflected by 45 degrees! This is a very powerful rock indeed.

Going back to the "OM" symbol, which is placed near the top of the boulder facing west—the place of the setting sun and setting stars. What is its origin? One of the possibilities is that it was given by un-recorded visitors from India hundreds of years ago. There is strong evidence from the South African archaeological record of trade links between Southern Africa and the East, ranging from the Indians (at Zimbabwe) to the Chinese (at Mapungubwe). One highly controversial researcher even claims that many of the Iron Age settlements (dating from 1,600 years ago to about 150 years ago) are in fact Hindu temples and that there are many examples in the Lydenburg area. Although the level of involvement of Indians with the local communities before recorded history is open to debate, it is clear that the Indians were involved in the prehistoric gold trade in the area. The town of Pilgrim's Rest, the site of spectacular alluvial gold finds last century, is almost within walking distance of Boomplaas. The gold mines in the area have been going for well over a hundred years and still produce a tidy profit for their shareholders.

***Above: These eroded carvings may be as much as 10,000 years old.
Below: Sketch of the same—Belt stars of Orion (left) and Sirius (right).***

Boulder has been pecked with many concentric circles and cupules.
Pooled rainwater serves as a natural mirror of the heavens.
OM symbol is located at lower right corner. See photo detail below.

Very faint OM symbol inside diagonal lines within inner ring.
(See Hindu Omkar, p. 155.) Outer ring may be a calendar.

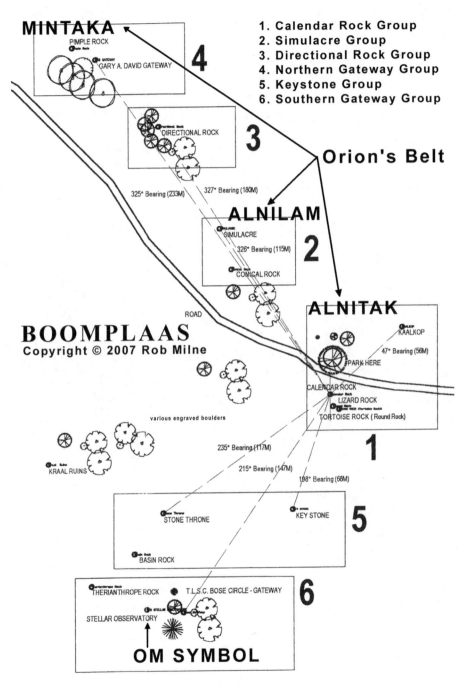

MINTAKA

PIMPLE ROCK

4

GARY A. DAVID GATEWAY

1. Calendar Rock Group
2. Simulacre Group
3. Directional Rock Group
4. Northern Gateway Group
5. Keystone Group
6. Southern Gateway Group

3

DIRECTIONAL ROCK

Orion's Belt

325° Bearing (233M)   327° Bearing (180M)

ALNILAM

SIMULACRE

2

326° Bearing (115M)

CONICAL ROCK

ALNITAK

KAALKOP

47° Bearing (56M)

PARK HERE

ROAD

BOOMPLAAS
Copyright © 2007 Rob Milne

CALENDAR ROCK
LIZARD ROCK
TORTOISE ROCK (Round Rock)

various engraved boulders

1

KRAAL RUINS

235° Bearing (117M)

215° Bearing (147M)

198° Bearing (68M)

STONE THRONE

KEY STONE

5

BASIN ROCK

THERIANTHROPE ROCK   T.L.S.C. BOSE CIRCLE - GATEWAY

6

STELLAR OBSERVATORY

OM SYMBOL

For more info, visit: www.robmilne.com

Appendix 2

Votan: Diffusionist Deity
Gary A. David

He Was Cosmo When Cosmo Wasn't Cool

In this appendix I will generally discuss variations on the myth (read "primordial truths") of Votan and specifically explore the influence of the American Southwest's version of this culture hero on the Hopi Indians, especially in regard to their pervasive and enduring snake cult. His presence in the South Pacific will be discussed, as well as his association with the Phoenicians of the Middle East and with the specific word *mas*.

I will furthermore show that Votan was not white, as he is commonly conceptualized, but instead was red, or at least a genetic mixture of the two. I will also talk about the northern version of Votan and, finally, describe his return vis-à-vis the figure of Quetzalcoatl.

One of the most clearly diffusionist legends comes to us from Mesoamerica. Votan, appearing as the bearded "god" clothed in a long, flowing robe, disembarked with his crew from a flotilla of ships upon the Gulf coast of Mexico.[1] He then ascended the Usumacinta River and established Na-Chan (or Na-Kan), the "City of Serpents," tentatively identified as Palenque in Chiapas, Mexico.

Votan is sometimes referred to as Lord Pacal, whose tomb was found in the Temple of the Inscriptions at Palenque. However, this famous Mayan ruler, who reigned between 615 and 683 AD, may have merely assumed the name of the much earlier deity.

The lid of Pacal's sarcophagus gained pop culture status, by the way, when in the late 60's Erich Von Däniken interpreted it as showing Pacal Votan seated at the control panel of an extraterrestrial spacecraft. We certainly live in strange times.

The actual name Votan comes from the Tzendal Maya of Chiapas. It literally means 'heart', and he was known as "the heart of the people." This deified human reputedly kept a record of the origin of the native races, which he gave to the guardians of a subterranean "Hall of Records" in Mesoamerica.[2] The whereabouts of this depository are still unknown. John Van Auken of the Edgar Cayce Foundation provides compelling evidence that it may be located at Piedras Negras in Guatemala, though this remains unconfirmed.[3]

Votan's mythological analogues include Kukulkan at Chichén Itzá, Gucumatz for the Quiché Maya, Itzamná in the *Book of the Chilam Balam*, Quetzalcoatl in the Aztec tradition, Viracocha in the Peruvian Andes [4], and Pahana among the Hopi.

In the Mayan mythological, historical, medical, astrological, and esoteric text called *Chilam Balam*, for instance, we find the following prophetic lines: "Itzamná Kauil shall rise. Our lord comes, Itzá. Our elder brother comes, <oh> men of Tantun [Island of Cozumel]. Receive your guests, the bearded men, the men of the east, the bearers of the sign of God, lord."[5]

Votan was the archetypal bringer of civilization, bequeathing hieroglyphic writing, the codification of laws, the use of a complex Mesoamerican calendar, the cultivation of maize and cotton, sacrificial offerings of flowers and fruits rather than humans, and such diverse sciences as astronomy, metallurgy, ceramics, and medicine. It appears that he was, so to speak, a quintessential Renaissance man.

Across the Ocean Blue
(Before Fourteen Hundred and Ninety-two)

For that time period, the cosmopolitan Votan clearly got around. But where did he come from? According to some authorities, he may have been a Phoenician from Carthage (modern-day Tunis). Author Adrian Gilbert, for instance, believes that the evidence for this rests in the friezes at Palenque. He says that the figures depicted there have large noses and that their facial features generally look Carthaginian.[6]

Researcher Andrew Collins, on the other hand, thinks that Votan was probably a Hebrew, citing the Phoenicians' lack of serpent worship as well as their mercantile motives for navigation that superseded any interest in empire building.[7]

This theory is contradicted, however, by the fact that a "...snake's egg... [was] hung up in the temple of Hercules in Tyre, encircled by the Agathodaemon, or the good snake that gives rain."[8] This Phoencian version of the *uroboros*, or a snake swallowing its tail, is a symbol of eternity.

Another name for the port city of Tyre is Tsur, which in Hebrew means 'rock'. The Hopi word *tsur* means 'wedged in a crack', and *tsu* means 'rattlesnake', which is also associated with rain. In addition, the Hopi *tsu'ki* refers to 'a hole inhabited by snakes'. The Hopi term *tusyap*, incidentally, denotes a 'flat rock'.

A winter solstice ceremony for the resurrection of the sun was held in the same Tyrian temple. This impressed the infamous Freemason Albert Pike:

> "The temple of Hercules of Tyre was reported to have been built 2300 years before Herodotus [that is, about 2,800 years BCE]; and Hercules, whose Greek name has been sometimes supposed to be of Phoenician origin, in the sense of Circuitor, i.e. 'rover' and 'perambulator' of earth, as well as 'Hyperion' of the sky, was the patron and model of those famous navigators who spread altars from coast to coast through the Mediterranean, to the extremities of the West..."[9]

In Greek mythology Hyperion was the Titan (a giant) who fathered Helios (the sun), Selene (the moon) and Eos (the dawn). His name literally means 'above' (*hyper-*) + 'going' (*ion*). It is possible that Heracles (Hercules), whose altars most likely reached west to the New World, was a variation on the theme of Votan.

On one of four journeys back to his homeland named Valum-Chivim, the demigod Votan witnessed the construction of both the "house of God" (that is, King Solomon's Temple in

Jerusalem, about 970 BC) and the Tower of Babel in Mesopotamia. Some authorities state that the latter was built about 1000 BC.

Pioneering diffusionist researcher Constance Irwin conversely provides a slightly later date: "Such was the Tower of Babel as *rebuilt* by Nabopolassar and his successor Nebuchadnezzar in the seventh and sixth centuries B.C.—a date, by the way, which corresponds better with the possibility of four successful round-trip transatlantic voyages."[10]

Citing a history of Palenque written by an 18th century friar named Ramon de Ordoñez y Aguilar, Collins further remarks on one of these voyages made by Votan: "More curiously, on a second visit to the 'house of God' Votan 'was made to traverse an underground passage which ended at the root of the heavens.' Moreover, that this 'passage was nothing less than a snake hole, where he entered because he was a Son of Serpents'."[11]

I can think of no better description of the portal located on the floor of a Hopi structure called a kiva. This round or rectangular semi-subterranean prayer chamber found throughout the American Southwest is accessed via a ladder protruding from a hatchway in the ceiling. The hole in the floor, which is termed a *sipapu*, is the passageway to the underworld.

**Ancient Hopi (Anasazi or Ancestral Puebloan) kiva.
The small hole to the left of the fire pit is called the sipapu.
Long House, Mesa Verde National Park, Colorado.**

The model for this structure may have been imported from the Old World. The late epigrapher Barry Fell cites Herodotus' report of the Troglodytes of Libya, who once lived in semi-subterranean "apartments." Fell writes: "This arrangement, seen in the mountainous desert to the west of Tripoli, and extending into Tunisia, may be the origin of the circular kivas of the so-called pueblo towns of the southwest United States."[12]

On a macrocosmic scale, the *sipapu* in the Hopi kiva corresponds to a specific travertine dome known as the Sipapuni. It is found at the bottom of Grand Canyon near the spot where the Little Colorado River flows into the Colorado River. This supposedly is the entrance to an underground conduit leading to the previous Third World—seat of the afterlife and the spiritual home of the *katsinam* (also spelled *kachinas*), or spirit messengers.[13] We are now at the end of the Fourth World, Hopi elders say.

Collins writes that Votan descended into the "snake hole" simply because he was descended from the lineage of serpents. It is significant that the biennial Snake Dance is still a major part of the Hopi ceremonial cycle in Arizona. If we can believe the stories of Votan's voyages around the globe, this sacred ritual may have come from elsewhere. (For more on this, consult my book *The Orion Zone: Ancient Star Cities of the American Southwest*—available from: www.adventuresunlimitedpress.com.)

Irwin says that Chivim, the name of Votan's terrestrial origin, is derived from "Chna," the English transliteration of the Greek word referring to Canaan, or the land of the Phoenicians. [14] The scholar Donald Mackenzie believes that Chivim refers to Tripoli, and that the name is a cognate of *Hivam* (or *Givim*), the Phoenician word for 'snake'.

The Hivites are descendants of Heth, son of Canaan. (Genesis 10:15)[15] In this regard, the theosophist Madame Blavatsky comments: "The names Heva, *Hivi* or Hivite, and Levi, all signify a serpent; and it is a curious fact that the Hivites, or serpent tribe of Palestine, like the Levites or Ophites of Israel, were ministers to the temples."[16]

Collins additionally argues that Chivim is related to the

Hebrew *chevvah* and the Arabic *hawwa,* both of which variously mean 'snake' and 'life'. More importantly, he stresses that these words refer to *awwim,* which is another name for the Nephilim. [17] These creatures were the "giants in the earth" from the Book of Genesis (6:4). They were, of course, the offspring of the so-called fallen angels and the "daughters of men."

A possible link exists between the Hopi *katsinam* mentioned above and these angelic "Watchers." As mentioned in Chapter 16, part of the Snake Dance ritual in the First Mesa village of Walpi is held in the kiva called Wikwa'lobi, or 'Place of the Watchers.'[18]

Nebuchadnezzar, the king who reconstructed the same Tower of Babel that Votan visited, received in a dream one of these Watchers, as the Book of Daniel (Chapter 4) records. In this context it is significant to note that the Hopi word *tawa* (phonetically similar to *hawwa,* the Arabic form of Chivim) means both 'to watch' and 'sun' or 'day'. The deified sun in his journey per diem across the sky is said to watch over the earth.

Furthermore, the Hopi word *hawi* means 'to come down', perhaps from the sky, and the word *mongwi* mean 'chief'. Put these together and you have the sense of "chief-comes-down-from-the-sky"—*à la* the arrival of the Watchers. It is perhaps more than a coincidence, then, that the megalithic structure on the South Pacific island of Tongatapu is called the Ha'amonga of Maui. This is not as much a digression as it sounds.

Tales of the South Pacific

On the island of Tonga the massive trilithon, as it is called, is constructed of two upright, rectangular pillars rising fifteen feet and weighing fifty tons each. A rectangular lintel eighteen feet long and weighing approximately nine tons was placed on top. Built perhaps as early as 1500 BC, this structure probably served a purpose similar to that of Stonehenge—as a solar, lunar, and stellar observatory. In fact, notches in the stones of the trilithon mark the summer and winter solstices.[19]

Barry Fell opined that legends of Maui were based on an

actual maritime explorer of Oceania, who sailed east from the Indian Ocean across the Pacific in 232 BC.

> "The word *mawi* in Egyptian means a guide or navigator, but it also sounds very like the Polynesian name Maui. In Polynesian legend Maui was a great sailor who, in the figurative speech of Polynesian tradition, was said to have 'fished up new lands' from the sea...—a poetic way of recording his discovery of lands hidden beneath the horizon."[20]

The Hopi word *maawi*, by the way, means 'to pick beans or fruit'. This suggests pulling up food from the soil in the same manner that Maui metaphorically pulled up islands from the bottom of the sea.

The key calendrical positions found on the trilithon are also used by the Hopi Water Clan. Its members are the traditional sun-watchers, keeping track of the solstice and equinox points on the horizon. The clan plays a large part in determining the agricultural calendar—sowing, cultivating, harvesting, etc. A calendar is absolutely essential for survival in their harsh climate.

Did the Hopi once use these same skills to navigate across vast stretches of ocean? This is perhaps the case, since another name for the Water Clan is the Houseboat Clan. Oddly enough, one Hopi legend describes them escaping a great deluge on bamboo rafts across the Pacific Ocean. They sailed eastward from one "steppingstone" (island) to another until they eventually landed on the western shores of Mexico.

The Water Clan then traveled north, either on foot or by boat, to arrive at the Baja Peninsula and the mouth of the Colorado River. After poling upstream they came to Grand Canyon. This served as their "Place of Emergence" (or Sipapuni—see reference above) from which they spread out upon the Colorado Plateau where they still live in pueblo villages made of stone. So, apparently these desert dwellers were once great mariners—or at least the members of the Water Clan were.

This clan possesses the knowledge that a culture hero such as Votan may have once shared. He was also known to have the ability to measure the earth[21], thus engaging in what best-selling author Graham Hancock calls "geodetic prospecting."

In his discussion of Rapa Nui (Easter Island) and other sites, Hancock describes the function of a worldwide grid system used by figures such as Votan: "What we are suggesting therefore is that Easter Island might originally have been settled in order to serve as a sort of geodetic beacon, or marker—fulfilling some as yet unguessed at function in an ancient global system of sky-ground co-ordinates that linked many so-called 'world navels'."[22]

The natives of Rapa Nui call their original homeland Hiva, an island that long ago sank beneath the sea like the legendary continent of —at the risk of using the 'A' word— Atlantis. We remember, of course, that the Phoenician name for snake is *Hivam*. We also recall that the Hopi still perform many of their sacred ceremonies in a kiva. In the Rapa Nui language, *kiva* means 'to keep a secret'. [www.rongorongo.org/vanaga/k2.html] On Mauke (one of the Cook Islands), the name *O Kiva* means 'ocean'.

And what can we make of the following? Easter Island is located on the same longitude as the final territory of the Hopi. Is this meridian alignment merely a coincidence? Or is it synchronicity—what psychologist C. G. Jung calls a "meaningful coincidence"?

Regardless of whether Votan was Phoenician, Hebrew, or of some other ethnic origin, he must indeed have been a potent force for worldwide cultural transformation.

The Red Man and the Sea

The Hopi Water Clan supposedly resided for a time far to the southeast of the Arizona desert in a mythical city called Palatkwapi. Southeast is also the general direction where the Maya live. It may be significant in this context that Palenque's stucco walls were once painted a brilliant crimson.

On the other hand, the Hopi name Palatkwapi, which actually means "City of the Red People" or simply "Red City," probably refers to its inhabitants rather than to building materials or landscape. Diffusionist proponent James Bailey writes in this regard: "The name Phoenician means Red Men. The name Red Sea then covered what is now called the Indian Ocean as well as what we today call the Red Sea and meant the Sea of the Red Men."[23] Herodotus (in *The History*, VII, 89) was the first to recognize the Red Sea area as the origin of the Phoenicians.

In his subsequent book Bailey takes this even further: "Amerindians are brown-skinned. The Greeks used the term Phoenician, meaning redmen, for the different clans of Western Semites. So the term Red Indian may have derived from this long period of Phoenician government across large parts of America."[24]

The renowned Atlantean scholar Ignatius Donnelly adds: "The ancient Egyptians were red men. They recognized four races of men—the red, yellow, black, and white men. They themselves belonged to the '*Rot*,' or red men..."[25] Hence, we now have another culture from which Votan may have originated.

Back in the American Southwest, one Hopi legend describes the chief of the Water Clan dividing pieces cut from the neck of Palulukang, the horned water serpent, in order to give to all those who once lived at Palatkwapi, City of the Red Men. This frightening creature inhabits bodies of water such as springs or lakes and has the power to bring rain.[26]

Again the snake raises its head from this dizzy-

Drawing of Hopi water serpent rising from ceramic pot, as it struggles with a "Mudhead" ogre or clown. **[Twenty-first Annual Report of the Bureau of American Ethnology]**

ing whirlpool of cultures.

To make matters even more confusing, the Hopi author Albert Yava makes the following politically incorrect statement: "One thing you hear from the Patki [Water Clan] people is that in ancient times they were white, not Indian color. They say, 'My ancestors had white skins, but because of evil things that happened, we lost all that.' They also say, 'The Patki people are the ones who are supposed to teach the Hopis good moral values, how to lead good lives.'"[27] (The above quote is also cited on p. 148 re. the Patki Clan.)

This might be evidence of the pre-Columbian merging of two peoples—the Amerindian and the Semitic/Hamitic. In the case of either the Phoenicians or the Egyptians, the self-designated racial classification of "red" may indicate that this process had already occurred.

I should furthermore point out that Votan and his men selected mates from the native population they encountered. It is almost as if integration and miscegenation were a spiritual imperative.

Perhaps for this reason we see a similarity between the name of the Patki (or Water) Clan and the Sanskrit word for Phoenician: *Pani* or *Panch*—especially if we attribute a hard "ch" sound to the latter term. The Tibetan usage of this term is especially relevant. The Panchen Lama, second in spiritual importance to the Dalai Lama, is derived from the Chinese word *banchán*. This word is a transliteration of the Sanskrit *pandita*, or pundit, literally a 'learnéd man'. We must remember that the Phoenicians were the ones who invented the alphabet.

At this point a number of questions arises: Did a "Red Man" or "red men" actually have something to do with the migration from the previous Hopi Third World (or era—now conceptualized as being spatially subterranean) into the current Fourth World (or earth plane)? Did the Hopi Mesas of Arizona become the New World Canaan, to which this tribe was ultimately led? Was the Old World seen as the antipodal underworld?

In his insightful research, comparative linguistics scholar

Gene D. Matlock describes a possible scenario:

> "**Maasawa** [Masau'u] agreed to aid and finance the
> departure of the Hopi. To lead them out of **Muski**
> [Maski, the underworld], he contracted the services of
> what the Hopis call 'white men,' known as **Bahanna**
> [Pahana]. Then, their Wind God, **Yaponche** [Yopontsa],
> blew them across a great lake to the Promised Land. In
> Sanskrit, **Vahana** means 'mover, transporter; ship; vessel,
> boat.' Panch was a Sanskrit name for **Pani** or
> **Phoenician**."[28]

The Hopi deity of death and the underworld is named
Masau'u (or numerous other orthographic variations). (See
drawing on p. 107.) He is also the lord of the earth. If some sort
of long-distance influence on the Hopi in general and the Water
Clan in particular did not exist, why else would we find
Massawa located on the eastern shores of Africa? This is, in fact,
the name of a major port on the Red Sea! It appears that
Masau'u, together with Pahana, assisted at least some of the
Hopi in their ancient journey to the New World.

More on the Massing of *Mas*

> The following are Sanskrit variations of *mas*:
> *mAs* – 'flesh, meat'
> *mAs* – 'moon, month'
> *maS* – 'to hurt, to injure'
> *mas* – 'to measure, to mete'

In Hopi *mas* (or *maas*) means 'gray', as in putrefied flesh,
or 'ghostly'. Their god Masau'u is the terrestrial equivalent of
Orion, the Hunter. Like Osiris, he metes out punishment in the
underworld. On the positive side, Masau'u, with his planting
stick and sack of seeds, taught the Hopi how to grow corn. This
is also part of the curriculum vitae of Votan.

This animal/plant dichotomy is reflected in a pair of related Hopi words: *puukya* means 'flesh', 'skin', or 'animal hide', while *piikya* means 'immature ear of corn'. In addition, agriculture naturally involves lunar cycles—one of the Sanskrit meanings of *mas*.

The English word "mass," which refers to common physical matter, is derived from the Greek word *mâza*, literally 'barley cake'. The word "maize" comes from the Taino word *mahis*, which means 'source of life'. The Taino, by the way, were the Indians that Columbus encountered on the Caribbean island of Hispaniola.

In the Bible one of the sons of Ishmael was named Massa. The term Masani, which literally means 'burden', refers to an Arab tribe near the Persian Gulf. (Did its members carry their burden to a new land?) The Hebrew word *masorah* means 'tradition'. In Ezekiel 20:37, it is used to denote 'fetter' or 'bond'. In addition, Massah was the place at Horeb where Moses struck a certain rock with his staff and water miraculously came out. (Exodus 17:7. Also in this same book of the Bible, we see both Moses and Aaron throwing down their staffs, which then turn into serpents.)

The official Website of the Theosophical Society [www.theosociety.org] contains the following definition of the word *Masben*: "The sun in putrefaction, used in modern Freemasonry with a direct reference to their 'word at low breath.'" The disturbing concept of putrefying flesh is very much a part of the Hopi god's purview.

The Phoenician term *mastruca* refers to the coarse skins of wild animals worn by the people of Carthage and Sardinia, both Phoenician colonies.[29] This word may be connected with the first Sanskrit definition of *mas* given above.

In Sudan at a place called Masawwarat es-Sufra, an archaic temple structure complete with colonnades and porticos was built probably in the late Ptolemaic dynasty (305 – 30 BC). It surprisingly contained carvings of serpents. Fifteen miles to the south on route to the Blue Nile was located a temple complex called Naga (which is the name of the serpent worshippers of India). This city featured a characteristically Egyptian pylon.[30]

The Egyptian word *maas* meant 'to slay, to kill'[31], thus reinforcing the connection Masau'u has with death. The ancient Egyptians were *mas-ters* of wordplay, so the word *mas* (*m's*) also had the meanings of 'to bring forth', 'to pass on or into',[32] or perhaps even 'to give birth'. It additionally carried the sense of 'to fashion a statue' (containing the *ka*, or spirit, of the person represented).[33] (See Chapter 16.)

The distribution of place-names containing the syllable *mas* ranges from Ethiopia (land of the Masai Mara tribe) up the Red Sea coast into Egypt and even farther north into Iraq.

South to North:

·Masaka, on the western shore of Lake Victoria.
·Ras (Cape) Maskan, south of Djibouti.
·Mawshij, on the western coast of Yemen on the Red Sea.
·Massawa, a major port city of Eritrea—what first keyed me into this region vis-à-vis the Hopi god Masau'u.[34]
·Masqat, capitol of Oman, as well as the nearby Island of Masirah.
·Mastabah (like the flat-topped burial pyramid?), on the coast not far from Mecca, as well as Masturah, a little over 100 miles to the north.
·Mashabih Island, off the coast of Saudi Arabia.
·Masak el Sharib and Masak el Rakhiyat in Egypt, west of the Strait of Gubal leading into the Gulf of Suez.
·Masara, on the Nile about a dozen miles south of Armana, where in the mid-fourteenth century BC Akhenaten built his city named Akhetaten.
·Al Mawsil (or Mosul, the northern Iraqi city).

This last site is, of course, located in the ancient land of Sumer—tragically embattled to this day.

In the Sumerian *Epic of Gilgamesh*, we find a reference to the "land of Mas" (or Mashu). Variously described as giants, spirits, demons, or fierce gods, a pair of "scorpion men" guards the entrance to the underworld.

> "Mashu is the name of the mountains. At last he reached them,
> Where every day they keep watch over the rising and setting
>   of Shamash, the sun god.
> To the zenith of heaven rise their summits, and downward
> Deep into hell reach their breasts. At their portals stand sentries:
> Scorpion men, awful in terror—their very glance is death,
>   and tremendous
> Is their magnificence, shaking the hills. They are the wardens
>   of Shamash,
> Both at his rising and setting. No sooner did Gilgamish see them
> Than from alarm and dismay was his face struck with pallor.
> Senseless, he groveled before them.
> Then the scorpion man to his wife spoke:
> 'He who comes to us—his body is the flesh of the gods'.
> But his wife answered: 'Only two parts of him are god-like;
> A third of him is human'."[35]

Is the Hopi underworld, which is named Maski, the same as Mashu? The mountains of Mashu apparently reach from the heavens deep into hell. The related Sumerian word MASKU means 'skin' or 'hide'. This semantically corresponds to the skin of the Hopi god Masau'u and *his* deathly gray pallor. (MASKU may also be where the English word "massage" comes from. Also, the Arabic *massa* means 'to handle'.)

In this context it is significant that Gilgamesh's "flesh" is two-thirds god and one-third human. The Sumerian demigod may indeed be a dead ringer for Votan himself.

In addition, the Sumerian phrase *Maskim Xul* refers to Evil Fiend, or Ambusher. Various legends attribute this role to the Hopi deity as well.

The Land of Mas was located in the Valley of EDIN. The Sumerian MASALU means 'to make equal'. Was Eden that paradise far in our shamanic past before the biblical Fall, when humans and animals could speak the same language and were equal? Of course, the serpent changed all that (in Chapter 3 of

Genesis). We recall that the Tigris and Euphrates in present-day Iraq were two rivers in Eden.

Members of the Yaresan religious sect of southern Kurdistan believe that the Masya was the first man, Adam, while Masyanag was the name of Eve.[36] Notice the syllable *-nag*, or 'snake', in her name.

The Armenians refer to Mount Ararat, where Noah's ark reputedly landed, as Masis. Some believe that the Garden of Eden was located somewhere near Armenia.

On our tour of place-names derived from the syllable *mas* (the root of the name of the Hopi god Masau'u), let's not forget Masada in Judea. This fortress atop a large mesa overlooking the Dead Sea was where the revolutionary Jewish zealots called Sicarii made their last stand in the first century AD. They were waiting there for the Messiah or, in Hebrew, the *Mashiah*.

Lastly, the Arabic word *masr* refers to either Cairo or all of Egypt, which brings us back to the "Red Men" that inhabited that land.

What exactly does "red" mean in this respect? A red place? The major city of Atlantis was Poseidon—traditionally known as the "Red City."

Red skin? We recall the Hopi site of Palatkwapi, or "City of the Red People."

Red hair? Members of the Hopi Fire Clan who lived with the Snake Clan in the northern Arizona cliff dwelling of Betatakin (now part of Navajo National Monument) were known as "redheads." In 1911 inside a cave near Lovelock, Nevada, guano miners found mummified giants with red hair. (Didn't the "giants in the earth," a.k.a. the Nephilim, also have red hair?) Some of the giant Easter Island statues called Moai have red topknots carved from blood-red scoria, considered to be a sacred sign of the high priesthood.

Red metal? (Copper, of course, defined the Bronze Age.) The Hopi word *voton* means 'coin'.

Red blood? Was Votan (or the Hopi version Pahana) red or white? The Hopi word *pala* means 'red', while *pahan* means 'white' (Anglo). In all probability he was both.

Nordic Trek

One god of Norse mythology shares with Votan many of the same attributes . Odin was the deity of prophecy, magic, and poetry. He invented the runic alphabet and sacrificed his right eye in a sacred spring to gain otherworldly wisdom. Perhaps he even strove to be, as Matthew 10:16 says, "wise as serpents."

He also hung on the World Tree named Ygddrasil, (literally, the 'horse of Odin'), for nine days and nights, wounding himself with his own spear—thus suggesting some sort of shamanic ritual. This is described in the "Hava Maal" of *The Poetic Edda* from Iceland.[37] *Hava Maal* literally means "Sublime Discourse," but notice the similarity to the Hebrew word *heva*, which (as previously stated) means 'snake'. An underworld dragon named Níðhöggr (or Nidhogg) gnawed at the roots of this cosmic ash tree. The dragon is, of course, a variation of the serpent.

Odin would also welcome slain warriors into Valhalla, the hall of the afterlife. Frequently carrying a staff like Moses, this bearded individual was furthermore associated with wandering and the hunt.

By the way, the Teutonic version of Odin's name is Wotan.

He rode an eight-legged steed named Sleipnir, which literally means 'smooth' or 'gliding' and is related to the English word "slippery." Indeed, Odin is also the master of cunning, deceit, and trickery. His miraculous mount could bear him swiftly across the sea or the air, but it also had the ability to journey to the land of the dead. In a word, he was mercurial.

It has been suggested that Slepnir's eight legs metaphorically represent those of four pallbearers. They may also be a kenning that signifies four pairs of oars on a Viking ship. A kenning is a type of circumlocution common in Old Norse and Old English poetry. Then again, Odin's horse just might be a means of *circum-location*, or circumnavigation.

Author Philip Gardiner explains kenning (also spelled "kynning") as an esoteric process: "This *kynning* is, of course, the origin of cunning, and originates from words etymologically associated with the wise serpent (can is serpent)."38

Arachnids (including "scorpion men" and spiders) are the only creatures in nature with eight legs. In this context I should mention a certain Spider *Woman* from Hopi legend. Revered as a guardian, Kótyangwúti helped their culture hero named Tiyo in his journey across the ocean to the island of the Snake People. (Nagas? See Chapter 12.)

One Hopi source talks about what happened when Tiyo went down into the kiva located on this island: "He entered the Kiva and saw the people all red there. They were painted red, and he happened to discover that they were confined in this Kiva as a set of Snake Priests."39 From these "red" beings he learned the aforementioned Snake Dance ceremony, which he brought back to Arizona.

One 18th century Icelandic depiction of Odin astride his usual mode of travel shows the god holding a double trident in his left hand. [See drawing: http://en.wikipedia.org/wiki/Odin.] This is similar to both the staff of Jupiter and the staff of Adad—the latter being the Babylonian god of thunder and lightning. This is comparable to the Hindu *vajra* that either Indra or Shiva wields. (Was this also like the staff-cum-serpent of Moses?) If one removes the barbs on Odin's staff, it becomes the zodiacal symbol for Pisces. The trident is, of course, associated with the sea god Poseidon, who was the supreme monarch of Atlantis.

Ultimately some sort of euhemeristic transformation probably took place in regard to Odin/Wotan/Votan, whereby an historic figure or group gradually gained the status of a god. If this were the case, ancient travel between continents apparently was the rule, not the exception. As we have seen, traces of global interaction still exist in both the tropical South Pacific and the arid American Southwest but especially in southern Mexico.

Return of the Snake-eye

"In the days of Quetzalcoatl there was abundance of everything necessary for subsistence. The maize was plentiful, the calabashes were as thick as one's arm, and cotton grew in all colours without having to be dyed. A variety of birds of rich plumage filled the air with their songs, and gold, silver, and precious stones were abundant. In the reign of Quetzalcoatl there was peace and plenty for all men."[40]

It sounds like paradise. But, as the cliché goes, all good things must come to an end, including the sovereignty of Votan (or, in his Aztec incarnation, Quetzalcoatl). Some believe that necromancers or evil priests overturned his original precepts of enlightened non-violence and instituted human sacrifice. One myth describes the god Tezcatlipoca ("Fiery Mirror") plying Quetzalcoatl with the intoxicating drink *pulque*, thereby causing the latter to fall into dissolution and moral decay.

The feathered serpent finally abdicated his authority in Mexico and sailed toward the rising sun on a raft of snakes. In another version he cast himself upon a funeral pyre, after which the eponymous *quetzal* bird with its brilliant plumage rose phoenix-like from the ashes. Quetzalcoatl's heart then ascended into the sky to become the Morning Star (Venus).

Before departing toward the east, however, he had promised to return one day for the purpose of redeeming the land and its people from the trials and suffering they were destined to endure.

In the early 16th century Hernando Cortés conquered –almost too easily– Moctezuma and his Aztec subjects at Tenochtitlán (now Mexico City). This rapid capitulation was due in part to the native leader's belief that the Spaniard was fulfilling the prophecy of the ancient god's return.

Whether we are talking about the Aztecan Quetzalcoatl or the Mayan Votan, the disastrous result was the same: magnificent cities with their soaring temples and pyramids were left in smoking ruins, while sacred codices with their accumulated knowledge were callously consigned to the flames or lost in the jungles.

It is interesting to note that one of the meanings of the Spanish word *votan* is 'a religious vow'. In this case the vow to convert all inhabitants of the New World to the Catholic faith resulted in the almost complete destruction of a fiercely brilliant aboriginal culture that had flowered for millennia.

Apocalypse Tao

The facts presented in this essay join the plethora of evidence for pre-Columbian intercultural exchange, ultimately producing a cumulative effect. An increasing array of distinct artifacts and customs found on separate continents seems to have mutual elements. Their sheer number and diversity belie any notion of independent invention in isolation. The only plausible explanation is that extensive maritime travel and trade were the norm prior to the Christian era.

Either the discovery of new methods of DNA testing or the refinement of current ones will soon make its results more conclusive. Scientists will then be able to find genetic evidence that proves "deities" such as Votan were diffused or dispersed across the globe beginning perhaps as early as the Upper Paleolithic. Very recent findings point toward this:

> "The DNA data...suggest a lot more to-ing and fro-ing than has been suspected of populations during the past 30,000 years in Northeast Asia and North America. The analysis of the dataset shows that after the initial peopling of Beringia [Bering land bridge], there were a series of back migrations to Northeast Asia as well as forward migrations to the Americas from Beringia, thus 'more recent bi-directional gene flow between Siberia and the North American Arctic.'"[41]

In light of this and other scientific data, the ivory tower isolationists are becoming increasingly tedious. Their tenuous arguments probably have more to do with professional tenure than anything else.

But these petty academic skirmishes pale in comparison to what increasingly looks like an impending Endgame. The

Hopi living on their isolated mesas of Arizona continue to perform sacred rituals in a desperate attempt to keep the whole world in balance. This is the basic reason that they maintain their ceremonial cycle: not for themselves but for Mother Earth.

Despite their heroic efforts, though, they are losing the battle. Because of the onslaught of modern society upon their traditional life-ways, many of the ancient ceremonies are dying out. Fewer and fewer youth are learning the Hopi language. It has been remarked that the Maya are the guardians of time, while the Hopi are the guardians of space (namely the Earth). As 2012 approaches, the Hopi are less and less able to be of service to the planet through their rituals. As a result, the world is increasingly out of balance. The only thing they can do now is to wait for Pahana's return.

Former Vice President and Nobel Peace Prize Laureate Al Gore said in his award-winning documentary film *An Inconvenient Truth* that the results of global warming looked like "...a nature hike through the Book of Revelations."

CNN recently broadcast a series about environmental degradation called "Planet In Peril." Daily reports of the deleterious effects of "climate change" (hurricanes, coastal flooding, record rainfall and snowfall levels, tsunamis, droughts, forest fires, Arctic/Antarctic ocean warming, etc.) all produce a siege mentality in those sensitive to the increasingly morbid condition of Gaia. Who among us –except chronic skeptics or those with their heads in the sand– would deny that we are facing a global crisis, a live-or-die situation of monumental proportions?

If we combine this with the contemporary reality of nuclear proliferation, terrorist suicide bombings, oil shortages, geopolitical instability, Developing World mass poverty, refugee camps, famine, and epidemics, the very fabric of our existence seems to be unraveling right before our eyes. Has Death finally won the game of chess? Is the seventh seal about to be opened?

Even in an era of nanotechnology, robotics, genetic manipulation, cell phones and cyberspace, we still await the return of some primary archetypal force that speaks to all religions, ethnicities, and philosophies. The ancient Chinese called it the Tao, or the all-encompassing Way. If our grandest dreams indeed prove real, then this purveyor of peace and enlightenment could ultimately save us from annihilation.

In the chaos of these times, the catalyst for our new beginning may be the legendary Votan, who comes back again to vanquish the legions of evil. We can only hope.

Endnotes for Appendix 2

1. The presence of non-Amerindian, bearded sculptures in such diverse Mesoamerican ancient cities as La Venta, Chichén Itzá, Monte Alban, and other sites too numerous to mention is well documented.

2. T. J. O'Brien, *Fair Gods and Feathered Serpents: A Search for Ancient America's Bearded White God* (Bountiful, Utah: Horizon Publishers, 1997), pp. 64-65.

3. John Van Auken and Lora Little, *The Lost Hall of Records: Edgar Cayce's Forgotten Record of the Human History in the Ancient Yucatan* (Memphis, Tennessee: Eagle Wing Books, Inc., 2000).

4. Graham Hancock, *Fingerprints of the Gods: The Evidence of Earth's Lost Civilization* (New York: Crown Trade Paperbacks, 1995), p. 103-104.

5. *Book of the Chilam Balam*, XXIV, translated by Ralph L. Roys, 1933, at www.sacred-texts.com.

6. Adrian Gilbert, Maurice M Cotterell, *The Mayan Prophecies: Unlocking the Secrets of a Lost Civilization* (Shaftesbury, Dorset: Element Books Limited, 1996, 1995), p. 202.

7. Andrew Collins, introduction by David Rohl, *Gateway to Atlantis* (New York: Graf Publishers, Inc., 2000), p. 340.

8. J. F. Hewitt, *The Ruling Races of Prehistoric Times In India, South-western Asia and Southern Europe* (Westminster, England: Archibald Constable and Company, 1894), p. 249. (Digitalized at http://books.google.com.)

9. Albert Pike, *Morals and Dogma* (Charleston, South Carolina: The Supreme Council of the Southern Jurisdiction, 1928, 1906, 1871), pp. 78-79, p. 591.

10. Constance Irwin, *Fair Gods and Stone Faces: Ancient Seafarers and the New World's Most Intriguing Riddle* (New York: St. Martin's Press, 1963), p. 102.

11. Collins, *Gateway to Atlantis*, p. 336.

12. Barry Fell, *Saga America* (New York: Times Books, 1980), p. 245.

13. Hopi *katsinam* (also spelled *kachinas*) are masked figures that can represent any object or energy in the universe. Like angels, they are benevolent intermediaries between the divine realm and the human realm. Every spring and early summer *katsina* dances are held in the plazas of ancient Hopi villages. The dancers imitate these spirit messengers and in the process actually become them.

14. Irwin, *Fair Gods and Stone Faces*, pp. 100-101.

15. Donald A. Mackenzie, *Myths of Pre-Columbian America* (Mineola, New York: Dover Publications, Inc., 1996, 1923), p. 266.

16. H. P. Blavatsky, *Isis Unveiled: A Master-Key to the Mysteries of Ancient and Modern Science and Theology*, Vol. II (Pasadena, California: Theosophical University Press, 1950), footnote p. 481.

17. Collins, *Gateway to Atlantis*, pp. 341-342.

18. Victor Mindeleff, *A Study of Pueblo Architecture in Tusayan and Cibola* (Washington: Smithsonian Institution Press, 1989, reprint 1891), p. 136.

19. David Hatcher Childress, *Ancient Tonga & the Lost City of Mu'a* (Stelle, Illinois: Adventures Unlimited Press, 1996), pp. 26-33.

20. Fell, *Saga America*, p. 262-3, p. 294.

21. James Bailey, *The God-King & the Titans: The New World Ascendancy in Ancient Times* (New York: St. Martin's Press, 1973), p. 206.

22. Graham Hancock and Santha Faiia, *Heaven's Mirror: Quest For the Lost Civilization* (New York: Crown Publishers, Inc. 1998), p. 224, p. 254.

23. Bailey, *The God-Kings & the Titans*, pp. 245-246.

24. Jim Bailey, *Sailing To Paradise: The Discovery of the Americas by 7000 B.C.* (New York: Simon & Schuster, 1994), p. 57.

25. Ignatius Donnelly, *Atlantis: The Antediluvian World* (New York: Dover Publications, Inc., 1976, reprint 1882), p. 194.

26. Harold Courlander, *The Fourth World of the Hopis: the Epic Story of the Hopi Indians As Preserved In Their Legends and Traditions* (Albuquerque: University of New Mexico Press, 1991, 1971), p. 77.

27. Albert Yava, *Big Snow Falling: A Tewa-Hopi Indian's Life and Times* *and the History and Traditions of His People* (Albuquerque: University of New Mexico Press, 1982, 1978), p. 62.

28. Gene D. Matlock, "Is the Hopi Deity Kokopelli an Ancient Hindu God?", ViewZone, at www.viewzone.com/kokopeli.html.

29. Anthony Rich, *A Dictionary of Roman and Greek Antiquities* (London: Longmans, Green, and Co, 1893), p. 413. (Digitalized at http://books.google.com.)

30. P. D. Scott-Moncrieff, M.A., "The Ruined Sites at Masawwarat es-Sufra and Naga," Proceedings of the Society of *Biblical Archaeology*, Vol. XXX, Thirty-eighth Session, Jan.-Dec. 1908, London), p. 196. (Digitalized at http://books.google.com/.)

31. E. A. Wallis Budge, *An Egyptian Hieroglyphic Dictionary*, Vol. I (New York: Dover Publications, Inc., 1978, 1920), p. 270.

32. Budge, *An Egyptian Hieroglyphic Dictionary*, Vol. I, p. 286.

33. W. J. Perry, *The Children of the Sun: A Study of the Egyptian Settlement of the Pacific* (Kempton, Illinois: Adventures Unlimited Press, 2004, 1923), p. 434.

34. John Philip Cohane, *The Key* (New York: Schocken Books, 1976, 1969), pp. 114-115.

35. Adapted from *The Epic of Gilgamish*, Ninth Tablet, translated by R. Campbell Thompson, 1928, at www.sacred-texts.com.

36. Andrew Collins, *From the Ashes of Angels: the Forbidden Legacy of a Fallen Race* (Rochester, Vermont: Bear & Company, 2001, 1996), p. 196.

37. Henry Adams Bellows, *The Poetic Edda* (New York: The American-Scandinavian Foundation, 1968), p. 60.

38. Philip Gardiner, *The Ark, The Shroud, and Mary: The Untold Truths About the Relics of the Bible* (Franklin Lakes, New Jersey: New Page Books, 2007), p. 160.

39. *Hopi Hearings*, July 15 – 30, 1955, United States Bureau of Indian Affairs, Hopi Agency (Phoenix, Arizona: Bureau of Indian Affairs, Phoenix Area Office, Hopi Agency, 1955).

40. Lewis Spence, *The Myths of Mexico and Peru*, 1913, at www.sacred-texts.com.

41. "New Ideas About Human Migration From Asia To Americas," *Science Daily*, October 25, 2007, at www.sciencedaily.com/releases/2007/10/071025160653.htm.

Bibliography

Adams, E. Charles, *The Origin and Development of the Pueblo Katsina Cult* (Tucson, Arizona: The University of Arizona Press, 1991).

Allen, Richard Hinckley, *Star Names: Their Lore and Meaning* (New York: Dover Publications, Inc., 1963, reprint 1899).

Anon. editors, *The World's Last Mysteries* (Pleasantville, NY: The Reader's Digest Association, Inc., 1978).

Baigent, Michael and Richard Leigh, *The Temple and the Lodge* (New York: Arcade Publishing, Inc., 1989.)

Bailey, James, *The God-King & the Titans: The New World Ascendancy in Ancient Times* (New York: St. Martin's Press, 1973).

Bailey, Jim, *Sailing to Paradise: The Discovery of the Americas by 7000 B.C.* (New York: Simon & Schuster, 1994).

Bauval, Robert, and Adrian Gilbert, *The Orion Mystery: Unlocking the Secrets of the Pyramids* (New York: Crown Publishers, Inc., 1994).

Bourke, John G., *Snake-Dance of the Moquis: Being a Narrative of a Journey from Santa Fe, New Mexico to the Villages of the Moqui Indians of Arizona* (Tucson: The University of Arizona Press, 1984, 1884).

Bradfield, Richard Maitland, *An Interpretation of Hopi Culture* (Derby, England: privately published, 1995).

Brady, Bernadette, *Brady's Book of Fixed Stars* (York Beach, Maine: Samuel Weiser, Inc., 1998).

Bramley, William, *The Gods of Eden* (New York: Avon Books/HarperCollins, 1990).

Burnham, Robert, Jr., *Burnham's Celestial Handbook: An Observer's Guide to the Universe Beyond the Solar System*, Vol. 2 (New York: Dover Publications, Inc., 1978, reprint, 1966).

Campbell, Joseph, *The Masks of God: Oriental Mythology* (New York: The Viking Press, Inc., 1962).

Capt, E. Raymond, *The Glory of the Stars: A Study of the Zodiac* (Glendale, CA: Dolores Press, Inc., 1983, 1976).

Chatelain, Maurice, *Our Cosmic Ancestors* (Sedona, Arizona: Temple Publications, 1988, 1987).

Childe, V. Gordon, *New Light on the Most Ancient East* (New York: Grove Press, Inc., 1957).

Childress, David Hatcher, *Ancient Tonga & the Lost City of Mu'a* (Stelle, Illinois: Adventures Unlimited Press, 1996).

Childress, David Hatcher, *Lost Cities of Atlantis, Ancient Europe &
the Mediterranean* (Stelle, Illinois: Adventures Unlimited
Press, 1996).

Cirlot, J. E., *A Dictionary of Symbols* (New York: Philosophical
Library, 1962).

Clark, R. T. Rundle, *Myth and Symbol in Ancient Egypt* (New York:
Thames and Hudson, 1991, 1978, 1959).

Collins, Andrew, *From the Ashes of Angels: the Forbidden Legacy of a
Fallen Race* (Rochester, Vermont: Bear & Company, 2001,
1996).

Coppens, Philip, *The Canopus Revelation: The Stargate of the Gods
and the Ark of Osiris* (Kempton, Illinois: Adventures Unlimited
Press, 2004).

David, Gary A., *The Orion Zone: Ancient Star Cities of the American
Southwest* (Kempton, Illinois: Adventures Unlimited Press,
2006).

Dockstader, Frederick J., *The Kachina and the White Man: The
Influences of White Culture on the Hopi Kachina Religion*
(Albuquerque, New Mexico: University of New Mexico Press,
1985, 1954).

Donnelly, Ignatius, *Atlantis: The Antediluvian World* (New York:
Dover Publications, Inc., 1976, reprint 1882).

Donnelly, Ignatius, *Ragnarok: The Age of Fire and Gravel* (New York:
University Books, 1970).

Ellis, Ralph, *Jesus, Last of the Pharaohs: The True History of Religion
Revealed* (Dorset, United Kingdom: Edfu Books, 1999, 1998).

Ferguson, William M., and John Q. Royce, *Mayan Ruins of Mexico in
Color* (Norman: University of Oklahoma Press, 1979, 1977).

Fewkes, Jesse Walter, *Prehistoric Pottery Designs* (New York: Dover
Publications, Inc.,1973, reprint of *Seventeenth Annual Report
to the Bureau of American Ethnology*, 1898; and *Thirty-Third
Annual Report to the Bureau of American Ethnology*, 1919).

Fewkes, Jesse Walter, "Two Summers' Work In Pueblo Ruins,"
*Twenty-Second Annual Report to the Bureau of American
Ethnology, 1900-1901* (Washington, D.C.: Smithsonian
Institute/Government Printing Office, 1904).

Fewkes, Jesse Walter, *Hopi Katcinas* (New York: Dover Publications,
Inc., 1985, reprint of *Twenty-First Annual Report to the Bureau
of American Ethnology*, 1903).

Freidel, David, Linda Schele, and Joy Parker, *Maya Cosmos: Three
Thousand Years on the Shaman's Path* (New York: William
Morrow and Company, Inc., 1993).

Gordon, Cyrus H., *Before Columbus: Links Between the Old World and
Ancient America* (New York: Crown Publishers, Inc., 1971).

Greaves, Todd, "The Tau (T) In Eschatology and In Religious Architecture Around the World," *Pre-Columbiana: A Journal of Long-Distance Contacts*, Vol. 3, No. 4/Vol. 4, No. 1, 2008.

Griffith, Ralph T. H., translator, *The Hymns of the Rigveda* (Varanasi, India: The Chowkhamba Sanskrit Series Office, 1971).

Henry, William, *Starwalkers and the Dimension of the Blessed* (Kempton, Illinois: Adventures Unlimited Press, 2007).

Hewett, Edgar Lee, *Ancient Life in the American Southwest* (Indianapolis, Indiana: The Bobbs-Merrill Company, 1930).

Johnson, Boma, *Earth Figures of the Lower Colorado and Gila River Deserts: A Functional Analysis* (Phoenix: Arizona Archaeological Society, # 20, 1986, 1985).

Kaiser, Rudolf, *The Voice of the Great Spirit: Prophecies of the Hopi Indians* (Boston: Shambala Publications, Inc., 1989, 1991).

Knight, Christopher, and Robert Lomas, *Uriel's Machine: Uncovering the Secrets of Stonehenge, Noah's Flood, and the Dawn of Civilization* (Gloucester, Massachusetts: Fair Winds Press, 2001, 1999).

Krupp, E. C., *Beyond the Blue Horizon: Myths and Legends of the Sun, Moon, Stars and Planets* (New York: HarperCollins, 1991).

LaViolette, Paul A., *Earth Under Fire: Humanity's Survival of the Ice Age* (Rochester, Vermont: Bear & Company, 2005, 1997).

Le Plongeon, Augustus, *Sacred Mysteries Among the Mayas and the Quiches* (Minneapolis, Minnesota: Wizards Bookshelf, 1973).

Mails, Thomas E., *The Pueblo Children of the Earth Mother*, Vol. I (New York: Doubleday & Company, Inc., 1983).

Malotki, Ekkehart, editor, *Hopi Dictionary: A Hopi-English Dictionary of the Third Mesa Dialect* (Tucson, Arizona: The University of Arizona Press, 1998).

Malotki, Ekkehart, *Earth Fire: A Hopi Legend of the Sunset Crater Eruption* (Flagstaff, Arizona: Northland Press, 1987).

Malotki, Ekkehart, and Michael Lomatuway'ma, drawings by Petra Roeckerath, *Maasaw: Profile of a Hopi God* (Lincoln, Nebraska: University of Nebraska Press, 1987).

Men, Hunbatz, *Secrets of Mayan Science/Religion*, translated by Diana Gubiseh Ayala and James Jennings Dunlap II (Santa Fe, New Mexico, Bear & Company Publishing, 1990).

Morley, Sylvanus G., *The Ancient Maya* (Palo Alto, California: Stanford University Press, 1947, 1946).

Norton, O. Richard, *Rocks From Space: Meteorites and Meteorite Hunters* (Missoula, Montana: Mountain Press Publishing Company, 1998, 1994).

Otto, Rudolf, *The Idea of the Holy: An Inquiry into the non-rational factor in the idea of the divine and its relation to the rational*, translated by John W. Harvey (London: Oxford University Press, 1971, 1923).

Patterson, Alex, *A Field Guide To Rock Art Symbols of the Greater Southwest* (Boulder, Colorado: Johnson Books, 1992).

Pennick, Nigel, *Sacred Geometry: Symbolism and Purpose in Religious Structures* (San Francisco: Harper & Row, Publishers, 1982, 1980).

Pike, Albert, *Morals and Dogma of the Ancient and Accepted Scottish Rite of Freemasonry* (Charleston, South Carolina: A. M. 5632, 1928, 1906, 1871).

Prescott, William H., *The Conquest of Mexico* (New York: The Junior Literary Guild, 1934, 1843).

Pye, Lloyd, *The Starchild Skull: Genetic Enigma or Human-Alien Hybrid?* (Pensacola, Florida: Bell Lap Books, Inc., 2007).

Roberts, David, *In Search of the Old Ones: Exploring the Anasazi World of the Southwest* (New York: Touchstone Books, Simon & Schuster, 1996).

Rudhyar, Dane, *An Astrological Mandala: The Cycle of Transformations and Its 360 Symbolic Phases* (New York: Random House, 1973).

Santillana, Giorgio de, and Hertha von Deschend, *Hamlet's Mill: An Essay Investigating the Origins of Human Knowledge and Its Transmission Through Myth* (Boston: David R. Godine, Publisher, Inc., 1998, 1969).

Schaafsma, Polly, *Indian Rock Art of the Southwest* (Santa Fe and Albuquerque, New Mexico: School of American Research and University of New Mexico Press, 1995, 1980).

Scully, Vincent, *Pueblo: Mountain, Village, Dance* (Chicago: University of Chicago Press, 1989, reprint 1975).

Sitchin, Zecharia, *The Cosmic Code: Book VI of the Earth Chronicles* (New York: Avon Books, 1998).

Sitchin, Zecharia, *When Time Began: Book V of the Earth Chronicles* (New York: Avon Books, 1993).

Sitchin, Zecharia, *The Stairway to Heaven: Book II of the Earth Chronicles* (New York: Avon Books, 1983, 1980).

Smith, LL.D., William, *Smith's Bible Dictionary* (New York: Family Library, 1973).

Stephen, Alexander M., and Elsie Clew Parsons, editor, *Hopi Journal*, Vol. I & Vol. II (New York: AMS Press, Inc., 1969, reprint 1936).

Stephen, Alexander M., "Hopi Tales," *The Journal of American Folklore*, Vol. 42, No. 163, January/March, 1929.

Thompson, Laura, *Culture In Crisis: A Study of the Hopi Indians*, foreward by John Collier, additional material by Benjamin Lee Whorf (New York: Harper & Brothers, Publishers, 1950).

Timms, Moira, *Beyond Prophecies and Predictions: Everyone's Guide to the Coming Changes* (New York: Ballantine Books, 1994, 1980).

Titiev, Mischa, *Old Oraibi: A Study of the Hopi Indians of Third Mesa* (Albuquerque, New Mexico: University of New Mexico Press, 1992, reprint 1944).

Turner, Christy G., II, and Jacqueline A. Turner, *Man Corn: Cannibalism and Violence in the Prehistoric American Southwest* (Salt Lake City: The University of Utah Press, 1999).

Walker, James R., *Lakota Belief and Ritual* (Lincoln: University of Nebraska Press, 1982, 1980).

Wallace-Murphy, Tim, and Marilyn Hopkins, *Templars In America: From the Crusades to the New World* (New York, Barnes & Noble Publishing, Inc., 2004).

Waters, Frank, and Oswald White Bear Fredericks, *Book of the Hopi* (New York: Penguin Books, 1987, reprint 1963).

Waters, Frank, *Mexico Mystique: the Coming Sixth World of Consciousness* (Chicago: The Swallow Press, Inc., 1975).

Whitley, David S., *A Guide to Rock Art in Southern California and Southern Nevada* (Missoula, Montana: Mountain Press Publishing Company, 1996).

Wolf, Eric R., *Sons of the Shaking Earth: The People of Mexico and Guatemala—Their Land, History, and Culture* (Chicago: University of Chicago Press, 1959).

Wormington, H. M., *Prehistoric Indians of the Southwest* (Denver, Colorado: The Denver Museum of Natural History, 1973, reprint 1947).

Yava, Albert, *Big Snow Falling: A Tewa-Hopi Indian's Life and Times and the History and Traditions of His People* (Albuquerque: University of New Mexico Press, 1982, 1978).

Zapp, Ivar, and George Erikson, *Atlantis In America: Navigators of the Ancient World* (Kempton, Illinois: Adventures Unlimited Press, 1998).

A native of Ohio and writer for over thirty years, **Gary A. David** has spent most of his adult life in the American West. He has published numerous volumes of poetry and the recent nonfiction book *The Orion Zone*. His master's degree in English literature is from the University of Colorado. For the past fourteen years he has lived with his wife and daughter in northern Arizona, where he studies Anasazi petroglyphs and ruins, and tries to learn the stars. His favorite maxim: "As above, so below."

Author's Website: www.theorionzone.com
His e-mail: islandhillsbooks@msn.com
Island Hills Books: http://islandhills.tripod.com

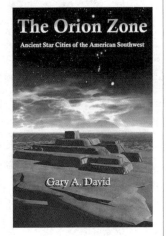